While Mem'ry Brings us Back Again

This collection of memoirs is dedicated to all Irish immigrants who came to these shores and especially those who shared their personal stories with us.

While Mem'ry Brings us Back Again

A Collection of Memoirs
Produced by the
Aisling Irish Community Center

NEW YORK

2006

FRONT COVER: MENU FROM THE S.S. BRITANNICA, APRIL 1957
COURTESY OF MARY CARRIGAN

BACK COVER: MAP OF IRELAND DRAWN WITH A MAGIC MARKER
BY MICHAEL CULBERT;
H BLOCK 4, THE MAZE PRISON, LONG KESH, NI. 1991
COURTESY OF DENIS MULCAHY

Compiled by Frances Browner, Aisling Irish Community Center

Edited by Patricia Hamill, Heron Moon Press

Photographs by Nuala Purcell

Aisling Irish Community Center
990 MCLEAN AVENUE, YONKERS, NY 10704
WWW.AISLINGCENTER.ORG
914-237-5121

ISBN-13: 978-0-615-13565-6

Table of Contents

Introduction

Established in 1996, the Aisling Irish Community Center in Yonkers, New York, is a not-for-profit corporation overseen by a Board of Directors, managed by a dedicated staff and supported by a large number of volunteers. The aim of the Center is to assist and support the Irish immigrant community. It helps new immigrants make their transition to life in the United States a positive experience, and it offers established members of the community a place to socialize, receive information, learn and share their knowledge and talents.

Among the many programs and classes offered, a "Young at Heart" group for seniors is hosted every Friday afternoon. In the fall of 2005, staff member, Frances Browner initiated a creative writing workshop. The members received this class with great enthusiasm. Thus, with pencils in hand, they embarked on a remarkable journey into their personal histories, which have culminated in this volume of memoirs.

It was not only an incredible trip through, but also an important lesson in, Irish and Irish American history. As a result the Center made a decision to put this precious information into a book, and it was also decided to include the broader community. Frances Browner conducted the additional interviews, transcribed the recordings into manuscript, and assembled the content into story form. The time span reaches from an ocean crossing in 1927 to a transatlantic flight in 1964. The ages of the participants range from 60 to 100 years old.

There are memories from those who worked for the rich and others who have become rich. Some describe living in the North of Ireland before the Troubles to living on small farms, small towns, large towns, and Dublin City. Included in the many occupations are telephone operators, waitresses, nurses, nannies, construction workers, police officers, transit workers, a banker and a teacher. There are several men who served in the U.S. military from the Second World War to the Vietnam War. There are some who took advantage of Frank O'Connor's GED class to others who graduated with master's degrees.

Immigrants such as these represented in this text also contributed greatly to the Ireland we have today by sending clothing and their hard-won earnings home. Hence, through their contributions to both the American work force and community and their monetary contributions to their place of birth, these people paved the way for succeeding generations in both countries. The Ireland they left behind does not exist as they knew it; the America that welcomed them has changed as well. This nostalgic journey of lives, which may have seemed ordinary in the living, has become extraordinary in the retelling.

The title is from a poem by Thomas Moore, "As Slow Our Ship." The cover is an actual menu from the SS *Britannica* on which one of the Center's members, Mary Carrigan, traveled in 1957. Both the line from the poem and the image of the ship inspire the reader to contemplate how voyages transport us to a vastly different worlds and how memory returns us to our roots.

The challenge of editing this collection has been to present each story as true to the recollection of the individuals as possible; however, the order of information in some of these tales has been arranged to provide a more linear exposition of events. Although the order of information in each story is not entirely true to the order of the telling, the memoirs have been edited as lightly as possible. A glossary is provided in order to identify the various names and places that may not be readily familiar to the reader.

The recordings will be stored in the archives of Irish America at Glucksman Ireland House, the center for Irish Studies at New York University.

Agnes Delaney,
Chairperson, Board of Directors

Message from the Consul General of Ireland Tim O'Connor

Ar son Ard Consulacht na hÉireann, is onóir mhór dom páirt a ghlacadh san leabhar ana-shuimiúl seo ón Aisling Center.

"While Mem'ry Brings us Back Again" is a brilliant idea. I first heard about it when I visited the Aisling Irish Community Center in May with my colleague, David Healy, at the invitation of Agnes Delaney. That afternoon, in the company of a spirited and fun "Young at Heart" group, we heard from Frances Browner about her simple idea of having them write down their memories of coming to America.

The result is this wonderful publication. I know from personal experience that you will not want to put it down until you reach the last page. Ordinary people, extraordinary stories - that is perhaps a cliché, but that is partly what the book is about. I say partly, because at another level the people involved are fundamentally not ordinary either. They all made the journey from their homeland of Ireland to a new world in America, far from their families, friends and everything they were used to. They overcame homesickness and the challenges of a new world and built fine lives for themselves in this great City that we all now call home. There was nothing ordinary about that.

The stories will delight, absorb and uplift you. They also underline the amazing story that is Irish America and the Irish in America – and just how good this country has been to millions of our people. The word "thanks" comes into play – to the writers themselves for the inspiration they are to us, America for opening its doors and its heart to so many of our people, and Irish America for never forgetting the Motherland and the communities they left behind.

We are building a new Ireland today on the island of Ireland, based on prosperity and peace. The United States, New York and Irish America have a made a huge contribution to both. We are very hopeful about the future, a future based on partnership between a new, resurgent Ireland and the United States. But we will never forget the sacrifices and struggle of so many in the past who made such a bright future possible. This book is about some of those people – we salute them all.

Finally, I want to pay tribute to the Center itself. Along with the other Emigration Centers, the Aisling has made a huge contribution to the Irish community in New York. The Irish Government has recognized this contribution and in the recent round of new funding, the Minister for Foreign Affairs, Dermot Ahern, TD, announced a significant grant for the AICC for 2006. I pay particular tribute to its Chairperson, the tireless Agnes Delaney, ably assisted by the Board, by the executive team of Orla Kelleher, Maura Jordan and Frances Browner and, of course, by all the volunteers who make such an important contribution. I also take this opportunity to thank the outgoing Director, Patricia Grogan, for the fine contribution that she made. David Healy and the rest of my colleagues at the Consulate look forward to a continued fruitful partnership with Agnes, Orla and their team.

Foreword

by Frances Browner

My task was to organize activities for the seniors group who meet every Friday at the Aisling Irish Community Center. Noticing a few gaps in the fall 2005 schedule, I casually suggested a creative writing workshop. "Will we bring our jotters?" Anne O'Connor was mischievous as usual. Thus our journey began.

For their first assignment the trigger phrase was – I remember. The kitchen suddenly fell silent, as the ladies ardently attacked their jotters. A barrage of memories was released unto the pages. *I remember my first day at school . . . I remember the first time I saw myself in the mirror . . . I remember the awful snowstorm of 1947 . . . I remember the thrashing and making the hay . . . I remember my first job . . . I remember coming to America on the boat . . .* The latter ignited a torrent of recollections from around the table – "I came on the SS America; the SS Washington; the Britannica; the Franconia; the Olympia; the Saxonia; the Georgic; the Queen Elizabeth; the SS United States." *There were that many boats?*

Our next project was thus born – write about the boat. Further discussion led to the job; the ballroom; the boyfriends; the beach at Rockaway; vacations in the Catskills and Cushman's cakes. Reminiscences even returned to childhood. They remembered the families, villages, towns, and parishes they left behind. They wrote, and they talked, then wrote and talked some more. The only sound in the room sometimes was the ticking of the Aisling kitchen clock, as the group began to write, and write, and remember. They remembered their first impressions of America. They remembered their jobs in Schrafft's restaurants, the New York Telephone Company, and B. Altman's department store. The dance halls came back to life—the Jaeger House, City Center, the Tuxedo Ballroom, the Laurel Eye and the Red Mill. Gaelic Park on a Sunday was vividly recaptured, as was the magnificence of a long ago Fordham Road. The Grand Concourse, Inwood, Highbridge, Kingsbridge, and Queens were transformed from unfamiliar enclaves into friendly pockets of Irish life. I was transported back fifty years and plunged into a place that was already forgotten by the time of my own arrival in 1987. *Why did I not know this before?*

"These stories have got to be told," Patricia Grogan, then Executive Director of the Center, proclaimed. Not only were they going to be told, the Board decided, they were to be recorded too, and the contributors sought far and wide beyond the confines of the Center. I met Oliver O'Donnell one day in Dr. Gilbert's Café on Broadway. "What year did you come, Oliver?" The first of many times I would pose that question. "1960". His blue eyes twinkled. "By boat?" I ventured. "The SS America," he declared proudly. Thus the first interview was conceived.

From then on the participants poured in – my friend, Evelyn Henry, nominated her neighbors, Jerry & Marion; Timmy Cahalan suggested his old friend, Jimmy Clarke. One of our seniors, Jean McPeake, selected her Auntie Rose, and my darts colleagues, Clare and Margaret, designated their parents, Jimmy & Anne. As my childhood in Dublin had been spent pouring over pictures of American cousins, I cajoled members of my own immigrant family. Uncle Michael in Miami feigned protest, but willingly submitted, godmother, Phil, and her husband, Pat Murray, didn't hesitate. Our photographer, Nuala Purcell, proposed her mother, Carmen; Consul General of Ireland, Tim O'Connor, told me I just had to meet Joe Cunningham; Patricia Grogan and her father, Patrick, conducted a videoed interview with Tom McCarrick; and members of our Board tendered their own contributors. Some participants presented themselves at the Center; others I lassoed. *So, when did you come?*

Along the way I drank wine - with Jerry and Marion at their home on Post Road; with Jimmy Clarke in his local bar, Shea's, and with Mike Cremins at the Riverdale Steakhouse, his favorite haunt every Sunday after Mass. Having savored one of Annie Chambers' famous dinners on Bailey Avenue, I left with a tin of 'Afternoon Tea' tucked under my arm. I lunched with Frank Bergin at Sidetracks in Sunnyside among a group of gambling revelers; and with Denis Mulcahy at Fitzy's on McLean Avenue. About fifteen cups of tea were brewed by Rose Cunningham the day I visited her and Joe on Bronx River Road; while coffee and chocolate covered almonds were served by Sean Fleming in a pictorial garden overlooking the Tappanzee Bridge.

Meanwhile, in my basement office on McLean Avenue, I ploughed through hours of interviews, transcribed the recordings into text, and then crafted their stories, all the while adhering to the individual voice of the speaker. References had to be checked, and citations researched. People had to be called over and over again to ensure accuracy of detail. "Don't worry," Bill Burke assured me. "Just tell them it was fifty years ago and our memories are a bit shaky."

What amazed me more that their memories was the courage and valor of these people who left their native homes and families at fifteen, sixteen, seventeen and eighteen years of age to travel thousands of miles to a strange land that was totally different from the one they left behind. "Could you imagine sending your sixteen year old granddaughter off on a journey like that?" I asked Denis Mulcahy, as we munched on grilled cheese and ham sandwiches. "I'd have a hard time letting go of my son," said Denis. "And he's forty."

The other facet that struck me was the love they all still hold for Ireland, despite the fact that they haven't lived there in fifty, sixty, seventy, even eighty years, and despite the fact that it is a very changed country from the one they left. And even though many of them were forced to leave because of extreme poverty, nobody resented the prosperity their homeland is enjoying today. "I'm delighted for them," I heard over and over again.

They wondered if families missed them after they left, and I wondered how they could not have. I thought of all the parents who said goodbye to sons and daughters, some never to see them again; and of a countryside bled of its people. Their hearts must have broken I was sure, and Ireland's should have been, I was certain.

"Do you think anyone will be interested?" Martin O'Malley seemed dubious. "Absolutely," I assured him.

I want to thank everyone who participated; for sharing your memories and your moments; for contributing pictures and mementos; for your patience and your hospitality.

A story does not need to have an elaborate plot, intricate language or sophisticated vocabulary. A story should simply come from the heart. And all of these memoirs come from the hearts of the people who lived them.

I hope you enjoy reading these tales as much as we have enjoyed telling them.

So, Jimmy, when did you come . . .

Jimmy Clarke, 1927

I came in 1927 when I was twenty years of age with a neighbor of ours who was home on vacation. My father paid for my passage and I had a girlfriend there at the time, but I didn't have the fare to bring her with me. She married someone else after I left. The ship was full of Irish leaving for the first time. I was sick for part of the journey but eventually settled down and enjoyed it. Tommie Hardiman who was a brother of the neighbor I was with came to the dock to meet us. I can't remember the name of the boat, but they took me off it down there on 58th or 60th Street and I went to stay with another neighbor of ours from home, Michael Hobbits, on 97th Street between Park and Madison in St. Francis de Sales Parish.

I was born in County Galway in the village of Castlenancy on July 23, 1906, to Charles Clarke and Margaret (nee Coen). Castlenancy is in the Parish of Mullagh, about seven miles from the town of Loughrea. There were only seven houses in the village and I was one of thirteen children; there was one girl and five boys before me and three boys and three girls after me. What were we all going to do in Ireland? Someone had to move. We always had to work hard on the farm, doing the tillage, making the hay. Then every now and then we'd bring the cattle to the fair in Ballinasloe, while the women did the shopping. We'd travel on the horse and trap, or the sidecar. That was the only way we had of traveling—or the bicycle. But, there were nine boys. What were we all going to do on a small farm? Back then you had to serve your time at something to get a decent job, but then you had to pay for that and we didn't have the money. Those days are over now in Ireland, Thank God. It's changed a lot over there, and sometimes I think too much. Ireland won't be Ireland after another while.

So I was the first to go and another brother came along the following year. The rest of them all stayed at home, which was unusual for the time, as most of our neighbors would have emigrated. Four of my brothers married locally and four of my sisters also married in Ireland. My oldest brother, John, was in the old IRA until 1923 when he became a guard and moved to Roscommon. Another brother had been arrested in 1921, as they had suspected he was in the IRA and he spent a year in prison in the Curragh. Upon being released he also became a guard in Cork City. He was the one who took me to Cobh the day I left.

Jimmy & Mae on their wedding day, January 8, 1933

My first job in America was in an apartment building down there on the East Side where I worked as an elevator operator. The best part about it was meeting all those nice Irish girls who worked for the rich families. Then, in 1933, I became a citizen and was able to take my first examination for the Transit Authority. In 1934 I passed the test and started working on the Independent subway lines, operating the trains. Back then there were three transit companies: the Independent, the IRT, and the BMT. Now they're all the one*. I was with the Independent anyhow until I retired in 1971.

I got married in 1933 to a girl I met through Mrs. Hobbits' aunt. She was Mary Treacy from Loughrea, not far from me at home, who had come out to her aunt, one of the seven Daly sisters from County Galway. I had gone up to visit them one night and I met Mae anyhow and I guess we fell in love. We started off on 78th Street and Third Avenue and eventually settled in 2534 Eastchester Road in the Parish of the Holy Rosary.

I remember the Great Depression. I can still see people sleeping out in Central Park, cold and hungry because they had no place else to go. I remember them shining shoes and selling apples and flowers on the side of the street to try and make a living. I was lucky, I suppose, because I was always working and I always had some place to live. I didn't make much money, but I always worked. I also remember the transit strike of sixty-six, but I was on vacation those ten days in January, and didn't really take an active part in it at all. They'd be calling me up on the phone to go down to the picket line and my wife would tell them I was not home. Mike Quill, our union leader and a Kerry native, was a great man and a great speaker and organizer. He did a great job for us, getting us more money I suppose and extra vacation days and social security and what have you.

Shortly after I arrived, I started playing hurling for Galway. That time we were out in Celtic Park in Sunnyside, Queens. That was a beautiful park with a beautiful stand and all. It wasn't until 1929 that we came up to Gaelic Park when John Kerry O'Donnell, P.J. Grimes and a man called Snow took it over. It was called Croke Park at first after the one at home, but Croke Park in Dublin didn't sell liquor so they had to change the name if they wanted to do so here. Not that they could legally sell it that time because of Prohibition. People went to speakeasies, which were in and around the same places that you'd have pubs today. You'd have to knock on a big iron door and they'd look out and if they knew you, they'd let you in. That went on until 1932 when President Roosevelt's reign ended.

They always had the hooch at Gaelic Park. People would make the poitín at home in the bathtub and sell it for a dollar a pint. Sometimes after a game they'd give the lads a shot of the stuff and it would nearly kill them. Not that I drank at the time, mind you. I never took a drink until I was forty years of age, but I'd see all the boys throwing back the shots in the bathroom. You couldn't be caught doing it, you know, or you could be arrested. They used bring it to the dance halls too. No, I never tasted a drink until someone spiked my ginger ale after a hurling match, and that was that. Now I love an odd scotch and soda, weak on the scotch, mind.

Gaelic Park was a great place, great for meeting people, watching the games, having a dance or two. You know when we came over here first, we thought America was the most marvelous place altogether. I had never even seen a bathroom until I came here. None of us had. And all the Irish were together back then, there was no such thing as being divided by counties, except on the playing field. We were all the one other than that.

I go home all the time, although I was here twenty-seven years before I went at all. On my first trip back with my four children in 1954, I saw great changes, but nothing like there is now. I was there two years ago for my brother's 100th birthday party. I always stay in Joe Fahy's Bed and Breakfast in Loughrea. Pat was the third of the boys that made the 100, and I'll be the fourth if I last until July. I wonder if that's a record, four out of a family of thirteen to reach a hundred years of age. When I was back in 2001 there were seven of us over ninety. The eldest one died at 94 and there are three more still alive. One of them is coming over for my party in Rory Dolan's in July, along with about twenty of my nieces and nephews. And to think that my wife's family didn't want her to marry me because I had consumption at the time and they thought I was dying. They thought I wouldn't last long at all.

Even my mother lived to be a 101. She died in an automobile accident on her way to a poker game. She had just bought two pairs of shoes at the local store and they were strewn along the side of the road after the crash. We were all mad about cards at home and played them all our lives. I still do. I love a game of twenty-five and still play here in Shea's for the Superbowl box every year. The game I used to play though was called Nine. It was like Twenty-Five except for there would be nine people sitting around the table and you'd have three partners. We used to play for fowl back then. There was a group of Irishmen who met in Central Park long ago for a card game, but they're all deceased now and that tradition died with them.

I wasn't into politics at all. I never even voted in Ireland, as I left two months after my twenty-first birthday. Cards and hurling was all I was mad about. I remember when Galway won their first hurling All-Ireland in 1923. I wasn't at the game, we didn't have the money that time, but I remember it well with the bonfires burning to welcome the team home. Jim Power and Mick Gervin were playing then, from the nearby parish of Tynagh, and Ig Harney. Galway didn't win again until 1980 and I cheered them on here in the Bronx. My own nephew, Iggy Clarke, who was an All-Star for the county in 1978, played great hurling for Galway – Father Iggy Clarke, in the Number Seven jersey, but, unfortunately, he didn't tog out for their second victory, due to injury. The game of hurling has changed a lot, though. It's much faster now, not as slow and as skillful as it was in my day.

I've been a member of the Galway Association here since 1930. We used to have the meetings in Bradley's Hotel and the Commodore. We were all over the place. I've never missed a Galway dance and I will be Guest of Honor this October at their 125th Anniversary. I was honored before, in their 100th anniversary year, at one of the dinners. They have two every year, you know. Anyhow, Bishop Casey was honored at the other one that year. He was a lovely man, a lovely singer; he made the party that night. He's a Kerry man I do believe, but we won't hold that against him. I'm glad everything has worked out well for him now. I wish him the best back in Ireland.

Jimmy with his mother on her 100th birthday, 1974

So that's it now. I never worked a day since I retired from the subway. All I do is make the dinner for my son, Brendan, every evening or we eat out regularly in Cornyn's Coach'n Four and Jimmy K's. And I'm here in Shea's every other Sunday for my Scotch and soda and to see the bartender, Timmy Cahalan. Timmy there is from the same parish as me at home. I went to school with his father and he was a great friend of my nephew, Iggy. Another great hurler was Timmy.

My wife died in 1979 from a heart attack, only a few months after my grandson was killed in an automobile accident. The death of my wife was sad, but that of my grandchild was tragic altogether. Mae and I had four children: Eileen is married to a Clare man and lives on Long Island; the twins, Brendan and Kevin, are still bachelors and my other son, James, lives up in Rochester. I have four wonderful grandchildren and nine great grandchildren.

I'll hardly go back to Ireland again. I'd hardly be able for it. They call me the Yank, surely. But, the thing to remember about them at home is that you have to be just the same as the rest of them. You'll get on fine if you buy them a drink and let them buy you a drink and leave it at that. You can't be seen to be better than them. They don't like that.

*the IRT, IND, and the BMT were merged in 1940

Interviewed at Shea's Emerald Bar,
Bedford Park, Bronx, New York;
February 26, 2006

At last! One hundred years!
Jimmy and children at birthday party in Rory Dolan's, July 23, 2006

Rose McGurk 1928

I came in 1928, I think, it should be in all my papers, but I think it was 1928 anyhow, on the Cameronia. I traveled on a train from Desertmartin, a neighboring village in County Derry, to Belfast where we picked up another train that took us to Cork. We stayed overnight in Cobh. There were so many going, there were four of us to a bed in the boarding house, and the landlady took us a cup of tea and a piece of toast into the bed the next morning. We were very lucky to get it. All the rooms were full up and we were the last ones to get in. The guesthouses were all closed with all the people traveling. Things were bad in the North back then, they were bad all over Ireland, I suppose, but we were coming from the North.

I come from Draperstown, County Derry, in the parish of Straw. It was a lovely place, nothing fancy, but we had a nice little house. There were ten of us altogether. We lived right in the country, out in the open, about two miles from the town. We used to go there once a week. We had two cows, churned our own butter that we brought to the town on fair day, and we grew our own vegetables. We used to tie up the corn and the lint. We had a lint field up on the mountain, you see. There wasn't so much trouble in our locality. It was mostly down in Cookstown and Maherafelt and that area. The Catholics didn't like the Protestants and the Protestants didn't like the Catholics. There was one Protestant fellow who liked me and he came to court me, but my father said if he came around again he'd cut his head off. My father was very strict about the Protestants, you understand. Then the boy went off to Canada and his parents sent a letter for me to come to the party, but my father interfered and wouldn't let me go. So he went to Canada and after many years he came down to New York where he located me in Brooklyn and I visited him at his home near the Bronx River Parkway. He married a nurse after, a Catholic nurse, so his mother must have been happy. Isn't life funny?

My aunt had sent me a ticket for America. I didn't want to come, but she sent the ticket, so I had to come. She had sent three tickets, but I was the only one who passed the medical examination. Another niece, who was her favorite, was turned down. She said it was diabetes, but she was not diabetic, it was her eyes. If you didn't have good eyes they wouldn't let you in; you had to have good eyesight, and good health.

Rose, aged 16, shortly after her arrival in Brooklyn

I came out first class because of my father. You know back in Ireland the way they were always fighting over cows? Your cow can't walk here, or can't walk there, or can't go someplace else. Well, my father had this cow and someone said she was eating their potatoes and my father got this lawyer who said that the cow was entitled to go wherever she wanted, to eat whatever she wanted. My father told the lawyer that I was going to America and he gave me a letter for the Captain of the Cameronia who let me travel first class. I was lucky all over, you see. My girlfriend used to come up and stay with me at night, a wee girl from Donegal, but she couldn't be caught there during the day. She died shortly after. I went to her funeral. I can't remember her name. I don't remember everything, you know. A couple of months later, my aunt demanded the money for the ticket, and I told her I never wanted it in the first place. But I gave her the hundred dollars anyhow, and I had luck with me all the way.

I went to an agency first for a job, but didn't find anything. Then I was out walking one night and I met this girl with a dog. I took a fancy to the dog and I asked her if I could walk with them. I told her I had no job, and she said come home with me and I'll get you a job. Her father was President of a bank, Kennedy was his name, and her mother had been to the agency the day before also looking for help, but they hadn't settled on anybody. So I went home with the girl that night, got hired straight away, and I stayed there until I got married. My job was to take care of the mother, dressing her for bed at night; she wore lovely silk nightgowns that I had to wash by hand and iron every day. I had to be so careful when I ironed them, and I put a fresh one on her every night.

Aunt Mary was mad at me for talking to strangers, but she got a job with the same lady later and she had four girls working for her by then. The daughter went off to Skidmore College and she was crazy about horses and she bought a big place up in Connecticut. She wasn't that interested in boyfriends or anything, but she was crazy about me and when times got bad and the mother had to let the other three go; she kept me on. I was lucky you see.

I must have been sixteen years old when I came, and I wasn't lonesome really because I was so active. Going to Church the first Sunday I met this girl, Helen, who was Polish, and she said to me I'm looking for a Catholic church and I said so am I. Then we met this man dressed head to toe in a white U.S. Navy uniform and a big white hat. He was a nice-looking man from Donegal and he worked in the Brooklyn Naval Yard. He showed us the way to the church and he gave us the address of his sister-in-law who lived nearby and invited us to visit her home that night at seven o'clock down in another part of Brooklyn. So Helen and I went to the bakery after Mass and bought a big bag of buns and went down to the sister-in-law's house that evening.

There was a whole bunch of people there and an accordion was being played and a fiddle and there were two fellows there from County Antrim and they walked Helen and I home. We didn't go out with them; they just took us home. One of them was called McCullough and he'd reddish hair. But talk about luck on that first Sunday. We often visited that woman's house after and remained friends with the man in the uniform. And Helen and I were the best of friends until she died a few years ago. I was at her funeral, and the church that we found that first Sunday, St. Cecilia's, was the one I got married in. Isn't life funny?

Then the Depression came. I can remember fellows knocking on the door of the house where I worked and do you know what they had on their feet for shoes? Burlap bags. I told them I couldn't help them that the lady was out. Of course, they'd tell me that I didn't know what it was not to have money, and I would say I certainly did. They were Irishmen who had walked miles and miles looking for work. They'd come down from Detroit and Boston. It was very bad. There was one fellow, a really nice looking Irishman who was looking for money and a job, and I couldn't help him. I told him that I wished I could help him but I couldn't. But I told him I'd say a prayer for him. He got a job on Staten Island later and he came to see me before he left. He told me I was one nice girl and always to stay that way and I never forgot that.

One night two men came and jumped off the roof of the house where I was working. When I opened the door the next day to let out the dog, there they were there dead on the ground. They had committed suicide. It was the Depression, you see. I remember when we used to go dancing and you couldn't take any money with you or it would be stolen. I used to put it in my shoe and sometimes pin the dollar bills to my bra. Nobody had any money back then. Nobody was working, you see.

We used to go dancing a lot, to Erin's Isle, and to this other place on Lincoln Road. And we'd go to the cafeteria for a cheese sandwich afterwards. That's all we could afford. That boy I met the first Sunday, McCullough, would call now and then and write, but we never went out. I wouldn't see him for weeks, even months, and then I'd bump into him at a dance and he'd walk me home and then nothing. Then I didn't hear from him in a long time and out of the blue two years later he wrote and said he had enough money saved to get married, buy a house and buy a bar and could he call to see me? He must have been waiting till he had some money, you see, to go courting a girl. I wrote him a note to say, yes, he could come to see me at my wedding the following week.

I married a fellow from near home, from County Tyrone. For a long time Helen and I had no boyfriends. Everyone we met was just not suitable. One night we were walking out from town, from the subway, and this one man we knew said he couldn't understand that we were not married. I said we can't find anyone who wants to get married. They all want to have sex, but they don't want to get married. So I said to him, "I'll tell you what to do. You invite a bunch of boys from Sheffield's over to meet us." Sheffield's was the milk company where all the Irish fellows used to work at the time. He said that Helen and I and Alice, my cousin, would have to cook the dinner. So he gave us some money to buy a roast beef and a leg of lamb and he gave us his house to cook it in. He then invited several fellows, single fellows, all good-looking from different parts of Ireland and we invited the girls and cooked the dinner. We sat them all at the table with one boy, one girl, one boy, one girl, and we didn't care if they knew one another or not.

When the dinner was all served and everyone had eaten, Helen and I decided to take someone up to dance. I walked across the room and asked this fellow and he said he had never danced a step in his life! Well I wanted the floor to open and swallow me up. I sat down. Then this big fellow stood up and said, "C'mon, I'll dance with you." And we did, we danced.

When it came time to go home, two other girls had their eye on this fellow that I had danced with and I had my eye on him too. When we got down to the street, this fellow that I liked said he was going to Brooklyn, and I said I was going to Brooklyn too. This other girl was trying to push me out, you see, but I went off home with him anyhow, and you know he only lived two blocks from my aunt. He asked for my number and said he would call, but explained that he worked nights in Sheffield's. A lot of the Irish fellows worked there when they came out from home first. They delivered milk, and they emptied the milk from a pump into the bottles, and then they sterilized the milk and boiled water in a big tub. He took me all around it later. They steamed the bottles, he told me. It had to be piping hot so the milk would keep, he said. Even though he worked the night shift, and wouldn't be off that much, I gave him my number anyway.

He called the following week and he said he'd be off for a couple of hours to go to church, so I met him after church and we had a cup of coffee. He never said anything about meeting me again, but during the week he called me and said do you want to do the same as we did last Sunday? I said alright but could we go to *Donegal Park after? Everybody back then went to Donegal Park; a place in Brooklyn called Donegal Park. No matter where you lived in the city you went to Donegal Park, an Irish park, where they played football, and everybody met. So we went to Donegal Park and do you know I married that boy? Edward McGurk was his name from County Tyrone, which wasn't too far from me at home, only about thirty miles.

He had worked in the coalmines in Scotland before he came out here. He had a brother in the cops and he brought Eddie out and another brother who died later from tuberculosis. We got married in April, I can't remember the year, right there in Brooklyn in the St. Cecilia's church where that man in the navy uniform showed us where to go that first Sunday. We had hardly any money and Helen cooked a leg of lamb and I cooked a ham and we took it over to my cousin's house and we sliced it up and that's the kind of wedding I had. The McCullough boy also from that first Sunday came and when he eventually opened his own bar in Rockaway, we went along to the opening night.

Eddie and I didn't have much money, but we had great times. We used to go on picnics; groups of us. One time we were up near Bridgeport, Connecticut and the bus driver asked if we knew who lived across this lake he was pointing to. We said no and he told us it was Helen Hayes, the actress. We swam over and there she was in this garden full of blueberries and she had a goat. She called me girlie and she asked me could I cook and I said I could. So my friend, Helen, made a blueberry pie and I made blueberry muffins. She invited the whole picnic party to join her; there was about twelve of us around a long table, and Helen Hayes served us and she had this old apron on her.

I had this other friend, Tessie, from Hungary and she taught me how to swim. She made a swimmer out of me, that girl. When I'd say I couldn't do something, she'd say, of course I could. She met one of the Chauffeurs on one of those trips we were on and she married him. And she died after, having a baby. She was very good to me. I mixed with all nationalities. That Tessie was from Hungary and she died after the baby and I missed her very much. Her family lived on 86th Street there on the East side. We used to go over to her aunt and she'd make Hungarian goulash, a sort of soup, a stew.

World War I wasn't long over when I came out, and the next thing the Second World War was upon us and Eddie was sent off to the army. He didn't let me work when we got married first, but I got a job in Montgomery Ward's department store once he was away. Then I got diphtheria, scarlet fever, and I was in bed for a long time and they wanted me to go to Ellis Island. That was where they sent you if you had a contagious disease, you see, and the neighbors were all mad for me to go there. And would you believe my luck, the doctor who came to see me from the Board of Health was from Belfast by the name of McGrath and he said to me, "No way are you going to Ellis Island, you're staying right here." He found this French woman who took care of me for a whole year until I got better and I always sent her a dress from the store every Christmas and every holiday until she died.

Eddie did his military service in Mississippi, a terrible place. There was all this red sand everywhere and terrible heat and the sand was full of bugs and it would eat your whole skin. When he came home after two years we had to put him in a bathtub with some sort of solution because his skin was all eaten up by the bugs. They used stick to his skin and get in under it too; nearly killed him; made him very cranky. I used bring him over to the Veteran's Hospital in the Bronx in a taxi to try and get him relief. Then he left Sheffield's and joined the Bank, the Federal Reserve, and went back to school night and day. He was always studying. He was very lucky too. He had this tailor, a Jewish man, who helped him, he loaned him money, and he had this Chinese man who pressed his shirts and he put up a Bond for him so as he could go to school. And then Eddie sponsored his wife and children to come over here. They all helped each other, you see. I went over to the party and all the Chinese people were sitting on the floor. They were so grateful to Eddie, you see. But you have to be nice to people. If you're nice to them; they'll be nice to you.

Rose (right) with niece, Jean McPeake, New Jersey, 1957

We started the Derry Society from nothing. A whole bunch of us came out together. Frank Daly was here and Laurence Hegarty, he was from near home and we used to get together on a Sunday night in one of the houses and drink tea and eat scone bread and talk about starting up. We'd talk about doing this and that. But we needed money so; finally, we decided to have a dance. The first one was two years after I came out, on the 16th, I can't remember when, I think it was March. Then my brother came and Barry Walsh came, and the McDaid's came. There were three of the McDaid's here. One of them was Kathleen and she died having her first baby. I went to her wedding and I went to her wake nearly in the same year. And the dance was the next night. Every year then we had a dance. But nearly all those people are gone now.

I belonged to the Tyrone Society too after I got married and we would march in the parade on March 17th. We used to go to the Tyrone dance too and the Donegal dance. All of the counties had dinner dances back then, just like they all had their own society, or association, too. I went to the Galway dance once, but I didn't care for it. There were all these fellows in big shoes; the floor would be jumping after them. Then one St. Patrick's Day Helen and I met these fellows from Fordham University at the parade. I was already married, but when they asked us where we were going that night, we told them to come to the Derry Dance and they did. And would you believe it, Helen married one of them. Isn't that something? Life is funny sometimes. Helen only died lately and her husband, the fellow we met that day, only died recently too. We were great friends.

Our Wedding Day

I want to tell you, I had two uncles who came here, John Boyle and James Boyle and they became builders on the Brooklyn Bridge. Then the Brooklyn Bridge collapsed. There was a big write up on the paper, and my aunt here still had a copy of it. About two hundred of them drowned, and one of my uncles, it was reported, held on to a branch on the side of the river, the Hudson River, but he must have got tired and let go, because he died anyhow.

About two hundred of them are buried in a section of a graveyard out on Long Island. I went to see it twice. Their names weren't put up individually or anything, or they weren't buried separately. They were buried in a group with no headstones. The names were put in a book and my husband and I went and looked up the book and located their grave. I sent a copy of the write-up to my father and I told him to keep it, that it was very precious, but he put it in the stack of turf outside the house and when I went home the first time it was gone. My mother must have burnt it in the fire with the turf. The Boyle brothers, one was seventeen, one was sixteen. One was James, and one was John, and they were my two uncles. My grandmother told me stories about them.

Times were harsh when they left. Donegal was a bad place. It was a very poor section of Ireland. The county is surrounded by water; and there's a lot of fishing there. Draperstown is not too far from Donegal. We used to go up for the day when we were younger. The school would have a tour and we'd bring sandwiches. We used to have the scone bread, and the potato bread. I didn't care for school much. I had a very cruel teacher called Bradley. She used to hit me with a big stick. I didn't care much for Derry City either. The people weren't friendly. Some parts of Ireland were very open and people would say, come on in and have a cup of tea. But in Derry they were very proud; they seemed to have a lot more money than others and they didn't mix.

I went home a lot, but it wasn't the same. People weren't as friendly as they used to be. And if you were tearing around, they'd be talking about you. Eddie and I traveled all over Ireland; it was very nice. We'd stay in farmhouse guesthouses and they'd give you breakfast and your dinner in the evening and sometimes there'd be music and we'd have dancing. I went to Galway and Mayo; Tipperary was nice too. One time we stayed in a hotel near Dublin Airport. We always had a good time. Eddie died from a heart attack about twenty years ago and that was the end of my good times.

I was glad in the end that I came to America. That aunt who was kind of mean sent the tickets. After I was here for a while she said to me, you never offered to pay me back and I said, you never asked me if I wanted to come in the first place. You sent me the ticket, I never asked for it. But I paid her anyway. Life is funny sometimes, isn't it?

* We cannot find evidence of a Donegal Park that was used for Gaelic games. There was a McGolrick Park in St. Cecilia's Parish in Brooklyn, called after a Monsignor McGolrick from County Donegal, and some games may have been played there.

Recorded at Schervier Nursing Care Center, Riverdale, New York; January 28, 2006

Frank Bergin, 1929

On June 10, 1929, my family and I boarded the S.S. Cedric, part of the White Star lines, at Cobh. We cruised into Boston harbor on Bunker Hill Day, June 17. I was only four and a half years old and at that young age a ship was hot stuff. All I can remember is playing on deck all the time. There were a lot of children on board and we all had a separate table and a special stewardess assigned to us. My father had a letter of introduction to a man in Boston whose obituary he read the day we arrived. Talk about planning! He bought a share in a cosmetic manufacturing business and it only lasted a few months, as the Stock Market crashed in October. We lost our house and he and his partner lost the business.

My father moved to Long Island City to two sisters who grew up near him in County Offaly. One of them had married an American, who was killed in World War I, and the other never married; she was a governess to a large Jewish family. They were like part of our family. We must have had some money because he bought another house, this time in Flatbush, Brooklyn, and we moved down to join him. Unfortunately, we also lost this house two years later, and moved into an apartment over a delicatessen. They were desperate times.

Dad finally got a job with William Archer who had drafted the New York State Workers' Compensation Law. Archer was the legal representative for various companies, but his most influential client was Patrick McGovern who was probably the wealthiest Irish man in this area. He was the principal contractor on the building of the City Water Tunnel Number Two that carried water from the Catskills right down here to Queens. Heavy construction like that involved a lot of injuries, and McGovern operated under the premise that no man who worked for him and got hurt would go without as long as he had anything.

Two other important clients were the Walsh Construction Company, who worked on the Queens-Midtown vehicular Tunnel, which I had the pleasure of walking through before it was officially opened, and George H. Flinn, who was the principal contractor on the Brooklyn-Battery Tunnel. My father traveled all over the east coast of this country taking care of people who had been injured on the job. I remember one time he took me with him on one of his visits to some place in eastern New York. He loaded the cab up with groceries. I must have been ten or eleven and we hauled all of these supplies up three flights of stairs in one of those tenements. These people had nothing, as there was no compensation that time for people who couldn't work. He brought me, not because he needed help, but because in his wisdom he wanted me to see how some people lived. And I've never forgotten that.

I remember a big open field in Flatbush where we used to watch football games back before Brooklyn College was built. The LIRR ran right through it down to the docks in Brooklyn Harbor. I remember this wasteland between the college and the tracks full of dug outs where men slept during the Depression. They were homeless and lived there in the ground. They had nowhere else to go. Sometimes my mother sent us out with pitchers of soup to them until she no longer had even enough for ourselves. These are little things that you never forget. The Depression was an international calamity. It affected everybody, even Ireland.

Dad came from a place called Fancroft on the Offaly/Tipperary border. In fact, my grandfather and his brother both had houses about fifty yards apart and one was in County Offaly and the other in County Tipperary. The estate also consisted of a grain mill, several out buildings and fourteen tenant cottages. In the book, The Great Irish Famine, by Canon J. O'Rourke written around 1880, it mentions Fancroft in the unabridged version. During the famine when the British were confiscating the food from the landed estates, the owners of Fancroft held out and wouldn't release the food declaring that it was needed for the people who lived in the area.

Although my father and grandfather would be regarded as coming from the elitist class, as had their ancestors for many generations before that, they were Irish and Catholic through and through. My grandfather sold his share of the property to his brother in 1903, I think, and bought a new home in Newcastle, County Dublin. Dad had attended the National School in Roscrea and ultimately went on to attend Mungret's College, a Jesuit boarding school in Limerick. He then studied law at the National University in Dublin, and according to himself, at twenty-one, he was the youngest person to be admitted to the Bar in Ireland up to his time.

He married Catherine Kavanagh in 1913, had two sons and, in 1917, decided to go to Australia to work at the Crown Law Office in Sydney. There he became friendly with a Dr. McAdams with whom he played cards every Friday night and whose assistant, Sister Kenny, developed a treatment for infantile paralysis. She was immortalized in a movie called after her with Rosalind Russell playing the title role. Dad's wife, Kitty died suddenly in 1921 from a heart attack. He was later floored with diphtheria and after a full recovery decided to return to Ireland with his two sons and a nursemaid.

Frank's passport photo, aged 4 years, 1929

He took the ship from Sidney and when it docked at Melbourne to pick up some passengers a young woman called Helen Victoria Hope came on board. She was born in 1891, one of five girls, and educated at the Loreto Convent in Melbourne before she subsequently studied nursing for a year in Hobart, Tasmania. The daughter of a dentist and a gentlewoman, according to their marriage certificate in 1880, she had lost her father, mother, and sister in the course of a year and had decided to try Europe for awhile. She was introduced to my father at a fancy dress party on board, where she'd been dressed up as the Australian flag and he a flagpole. By the time they reached the west coast of Africa they were engaged. A year later, in 1923, they were married at Our Lady of Victories Church in London. Helen Hope was my mother.

Upon his return Dad had joined the Free State Army, which had just been formed in Ireland after the Anglo-Irish Treaty, where he was appointed to the legal department. He took his basic army training at the Curragh; was assigned to Athlone in County Westmeath; and was eventually transferred to Collins Barracks in Cork where I was born in 1924. He was a commandant under John Hearne who was the Attorney General of the Irish Free State, and who later became my godfather. Hearne was the first Irish Ambassador appointed to the United States in 1950 and he came to see us at our house when we lived in Brooklyn. I remember once, at St. Rose of Lima, our local church in Brooklyn, my father had quite a nerve-wracking experience relating to his tenure in the Free State Army. He was an usher for the ten o'clock mass and one Sunday saw a man in one of the pews that he had court-martialed back in Ireland. The man recognized him too.

In Ireland, we lived on the Lower Road in Cork City. I remember going to St. Patrick's church and, after mass, going to a sweet shop called Hajji Beys — Hajji means a person who has made the pilgrimage to Mecca, he who made the hajj. I also remember my mother taking me on a picnic once out on Bantry Bay, in Glengarrif. When my wife and I went back years later we drove up and down every road in that area looking for Roches Hotel where I had enjoyed that memorable picnic on the grounds. But the girl in the store told me that it had been knocked down years before.

My mother loved Ireland, as her mother had been born there. Her father was Scottish. She didn't appreciate America until after the war when she realized what Europe had gone through and how America had helped them. She had strings of relatives all over the place and one family in particular had to flee Holland and escape on a boat to England when Hitler invaded. My sister, Mary Teresa was born in Cork in March 1926 and my younger sister, Helen Hope, was born there in August 1927.

There was a reduction in forces in the army in 1929 whereby my father received a comfortable settlement; so he packed up and brought us to America. Our maid, Mary, accompanied us with the understanding that she would stay under our employ for one year. That Christmas she paid a visit to her sister in Philadelphia from where she sent a telegram to my mother that stated, "Mrs. Bergin, I ain't coming back."

I attended the local elementary school, St. Jerome's, in Brooklyn and graduated from Bishop Laughlin High School, called after the first Bishop of Brooklyn. A few weeks after I got out, I was drafted into the army. Although I was eighteen the October of my final year at high school and eligible for service, they had to let me finish out the school year. I took my basic training in Fort Riley, Kansas, in the horse cavalry. Now up to this the only horses I had seen were the milkman's and that of a mounted policeman on parade. It was boring as hell. Upon completing basic training I was assigned to the 29th Recon Squadron and I never saw an army horse again. I had already been a member of the State Guards when I was in high school, which was full of old fogies and young kids. I'd had six months training with them so I knew that's what I wanted to do. I requested transfer to Infantry. At least I had some idea where the bullets came from, and was assigned to the 70th Infantry Division. Having spent some time in Oregon and Missouri for overseas preparation I left for Europe and arrived in Marseilles on December 1st, 1944. By Christmas Eve I was on the frontline.

Being in combat is hard to describe. It was scary as hell being down in those little foxholes that we dug out ourselves. Sometime we would be hunched down for hours on end watching the bullets dart by and seeing people pop off all around us. We were always on the move, following the German army, directed by the people above, whoever they were. Shortly before we had arrived the Battle of the Bulge had started in the French-Belgian sector. Our outfit was sent to Alsace to help quell the last outbreak of the Germans in what they called Operation Northwind. Our objective was to retake the town of Winger, which we did, but after suffering heavy casualties, both from the Germans and the cold. Many of our men were disabled by trench foot, often losing toes or most of their feet.

I was shot on March 4th, 1945. My outfit was approaching the German-French border and, after seventy days in combat, we were clearing the town of Stiring-Wendel, in sight of Saarbrucken. The bullet went right through my wrist and came out the other side as big as an egg. The shattered bone looked as if it had been hit by a hammer. I was quite an attraction to the local kids for some time. I spent two months in the hospital in Nice, on the Riviera, and four days after I returned to duty, the war ended. The departure of our train was delayed so as we could hear the announcement of the German's unconditional surrender.

Troops were sent home according to the number of points they had accumulated. The points were based on how many months they had been in service or in combat overseas, if they had been injured, if they had a wound or a medal, and so forth. I had gathered up only fifty points, and some of the guys who had gone overseas two years before me had about two hundred points. So, I had to wait a while. I was assigned to a signal outfit working on a machine much like a typewriter, which was used to transmit messages over wires. It was our job to salvage the Teletype wires, which were in danger of being destroyed, as the cables had been hung over trees during the war instead of between poles. I was on the Rheims to Paris line. Half of my hand was dead, however, so my typing was not that great.

I was given two weeks leave to be spent anywhere I chose, so I returned to Ireland for the first time in sixteen years. I stayed with an aunt in the little hamlet of Dalkey in South County Dublin and really went nowhere else—not to Fancroft, or Cork, or any of the places of my past. My aunt's husband, who had fought in the Boer War, was by then one of the top executives in the Irish Railway. Their house was called Rockmount, one of four in a row on the way up Killiney Hill where I spent my days walking and looking down on to its beautiful bay, the beauty of which they say is only surpassed by that of Naples.

In Germany with U.S. Army, July 1945

My first day back in France was cold, wet, and raw and I didn't want to go out in that lousy weather picking up those lousy wires. I told them my hand was paining me. The doctor asked me to place my hands behind my back, and then said, "Can you feel that?" I couldn't feel a thing and was surprised to discover that he had put a needle right through two fingers. He then asked me if I'd like to go home. I said, "I like how you're talking." We sailed back to the states on the USAH Wisteria, which we rechristened the USAH "Hysteria" after it broke down fifty miles out of New York. We wound up on Staten Island where I spent the next five months in Halloran General Hospital. After a four and a half hour operation to open the arm, I had to undergo four months of physiotherapy. My hand became somewhat serviceable again although I still have a loss of some sensation to this day. At this point I received a medical discharge. I don't remember if there was a hero's welcome for us when we arrived back in America; there was definitely one when I got home to Brooklyn.

As soon as I could, I went right into Fordham University to study business administration. I was twenty-two years old. I got my degree in

May, 1950, and the Korean War broke out in June. This time I enlisted into the army, but it turned out that I still wasn't a citizen. I had processed papers in 1935 under my father's name and had received temporary citizenship, but that seemingly had expired when I was eighteen and I didn't know. I'd entered the army and wasn't even a citizen. To think that I had been drafted in 1943 and had spent some time serving in the Second World War and I wasn't even considered a proper citizen. I had to file again and this Indian guy in my division sponsored me. I got my commission in June or July and then got my orders to report to Fort Benning, the infantry school in Georgia. That was infantry to the highest degree. It was a real spit and polish joint. Everything had to be shining.

With wife, Laurina, and daughter, Kathy, Mt. St. Mary's College, MD, 1974

I needed some sort of a refresher course, as I'd been out for four years, so I was assigned to basic training again in Fort Dix in New Jersey and then got orders to go overseas. But by this time, though, through certain machinations between my mother and my future mother-in-law who taught in our local school, I met my wife, Laurina O'Brien. We were all from the same parish, St. Jerome's in Brooklyn, and the two women nudged things into place and that was fine with me.

Laurina was a graduate of Good Counsel College in White Plains, New York, with a degree in chemistry and was then employed as a microchemist in Bell Laboratories. We began dating before I was called out in February and she sent me a St. Patrick's Day card. After that I decided I was going to get her, and she had the same feelings. In April I asked her to marry me, and she accepted. We set a date in October, but, in the meantime, I got my orders to go to Korea. In two weeks she organized the whole wedding. She did everything. She ordered the invitations and booked the photographers, caterers, and the church. We got married on August 8, 1951, in St. Michael's church in Cranford, New York and spent our honeymoon in Vermont.

Two weeks later, when I called home and told my parents to set two extra places at the table, my father informed me that they'd received a telephone call from the army to say that I wasn't going to Korea after all, but back to Fort Dix. All of my stuff was in Washington State ready to be shipped out. Apparently, my medical records had caught up with me and I had the option of returning to civilian life, which I refused. I had to go before the Medical Board and they asked me to sign a request for retention on active duty, so I signed it. As I result I got to stay in Fort Dix for the next two years and could go home every weekend. I came out of the army again in 1953, two years to the day of entering.

We settled in New Jersey where my business career began with Blue Cross and Blue Shield, the medical insurance crowd, where I was Assistant Claims Manager. From there I moved on to Forbes magazine as Fulfillment Manager reporting to two Executives who didn't seem to like each other very well. After two and half years I was fired. I would have fired me too, if I had been my boss. A dispute arose between my two superiors, who were always fighting with one another and I didn't handle things properly. It was just stupidity. After that settled, I became an office manager for the Beecham Group. I held a lot of responsibility but no authority. There was too much in the way of politics, which I didn't like, and someone suggested I try the insurance world. So I did and have been in that business ever since 1967. I also sold mutual bonds on a part-time basis, and only gave that up recently. Now I am a licensed real estate broker and I sell real estate in Florida.

The Irish Business Organization (IBO) was started in 1972 with twenty fellows who used to meet for lunch once a month, all Irish, and they first formed the Irish Insurance Organization, which then became the IBO. I didn't join until 1977 and still have the original papers. It had been quite informal prior to that and then they decided to semi-formalize it and asked my buddy, Leo O'Dowd, and I to join. We were member numbers 15 and 16. We were also president for one year each. The meetings initially were held in O'Lunney's on Second Avenue, then we moved to the 140 Club down on Fulton Street, before moving up to the Old Stand on Third Avenue. That was a great place; the people there were very good to us. John Lyons and Paul Donohue were two great bartenders. I traveled over to Ireland to John's wedding in Athlone. Then the president at the time changed the venue without consulting any of the members and moved us to The Shelbourne Hotel. Nowadays we move around all the time, but I was very disappointed to leave the Old Stand.

It was the uniqueness of the IBO that attracted me at first. To be a member one had to be Irish born and conduct business in the metropolitan area. Discussions on politics and religion were forbidden. Then it started to change, as we became too liberal with whom we let in. The members no longer had to have been born in Ireland and people were joining just to see what they could get out of it. I hadn't missed a meeting for fifteen years, not even when my wife died, but then I disassociated myself from them for a while. However, I like the tenure of it now and I've been slowly edging my way back in. I am an Honorary Life Member and for several years I was the only Life Member. If you ever read the Irish Echo you will notice regular letters from a John Rogers who was one of the founding members.

There are a lot of young people in the IBO now, which is good. I am hoping that this Kennedy McCain Bill is passed, which will enable many more to stay legally and succeed in this country. I attended a meeting in Woodside in St. Mary's Church last night with about nine hundred other people. There were a lot of speakers, including Senator Charles Schumer who was a huge asset, so let us hope that something gets done. What people forget about the immigrants is that they have the gumption to get up and leave their countries and do something about their lives. They are, for the most part, decent, hardworking people who should be given recognition for that. The number 7 train in Flushing is known as the "Orient Express" now. Sometimes I am the only white person traveling on it, but I think that's great. This is a great country for people to succeed in. Nobody cares where you come from, just what you can do. It is truly the land of opportunity, probably more so than any other country in the world.

I believe the war today was necessary if we were to avoid another world war. If we had taken positive action against the Germans back in the thirties, we would never have had World War II. Hitler could have been stopped by the French and the English for breaking their treaties. I think President Bush has goofed on a few things, but as far as this war is concerned, I think he's right. There is a very radical element in the

Islamic world that causes terrible damage. There are too many decent Muslims who are scarred by them. If America hadn't invaded Afghanistan and Iraq, we would have been heading towards World War Three.

My wife and I eventually made it to Ireland in 1987. I had always wanted to take her back, but she kept interrupting my plans by getting pregnant - six times - with Kathleen, Anita, Bob, Jim, Brendan and Monica. After our youngest graduated, we were able to go and it was absolutely delightful. We met lots of family and we visited Fancroft, and met its new owner, Bill Murray, who is in his late nineties now. He is distantly related to someone in the Bergin family through marriage and he ended up buying it from one of my distant cousins. I have been back several times since and always take him a bottle of Jack Daniels, as he likes the occasional drink, and he has told me a lot about the history of my family's home.

My father died in 1966 and had never returned to his homeland since the day he left. My mother died on January 12 of that same year. Laurina and I were blessed with our six children and eleven grandchildren, of whom she only knew four, as she died on New Year's Day in 1987. I subsequently lost my third son, Bob, to lung cancer in February 2001, when he was only forty-five years old. All of our children graduated from St. James Grammar School in Red Bank, New Jersey, from Red Bank Catholic High School, and from various colleges. Laurina also taught in the Union Beach, New Jersey, Adult School, to students who had never graduated from high school. She was absolutely in love with the work she was doing. And more than anything, I was and still am deeply in love with her. I was also particularly blessed with parents who taught me primarily how to cope with adversity and with success. They were both deeply, but unobtrusively religious and could have a good time with the best of them. I've been asked when I am going to stop working and my reply has always been, "When they put a shovel in my face." I've already made plans for my 100th birthday party in 2024.

Recorded at Sidetracks Bar & Restaurant,
Sunnyside, New York; February 18, 2006.
Hand written materials received from
Frank Bergin, June 2006

Joe and Rose Cunningham, 1929

Joe: I came to America in 1929 from the Parish of Crusheen, in County Clare. There was no other way over than by boat, but I don't remember the name of it. I was mystified that there was so much milk to drink and I couldn't figure out where they kept the cows. I looked all over that boat and still couldn't find them. Sure I knew nothing, I was only seventeen. It was like the first time my mother took me to Dublin when I was only nine years of age. It was the 4th of July and she bought me an ice cream on the corner of some street and I couldn't understand how they kept it so cold on such a hot day.

I had two brothers here and aunts and uncles and my parents had also been here from 1898 to 1902. They were married in New York and very shortly after them returning home, my sister was born. I came along much later, on April 11th, 1912, three days before the sinking of the Titanic. I was the sixth of seven children. My mother always wanted to come back here, but my father didn't. She was about the same age as DeValera, born in 1882 or something like that. Her parents had a lot of land, but the English government was running the show then and they warned her father that because he was not utilizing the farm, they would have to divide it up between five of the neighbors. It was eventually sold back to my brother, the only one who stayed at home.

I came to America because my parents wanted me to. That's the way it was, we did what we were told. My three sisters all became nuns and three out of the four boys emigrated. I started off in Mount Vernon and got a job as a clerk in a Daniel Reeves store up in Scarsdale. My brothers already worked with the same outfit. Reeves, also a native of Clare, was a protégé of James Butler, a Kilkenny man who came here in the 1880's and made a fortune in the grocery business. He got a horse and wagon and loaded it up with provisions and went around from house to house delivering the fare. When he had that route up and running, he handed it over to another Irish lad and bought another horse and wagon and developed another route. He kept doing that, building on the business, and eventually he opened a store and did the very same thing until he had opened a chain of them. Then four brothers from Clare, the Reeves, came over to work for him and eventually opened up a chain of their own of up to 800 stores.

After about a year I was let go because business was bad, but in reality it was because I was caught playing football with a rolled up apron when I should have been taking care of my three-wheeled wagon of foodstuffs. A man named McCaffrey from Cavan who started up the Mount Vernon American Irish Association, of which I soon became a member, offered me a job. And where was it only in one of the Butler's stores where he was a supervisor. So I was back selling groceries again. He kept me working all through the Depression though, even if it was only three days a week for $9. I was glad of it. Eventually they made me a Manager in the branch in Poughkeepsie. President Roosevelt's mother was one of my customers, Sarah Delano Roosevelt. Some day I am going to figure out how many Presidents I've lived here under.

I was also a member of The Knights of Columbus. It was set up by a man called McGibney to take care of the spiritual needs of the Catholics, along the same lines of the Masonic Lodge, which took care of the physical needs of the Masons. I joined the chapter up in Rye in 1933. It was great for me, as there was a bunch of youngsters there and we would meet up for social activities. We used to play cards on a Tuesday night and Matt, a colleague from Daniel Reeves, would come with us, a nice guy even though he was Russian and an atheist.

One night I had to go to the Mission in Rye first. It was being given that year by DeValera's stepbrother, a Father Wheelwright. DeValera's mother stayed here, you know, and she sent him home with her sister to be brought up in County Limerick. Anyhow she had this other son over here who became a priest. He died some time later when he was stung in the eye by a bee on his way to Philadelphia. Anyhow at the end of his Mass all of the congregation were going up on the altar to have their beads, statues, prayer books, what have you, blessed. That was the usual drill. On the way out I asked Matt, my Russian friend, how he liked it. I was hoping I had a convert here, you see. "It was alright," he said, "but that guy should be a salesman. Did you see the way they all rushed up to buy that junk?"

My brothers were in boarding houses when they came over first, but when I arrived we got an apartment along with another neighbor from home. One day he bought a little accordion. After a while my brother got word that my parents needed him at home to do up the house, and the neighbor talked my other brother into going out to Detroit to get a job in the automobile industry. It was the Depression, remember, and work was scarce here.

They left me all alone, and I only a young kid. When they were gone I discovered the accordion thrown on the bed. I had always loved music, so I picked it up one day and got someone to show me a couple of tunes, and then I took lessons from James Morrison, the great Sligo violinist. I saw the ad in The Irish Echo—music lessons a dollar an hour. He started me off with some theory and then gave me a few simple tunes, until I progressed and could learn anything I chose. Jim was the most beautiful person. It broke my heart when he died of cirrhosis of the liver when he was only fifty-three. Next year I am going back to Rivertown in County Sligo for the official opening of a music center called after him. Anyhow Denis McAuliffe from Kerry played in the halls then and when I'd come into the dance he'd wave me up to the stage and put an accordion in my lap. Then he'd go to the bar and leave me playing. If he had extra jobs, he'd pass them onto me until eventually he retired and left it all to me.

The Joe Cunningham Band played the New York circuit for sixty years. I didn't want to call it anything fancy. What's better than your own name? There were twenty-eight ballrooms in the area that time. During Prohibition there was nothing else to do, so these smart Irishmen opened up dancehalls, because the Irish love to dance. Sure there were speakeasies, always in the basement, and I often frequented them myself. It was in one in New Rochelle that I met the fiddle player, Michael Coleman, with another Sligo man by the name of White. Coleman played reels that nobody could touch. His most famous was "The Rose in the Heather." The two of them stuck out like a sore thumb up there and I got them to come down to the city and do a few gigs with me.

I played at the Al Smith Dinner around St. Patrick's Day every year, which that great New York Governor started to help the homeless in the Bowery. It is still one of the most prestigious annual events in the city to this day. It was on a very small scale then, and, after Smith died, Judge Goldstein ran it. I remember one year Paddy Sweeney, a celebrated violinist from Sligo, was playing with me. There was a blank card at every place ready to be filled out for a donation. After dinner Judge Goldstein addressed the audience and he said the beer was green, the cabbage was green, and the money was green, but the corned beef was kosher.

The Rose in the Heather – Our Wedding Day 1948

I often had three, four, or five playing with me and one time there were as many as twelve or fourteen. I got them all from the union, the 802, the musician's union. You couldn't work unless you were in the union. If a band came over from Ireland and took over your spot, you still had to get paid. Dermot O'Brien came out one time and they had to pay my band as well as his. What else could you do? It was our livelihood they were infringing upon.

I opened the Jaeger House on September 29, 1953. There were four of us and we got $120 for the night. A Dublin man, Harry McGurk, had leased the space down there on 86th Street and started up the ballroom along with two Sligo men. I was playing steady in this bar, The All Ireland, on Third Avenue and 76th Street, at the time and Harry wanted me to take three nights in the Jaeger House, as he initially only intended trying it out for three week-ends. But I would have had to quit a steady job and who knew if anyone was going to come to this new place? It was very good the first night, even better the second, and the third was phenomenal altogether. Soon all the bands in town wanted to play there. I knew Ruthie Morrissey well; she was a lot of fun. She was in the Navy and she was a dancer at first, and when she came back from the service Mickey Carton started her off singing.

My band were playing at a sweet sixteen up in the Catskill Mountains one time, in Mary Carolan's, and she told us how her daughter had heard this great song at a party and she wanted me to hear it. What was it? Only "Lovely Leitrim." This fellow, a New York policeman, had written it to the air of "The Moon behind the Hill." A few years later he was sitting in a bar on Third Avenue and these guys broke into the place, took his gun out of his pocket and shot him dead.

Then this fellow from Drumkeerin in County Leitrim, a teacher up in Boston, was interested in recording a song from every county in Ireland. He heard about "Lovely Leitrim" and came down to Carolan's to record it. But the machine went up in flames after four verses and that was all you heard of it for years. I often played it with Mary, but when she heard that Ruthie sang it one night, she was spitting fire. Mary was a great fiddle player though, but she only played Irish music, like Coleman and Sweeney, so she was no good to me. I only took them to places that were strictly Irish. Mickey Carton and I catered to the American audience too; we played the same circuit for forty years.

One night I was playing at this dance in the Carmelite Hall and someone gave me five dollars to play some American music and after a while this girl came up and asked me for "The Stack of Barley." She was just beautiful. I followed her with my eyes for the whole rest of the night, but I didn't know anyone she talked to. A couple of weeks later I went to Mass in Our Lady of Good Counsel Church at 90th Street and Third Avenue. I was a little late and there were no seats so I was ushered all the way up to the top. When I sat down, who was in front of me only that same girl? During the Offertory, she turned around to ask her brother for money, but he had moved up to give me his seat. "Do you have any money?" She looked straight into my eyes. That was fifty-seven years ago and she's still asking me for money.

By this time I was doing well in the music industry and I had spent some time as a driver with Cushman's Bakery on their Rockland route. There was no Tappan Zee Bridge back then and I would have to take the ferry from Tarrytown to Nanuet. At my last stop my last customer, a lovely lady, always brought me in for tea and a slice of Cushman's cake and one day she asked me if I liked my job. I told her I didn't mind it except for the pay, I was only getting $30 a week by then. She arranged for me to get into the Metropolitan Life Insurance where her husband worked and I ended up staying there for thirty-seven years. I started off as an elevator operator, but went back to school in the Bronx and qualified as an electrician. I was now ready to take a wife.

My mother always said, "Never marry until you have security, never bring a girl into misery." She always gave great advice. I would have met beautiful girls, but as soon as they showed interest, I looked the other way. I didn't have anything to offer them, when I didn't have a secure job. I was playing at a house party up in Rye one time and I walked a girl home. The moon was shining through the trees there on Purchase Street and we had to walk a long while and I carrying a heavy accordion. Anyhow next thing she started saying the rosary and I became mildly offended. "Are you afraid of me," I asked her, but she never answered. She just kept on praying. Twenty-five years later I was driving from Limerick to Ennis and four girls waved me down on the road for a lift. Next thing they started saying the rosary with the one beside me calling it out and the three in the back making the responses. I asked them why they were doing that, thinking again that I had scared them in some way, and they said it would save them the time before they went to bed. I figured that was what my companion in Rye had been doing all those years ago too. I had waited twenty-five years for the answer to that one.

Anyhow after two dates with Rose I knew that if I ever had children I wanted her to be the mother of them. What a mother she was. Every night when I returned home from a gig, she would be kneeling by one of their beds saying the Rosary with them. I always credit that for how well they turned out, because none of them ever got into trouble. That and all the prayers my three sisters, the nuns, would have said for us.

My two eldest sons run their own band now, The Cunningham Brothers. I taught them the music and to stick to their own name. I gave my other son six years of accordion lessons and nothing happened! But he has a great job now on Wall Street. There's only two higher than him. He was always a bit different. The others all worked in this butcher shop on Fordham Road when they were in High School. Cathy started off first, and then Joseph used to deliver the orders, then Jimmy. When John's turn was coming up I told him it was time to go into the butchers now, as that was where his brothers did their growing up. He squinted up his eyes at me and said, "I'll grow up somewhere else!"

Cathy now teaches in The Business School at Fordham University. So they're all doing well. We did lose a beautiful daughter to breast cancer twelve years ago. Her name was Mary and she left three lovely children. That was devastating for us. I thought we would never get over it, but we have to accept the will of God and He blessed us with fourteen wonderful grandchildren, so we have to be grateful for that.

Rose and I got married on Park Avenue & 84th Street, in St. Ignatius of Loyola Church. Twenty-five years later the children brought us there for an anniversary Mass. After it was over Rose nudged me and whispered, "That was the Mass for the Dead." It seems that the Priest thought it was the anniversary of our death! But that didn't matter. We are very devout and Mass is still Mass regardless of the intention. We attend the five o'clock every Saturday evening up there in St. Barnabas. But isn't it funny that we met at a Jesuit church, married there and since then three of our five children graduated from Jesuit institutions, Fordham Prep and Fordham University, and seven of our grandchildren attended Jesuit Colleges: two in Georgetown; three in Maryland; and two in Fordham. Without that chance meeting with Rose my life would have been a different story altogether.

Our first home was in 1575 McCombs Road in the Bronx, but they threw us out during the construction of the Cross Bronx Expressway, as they had to tear the building down. They gave us no compensation or nothing, just notice to get out. As Rose says, they literally told us to take our coats and run. Then we moved on to 2382 Webster Avenue, and we are now on Bronx River Road, so we've spent most of our married life in or around the Bronx.

It was playing the music though that acclimated me to this country and I would never leave it after that. I made my own happiness. What I had missed about Ireland at first was the companionship and the camaraderie of home. I had nobody to talk to. I had nothing in common with anyone here. I was used to the big family atmosphere in Ireland. The families were so huge that time. I knew a fellow who was one of twenty-two. They had to try and build up the population after the Famine. The bigger ones were often sent out to aunts and uncles and grandparents to live. That's why my sisters became nuns, I'd say, for somewhere to stay. I remember the one room National School, with girls on one side and boys on the other and we each had to bring a sod of turf to keep the fire going. There was a night school in Crusheen one time, now this is going back sixty years, and in it was a young boy who had been born here and then taken back by his mother, like DeValera. He had been to school in the States and he kept interrupting the class because he was smarter than the rest of them, I suppose. One time the teacher got fed up with him and asked him to leave. "No," said the boy, "I won't go until my turf is burnt."

I remember DeValera running for election. He was campaigning in Cooraclare and there was a mob there and the local guards were trying to keep people back shouting, "Don't you know he wants liberty?" That was a big joke around our place for a long time. Another time I saw him give a speech in Ennis just after his release from prison where he had been interned under the Public Safety Act of 1923. He got up on the very same podium where he had been arrested ten months previously and proceeded, "As I was saying before I was rudely interrupted." I can also remember being out in the yard one day when someone passed by roaring, "Collins was shot." I can hear that today. Of course, we were delighted because we were all Republicans. We didn't know any better then. I've changed my mind since. Collins was a great man. He would have straightened out the North if he had lived. But DeValera didn't know any better. He should have gone to England with him.

We always had a place to go home to, which was great. My brother used to see people all the time coming back from America, passing up the lane to visit their birthplace and looking in over a gap in the hedge at a run-down, derelict, old house. Their cries, he said, could be heard all over the valley. It would break his heart, and he promised that none of his family would ever have to do that. And we didn't. We always looked after him too, sending money back, and I looked after his wife until she died twelve years ago. But they all have money there now. They're all doing great. Two of his grandchildren play the fiddle and accordion and I sent one of them my accordion when I was finished with it. It was worth about two thousand dollars. He was delighted.

People don't seem to dance now as much as they used to. We could all dance back then. There was a McKenna fellow here from Kerry and he had dancing schools all over the area. He wasn't a great dancer himself, but he was a great teacher. Tommy Hill was another dancer and a teacher. Then there was Jimmy Cronin, and he was a beautiful dancer, but he wasn't a good teacher. Danny O'Donnell from Donegal, not the young kid they have now, the original Danny, was a beautiful fiddle player. He and his brother worked on the construction of the George Washington Bridge and their big Irish coppers would be weighing down their pockets until they wore through and dropped into the foundation. They say that's what's holding up the Bridge to this day—Donegal pennies. He came from a family of twenty-two and when his father got married his grandfather gave him a strip of a mountain in Dungloe and said, take this and raise your family. And he did. A lot of them went to Scotland and two of his sisters became nuns out in Cleveland.

Anyhow I was playing at a wedding in Bayonne one time and this man came up to the stage with his fiddle and asked could he play with us. I said fine. It turned out to be Danny and boy what a player he was. We played a lot of gigs together after that and he even moved in with us to our six-room apartment. One night we were practicing and my

The Joe Cunningham Band, Rockaway Beach

son, Joey, who was only three, started swaying to the music. Look, Danny pointed at him, he's got rhythm already. And he has it to this day. He's the one who knows what to play that the people will dance to. He's a genius at that. The floor is always full when he's playing, always full. But Danny O'Donnell was the first to notice it. Danny won the All-Ireland fiddle championship at the first Comhaltas Ceoltóirí Eireann in Dublin in 1951 and always carried the medal around in his pocket, but never talked about it, no, never bragged about it. He left after two years to go to San Francisco, but said he was stopping off in Cleveland to see his sisters, as they were leaving the nuns. But where were they going, only into an enclosed cloistered order?

Another time I was playing in Germantown, Pennsylvania and a guy came in late, walked straight up to the stage and requested that we play 'Kevin Barry." I told him we'd already done it and we had a policy to only sing a song once in the night. He came up three or four more times almost demanding that we play it and each time I refused. After another while he was waltzing past the band stand with a lovely young lady in his arms and without saying a word he just flipped back the end of his jacket and what was strapped around his waist only a gun. Needless to say I sang the song. I'd say he was harmless enough though; he was probably just a young cop on his way home from work. It just shows you though how they loved the Irish music back then, even the Americans; they wanted it that bad.

I played at all the Irish weddings over here. One time I was in Leitrim visiting some of Rose's people, and I went into a neighbor's house and there was a picture of me up on the piano playing at one of the daughter's weddings. I played in Gaelic Park on a Sunday afternoon when the ball games were over, played for a year and a half straight, on a contract, and then off and on when there'd be fundraisers. All the halls were the same to me. All the Hibernian halls, the hotels, the Knights of Columbus, were all the same. I never got tired playing though, as it was only for four hours at a stretch. It was the music that raised our children; that put them all through college.

I opened the City Center ballroom too, a couple of years after the Jaeger House. That went over big too. The Kerry man who was married to Carmel Quinn was running it and when another ballroom around the corner closed down soon after, he took their band, so he didn't really need me full-time. Carmel sang with me a few times, as she did with Tom O'Duffy, a musician from Derry who drove the buses here. He stopped the bus one day and gave out to these people who were flying the Union Jack and told them to replace it with the Stars and Stripes. His brother Michael was a well-known singer at home and one time he was going to be on the BBC and Tom asked a Protestant neighbor if he could go in and listen to it. "You can," she said, "but I won't be here." She'd let him in all right, but she wouldn't stay with him, you see, because he was a Catholic.

Why did they allow those marches in Dublin last weekend? It's such a sensitive time trying to bring about peace. They shouldn't have let the Loyalists march down South. Why didn't they have it up in Belfast first and see how they'd react? Do you think they did it on purpose to upset the apple cart? Look at this country, it used to welcome everyone with open arms; Catholic, Protestant, we loved them all. The war in Iraq is disgusting. Everybody used to love this country, but when President Bush said, "If you're not with me, you're against me," he lost a lot of friends. His rating is down terrible, you know? He's stopping in Clare next week again, I see, to refuel, they'll probably be out protesting against him again. But I don't like that either, I don't like to see Ireland against America. I don't like to see them fighting this country.

I don't know if I'm glad or not that I came to America; I don't know any different. I don't know what it would have been like if I'd stayed in Ireland. How would my life have turned out? As Kennedy said the day he was in Wexford pointing over at a nearby factory, if my ancestors hadn't left I'd be working over there.

There were hard times in Ireland. The best politician they had was Parnell. It took him a long time to get up there, but he went down fast. I didn't know anything about Irish history when I came here. Then I used to meet up with some group in a hotel in Manhattan. There was a Kerry professor who used to teach history, O'Leary, I think, and that was the first time I heard about Kitty O'Shea. I'm reading a great book about Commodore John Barry. If you ever get a chance, though, talk to old people. That's where you learn history, not from books. My grandfather was born in the 1820's and he lived until he was ninety. I knew him well. I was at his funeral. If only I had the sense then to ask him how he survived the Famine, but I never did.

I remember the Civil War. My cousins from Gort, the Loughnane brothers, were murdered. They were in one corner and the Black and Tans in the other. One of them heard one of the Tans make a nasty remark about the Irish and he went over and hit him in the face. Then he had to run and his brother with him, and some time after they found them in a swamp, burned, with their legs sticking up. They were my cousins. Shenaglis, was the village.

Their house was right across the street from the church where Bishop Casey is going to live now. I used to go over to visit them when I was only eight or nine years old. Mrs. Harte from our village whose husband was on the run, would give me a mug of milk and a cut of bread, and she'd put a note in my shoe. I'd be shaking passing the barracks. I was going another night for a can of spring water from the well and I heard these steps coming after me. When I turned around I saw a man in a trench coat. I knew he was Republican because they always wore a trench coat, and he asked me were there any Republicans around and I said sure. They nearly killed me at home, as he could've been a Free State spy for all I knew. Everyone around us were Republican, rural areas were more so than the cities.

Paddy Killoran, the great fiddler, told me he did the same thing, carrying messages, and he'd be riding a donkey. Do you know where they hid the notes? They hid them in the donkey's ear. I guess everybody did something. There were hard times. All those beautiful buildings in Ireland that the English built, but the poor peasants did the labor and they didn't get paid. Bacon and cabbage was our staple and potatoes. We also ate the fat and now we're told that causes cholesterol. Do you know what I think? It was all the oatmeal we ate. We called it stirabout. And we walked a lot. I think that balanced it out.

The doctor tells me walk, walk, walk, but I never get there. We don't drink; it's not good. We have enough of trouble walking when we're sober. I used to take a drink, but I don't anymore, because I could get used to it and I don't want to get used to it. I remember going to a lunch wagon out in Brooklyn with my two uncles when I came over first, and they were drinking root beer. I drank some and thought I'd broken my pledge. I still have 20/20 vision and I still drive. I had two cataracts removed two years ago when I was 92. I taught myself how to type, but the mind skips now and then. Nevertheless, I have built my speed up to twelve words a minute with sometimes no mistakes. I have taken some computer courses in the Aisling Irish Community Center and I like to stay in touch with people through E-mail. I check in on the Irish newspapers every morning over the internet and listen to the RTE news. I like to keep up with everything so as my brain won't go soft. I am also a member of the Ancient Order of Hibernians and I am a district leader and County Committee Chairman for the Yonkers Democratic Party.

When I retired at sixty-five, I didn't know what to do and the nest egg started to dwindle fast, let me tell you. Six years later I started up my own business as a chauffeur and companion to the elderly. I ferried around senior citizens, some younger than myself, in my 1985 Buick Skylark, taking them to the supermarket or to a doctor's appointment. I had one regular client whom I drove to her weekly session in a beauty salon in Eastchester. When necessary, I would even cook and do their shopping for them. It was a great outlet for me and brought in a nice income too. Now I only have Rose to carry about.

One of the best insurance policies for a good marriage is to marry into your Religion. That is the best way because at least you'd be together on something. I wouldn't advise against getting married; you don't need to when you're young, it's when you get old that you need somebody. It's too bad that there are so many good people of both genders and they never meet, they never meet. I think that's sad. I cook dinner for Rose every night, that way she'll never leave me. I said that jokingly to a woman in a shop in Eastchester one day and she looked at me blankly and snarled, "Where the hell would she go?" I make a lovely soup and I have a great recipe for chicken and fish. I place the filet in a little water in a baking dish with tin foil over it and bake it until it comes out soft the way Rose likes it. She'll never leave home after that she tells me. But, her memory isn't too good anymore, and that's a pity.

Rose: I came from a family of eleven in Drumkeerin, County Leitrim. Nobody stayed home that time. As soon as we could move, we left. Everybody in the towns left when they reached a certain age. My mother had come here when she was twelve years of age to her people up in Troy, New York. She went to school there for a while until she was of the age to work. Then she went home one time on a visit and met my father. He lived about twelve miles away in the parish of Creevalea. It was a long walk to look for love I used to think. His parents were in the market business; they would bring their produce from the farm – eggs, butter, potatoes, everything you could eat – and sell it once a week in the town. And that's where he met my mother. Her people here were very generous and as soon as they wrote for one of us, we'd come. Not that we were that poor or anything, because we always had food from the farm. My father would kill a pig and someone would come out from the town and preserve it for them for the winter so that we always had meat.

Anyhow, when I was sixteen my brother, Tommy, came home from New York and I had a great time tearing around the country with him. I had my hay day when Tommy came home. He bought me a bicycle before he left. It was 1932 and my cousin, Woodford, was home from Canada at the same time for the Eucharistic Congress. His family had left Ireland when he was a baby, and had a thriving grocery store over there. He also had a ranch with horses and a huge apple orchard; he was into everything. He was about the same age as Joe is now and he asked me if I'd like to go back with him. Tommy offered the money for the fare, so it was decided that I would accompany Woodford back to his home on 623 Richmond Street, London, Ontario. It was about 150 miles from that other big city, Toronto.

I had to go to school because I was too young to work. I took French and the Latin verb and math at St. Angela's College in London, Ontario, but I forget all that now. I had more schooling than I had brains; I can surely confess to that now. I had liked school back in Ireland, mainly because of who was there. Master McLaughlin was our teacher and he was a very good man. He had his own children that used to go there too, to our school. You see some of the teachers used to abuse the pupils, but I don't think that he ever hit anyone. He was a very, very nice man. And if you were anyway bright the teacher liked you. Because when the Inspector came they used to put the knowledgeable kids in the front row. The Inspector didn't know that. And the ones that didn't know so much had to go in the back. It was from the Master too that we learnt all of our Irish. My grandmother was from Drumshambo, the back of the cow in Gaelic, and I spent more time there than I did in Drumkeerin. Ah! We had a good home and we left it!

It was my dream to be a nurse, but I had to wait until I was eighteen. In the meantime, I came down to New York to visit Tommy and my dreams took another path. I decided there and then that this is where I wanted to be and so I stayed. I became a waitress at Schraffts restaurant and made some good money. The tips weren't great that time; you'd be lucky to get a dollar, but we had great fun and I made a lot of friends. I had a lot of good friends in Canada too, but they're probably all gone now. I went home on a visit one time and brought a bunch of my brothers and sisters back with me and then I met Joe and had hardly any time to spend with them. Joe was very solid; I knew that from the word go. Sure he was away a lot with the music, but it was our income. I would have been a spoilt cat if I had complained.

Interviewed at their home on Bronx River Road,
New York; March 3, 2006

The Irish Music and Social Club
of Greater N.Y. Inc. March 23, 1947

Thomas McCarrick, 1948

In May 1948, after spending a couple of years in England, my brother and I boarded the S.S. Washington. It was a mighty liner, a troop ship during the war. We went out to meet it at Cork Harbor and the tender was like a midget in the sea beside it. The accommodation was very nice, with excellent food, and the whole experience was just lovely. We left Queenstown on May 8, and we docked at New York harbor on the 14th. I was twenty-one years of age.

An uncle and his wife, and my sister, who was here about nine months at the time, met us at the boat. We spent the first couple of weeks going to parties. There was one in a different house every night, between all the relatives. I used to play the flute, so of course I was in great demand. As a youngster when everyone else was dancing I would be up with the musicians, as I had untold admiration for them. To my young ears there was nothing like the sound of the flute and the fiddle and Sligo is famous for both.

My uncle owned a bar, Jack's Tavern, out in Corona on Long Island, and he thought I should work there for a while. So I started bartending at night. I lived with him initially, but then moved on to Northern Boulevard, to people my uncle knew, but that didn't work out too well. Then I moved on to Junction Boulevard, which was only about two blocks from the bar where I worked. I stayed with a German family and they were very nice. I had a little problem with the German food, but otherwise it was very good.

Corona had a mixture of everything, but it was predominantly German. There weren't many Irish there. That didn't bother me though, as I had met a lot of German POW's working on farms in England so I was well used to them. However, the type that hung out in the bars weren't the cream of the crop or anything. Besides I didn't want to come into work at six o'clock at night and work until four o'clock in the morning and work weekends and everything. It was tough. Anyhow business in the bar wasn't that good. The old man was getting close to retirement, so it was time for me to move on.

I had an old friend in the bus business, Connolly, a neighbor of ours at home, who was a bus operator for twenty something odd years. I went to see him and he took me into the headquarters of Service Transit Incorporated down on Third Avenue at 129th Street. I was only a year in this country when I got hired as a bus driver in May 1949. I moved to the Bronx, to the Concourse at Fordham, and I used to get off the subway and stand on the corner and look around and wonder which way I should turn to go home. And I the bus driver? There was a wide range of people on the buses that time because we went through several different sections of the city. You were assigned to one garage, but as a new person you were moved from one bus to another. Some of them went through white-collar areas; some of them through Harlem, and all the ways in between. You never knew where you'd end up.

Willis Avenue in the Bronx was a great old Irish neighborhood. At St. Jerome's Church on a Sunday you'd see nothing but a sea of men in peaked caps. Then the Korean War broke out in June 1950 and in August, when I was fifteen months on the buses, I was called into military service. And, guess what, I was stationed in Germany; surrounded by Germans again.

For the next fifteen months I froze my rear end off along the border next to the Russians. I landed in Bremerhaven, a major port, and was posted to a perimeter west of Berlin and about ninety minutes east of Frankfurt. We were mainly doing patrol work along the German borders. I will always remember traveling by train towards Austria and looking out the window and seeing this gigantic "ice cone." It was the Alps.

Germany gets cold though in the winter. I remember one night on patrol something was stabbing me in the face and I didn't know what it was. It was like someone was jabbing me with a needle. We were parked beside an old castle and you could be there for twenty-four hours on end. It was bitter cold and there was a fog so it was hard to see in front of you. However, I gradually realized that it was the actual atmosphere that was freezing in the air and that's what was prickling my face. The water in the canteen would freeze on your hip. I remember Christmas night we pulled up beside an old church out in the country to have our evening meal; our Christmas dinner. But when we took out our rations, they were frozen. We then tied the food to the exhaust pipe of the vehicle we were traveling in, and thawed it out. So we were used to frozen food long before it became fashionable. The good thing about being in Germany was that after nearly four years away from Ireland, I got home on leave for nineteen days, swapping one border for another.

I was born in a thatched cottage in August 1926 the fourth in a family of twelve. The towns land of Carnaleck was on the side of the Cloonacool Mountains, which were situated on the Sligo and Roscommon border. There was a long, winding, hilly road leading up to the cottage and in 1930, when I was only a few months short of my fourth birthday, my father built another house nearer to the public road. Six of us were born in the old home and six of us in the new. I don't remember much about the old house except that my Granddad lived with us then, and actually died there before we moved. I remember playing by the fire one day with my cousin who was home from America with his mother, and we were both agreed that we did not like my elder sister. We had no reason in the world for it, but that's what we were at anyhow. And I can remember standing at the kitchen table one time and my mother was pouring the tea and the wind was so strong that it was blowing the thatch in tufts off the roof.

My father started off with a small farm, although by the time he died, he had quite a good holding between distant cousins leaving him a few acres here and there and buying the place next to us. We had a good deal of cattle so we had lots of milk and the hens laid almost a hundred eggs a day between them. Then we'd plant potatoes, that was the staple, especially during the war, as you didn't know if you were going to get bread or not. Wheat and flour and bread itself was very scarce that time. My mother was a great baker. She'd normally turn out four or five loaves a day. There was a field in front of the house, I guess the good Lord designed it that way, and down the far end of the field ran a river that sectioned off a small patch where we grew vegetables—carrots, parsnips and onions—and we sold the produce from that patch every year. The turnips were grown in another part of the field and the cabbage garden was separate too.

As children we worked like slaves on the farm and we had to help turn the turf on the mountain too. My father would take us up to the bog and he wouldn't see the turf again until it was stacked up in the yard. We would spread it out, foot it, bring it to its assembly place on the mountain and then draw it home on donkeys and creels. We'd light a fire every day and boil water for the tea, which we'd bring with us, as the mountain water you couldn't drink. My mother would give us a loaf cut in four quarters with slices of bacon inside and God that tasted good! We walked about half a mile to school and you could say my formal education took me up to the equivalent of the eighth grade today.

Tom in his Surface Transit Incorporated uniform

In Ireland we got a sound education and a good moral upbringing too. We would walk a mile and a half to Mass. My mother's brother was a curate there one time, before I came along. You'd be fasting in the morning from the previous midnight. There was one particular man and he was a short, little man, and all of his sons were tall. And he never owned an overcoat in his whole life. He lived another half a mile further up the mountain from us, and he would walk every Sunday to Mass and all the way home again, in the bitter cold sometimes, with not a bite to eat. Work was very scarce then and money was small. It was bare bones, bare bones. So the people had to go. It was a disaster then, a complete disaster all the people leaving County Sligo at the time. But we were raised with that concept. We had all kinds of relatives here and we had to follow the mob.

Everyone in my entire family, except one, emigrated at one time or another. Some of them went back. Francie went back from England and settled in the North. Marty, the youngest, also went back and built a beautiful house there. Mary went home from the States and married a farmer. They're both dead now. Pat was in England when my mother died and when he went home my father gave him the land. But I stayed here. I didn't socialize that much, as I was working that hard and I didn't drink. In fact, I was a teetotaler until I went to Germany and tasted Cognac and Coke.

When I got out of the service as an "Acting Sergeant" in 1952, having declined three commissions, I returned to New York, and went back driving buses again for another nine years. I went dancing a few times to the Tuxedo Ballroom, the Leitrim House, and the Caravan. That's where I met Kay, my wife, and where we had our first date. We got married in 1955 and bought a two-family house in the Bronx, in St. Francis de Chantal parish, under Monsignor Halpin. We bought a second home as I made my way up through the ranks.

In due course I made it into the Safety and Training Department, first as an instructor of new bus-drivers and then as a dispatcher, and after taking a competitive examination in 1967, where I was placed sixth on the list, I was promoted to Senior Dispatcher. In 1969 I was made chief of the West Farms depot in the Bronx, managing 420 drivers and 40 dispatchers. I kept on climbing up the ladder of success to Assistant Division Chief in Manhattan and then Scheduling Chief of Manhattan and the Bronx, supervising 6,000 people.

Throughout this period, I became a licensed real estate broker selling houses in Throgs Neck in my spare time, and raising seven children. I would knock off the buses at around four o'clock, come home for a short time to see the children in from school and then I was out again. If any of them every got a star or did well on a test or a report card, I would bring home donuts as a treat. That was our way of showing them that we appreciated their hard work too. When I was growing up our lives revolved around school, church and family, and when I was raising my family here we repeated the exact same pattern. When the children were growing up, our lives revolved around school, church and family. It was repetitious. They all went to school in Throg's Neck and got scholarships to High School.

Meanwhile, I received a double promotion in the Transit Authority and was made Director of Labor Relations and Personnel. Upon investigation I rooted out corruption in the payroll department where forged records and lost timecards were posing many problems and an attempt was even made on my life. One morning on my way to work a large steel bar was dropped out of an overhead window and landed on the sidewalk beside me. I just dusted myself off and kept walking.

I was eventually made Transit Superintendent of the Bronx; and finally General Manager in 1983/84 operating a budget of $160 million. Before I retired I was the highest ranking Irish-born man in the buses. Not bad for a guy with only a national school education from the parish of Tirnacoon.

I still dream of the buses at night. I was thirty-nine years with the MaBSTOA, the Manhattan & Bronx Surface Transit Operating Authority, a subsidiary of the Transit Authority. I was with them for the first transit strike in 1966, when Mike Quill, a Kerry native, went to jail. Quill and Mayor Lindsey were always at loggerheads. I had a company car when I was CEO and worked with people like Dan Scannell and Bob Kiely. Scannell was head of the whole Transit Authority and my idol. He was straight, honest, compassionate, and patient. I loved him. He wasn't an Irish native, but of Irish descent. Being Irish was not really helpful, as we had the monopoly and that caused a lot of resentment. Then in the sixties the minorities started coming into the system. The Irish were there en masse, but the African Americans were filling the retiree positions. I had a brother who also worked in the buses, but he died in 1973 at the age of fifty, leaving seven children. He worked very hard.

It was hard for everybody at first. We had to become acclimated to the heat, as it would sap all of your energy. It's amazing though how you get used to it. Air conditioning didn't come in until the sixties. We had refrigerators alright, and before that my mother-in-law had an ice box, which was a wooden box with a lid on top and the iceman would come every day and drop a big block of ice into it for twenty five cents and that would keep everything underneath cool. There were times when people were worse off here than they had it at home. I knew this fellow from Mayo, and he married a Mayo woman. They had a very nice family. And I guess he was very young in this country at the time when he started working with the Public Works when they were building the park beside Orchard beach over in Pelham. There was a bus that would have taken him from Fordham Road on the Concourse there for a nickel out and a nickel back. But he walked it every day to save the two nickels.

Even though most of us came from farms, we ended up in the cities, doing work we weren't used to. I only knew one particular guy whom I helped get a job as a bus driver and he went out to the Midwest eventually; to Montana or Idaho, where the government sold him land for something like twenty-seven cents an acre. He said they had a bunkhouse and a Mexican cook, just like in the cowboy movies, and the people worked the land year round. The snow used to get so bad that it covered the fences and they would just walk right over them, not knowing they were there at all. It was unusual though for an Irish person to go off like that even though we may have had agricultural skills, we didn't tend to use them over here.

I never lost touch with Ireland even though I didn't go back for years and years. From the time I was a child I loved home and I loved the farm, and I had a great mother whom I was very attached to. I was so attached to her that when I was at school I would ask permission to go to the bathroom. "Bhfuil cead agam dul amach?" I would request of the teacher in that age old refrain learned by every school-going child in Ireland, even though I didn't want to go at all; I just wanted to see my mother. I would stand at the gable end of the school, from where I could see our house and could watch her going in and out. I just wanted to see her. And I had those feelings all of my life. But you cannot go back; no you can never go back.

Initially interviewed on video by Patricia Grogan and her father, Patrick, in Mamaroneck, New York. Interviewed by Frances Browner in Rory Dolan's, Yonkers, New York; March 25, 2006

Michael Browner, 1950

My flying odyssey began at a place known as Rineanna. About forty hours later it ended at a place called Idlewild. Today, one flies from Shannon to Kennedy in about six hours. I prefer the old names.

It was raining, no surprise, pouring out of low-flying gray-black clouds that blended seamlessly with the flatness of the Shannon estuary. The tarmac was ominously empty, but, surely my escape would soon appear, ghostlike, out of the overcast. Not yet. We (my entourage and I) waited, and waited. Then there was an announcement. The flight was delayed...and delayed...and...delayed for twenty-four hours. I was taken to a hotel near the airport.

It was still raining the next day. My plane was on the ground, looming, monstrous, gray in the gray dusk. A flying whale I thought it was. I made a quick phone call to Kirby's, the local grocery store in Limerick; someone ran to get my mother. "Write soon son." I will. "Don't forget to say the Rosary." I won't. "Good bye, son." I never heard her voice again. "Good bye mother." I remember the maudlin song "I Left Ireland and Mother Because We Were Poor." A cowardly fellow; I should have stayed. I trudged to the plane in my new suit, new overcoat, new shirt, new tie, new blue and white scarf, new shoes, new haircut, but the same old volcanic acne eruptions were still with me as I flew to the new world at twenty years of age.

I was snugly comfortable in the belly of the whale. Unlike Jonah, who must have been mighty uncomfortable? I was ushered to my comfy seat by a gorgeous stewardess who smiled gorgeously as she took my coat. (Is she real?) Take off. Ireland was gone. She disappeared under the clouds, and I would not see her again for ten years. I was air sick, home sick, soul sick. The steak dinner was not to my liking; nothing was. The German doctor besides me suggested that I put my head between my knees and breathe deeply. I wondered if I would then be able to look back and see the Shannon.

In Gander the weather was still bad, but at least now it was sparkling, drifting snowflakes instead of rain. More delay. Many whales were grounded. It must have been about ten o'clock in Limerick. I wondered what they were doing. Don't go there, I warned myself. As if I could not. The lounge was crowded. I saw navy blue uniforms, wings pinned on the left breast seemingly ready to fly off, braided caps rakishly set, manly snow white smiles, and manly long-legged strides. Were they a different race? No plane would dare crash under the command of such gods.

The stewardesses were in smartly tailored, knee-length skirts, blue as the sky I hadn't seen in days. They had matching jackets over snowy blouses, pert and pertly work caps. Their legs were so long I wondered if they were made to order in high heels that were calf defining or, in a word, sexy. Sexier smiles painted red and white. They were the goddesses to serve the gods.

My God was unresponsive. I half heartedly called on St. Pat. No luck o' the Irish. Finally I realized my mistake—I needed St. Jude, hopeless cases, of course. "Please," I begged, "get me back to Ireland, to dull dreary delightful Limerick, to the girl I left behind me." I waited. I listened. I heard my name called. A man approached. It's St. Jude complete with halo. But no, it was only a uniformed capped official. My flight was about to leave; I must hurry. And that was the last time I prayed to St. Jude. Kissed him off I did.

The flight from Gander to New York is not even a blur; it's a blank except for one mesmerizing experience. Back in those innocent days, before metal detectors, waving wands, shoeless searches, and locked cockpit doors, passengers were actually invited to visit the holy of holies—the cockpit itself. I stood behind and between the pilot and co-pilot staring at a vast array of dimly lit, indecipherable instruments. Then I looked out the cockpit window into the blackness of the cosmos. I saw the pinpoints of light, millions I suppose, some in friendly clusters winking conspiratorially, others severely alone and aloof in their solitary, cold beauty. I stood there forever until, gradually, I diminished, I dwindled; I become a speck, a single atom of matter, less than that, and I was gone. Gone from Ireland, gone from Limerick; gone from St. Munchin's Parish in Thomondgate; gone from everyone and everything I ever knew. I was without an anchor in a strange, unfriendly, dangerous ocean.

It was early morning, about seven. We were safely down. The whale disgorged me and I was grateful. I went down the stairs into the biting, unwelcoming cold of New York City. As a lover of ritual, I kissed the American soil to show my politically correct attitude and my profound gratitude. I looked around. There was no soil, just a dirty, slick, oil-stained tarmac. I'd heard that the streets of America were paved with gold. But not the Idlewild tarmac. No soil. No gold. No kiss. I had arrived.

For two months I job searched every day. Nothing came of it except frustration, depression. I was, as we say now, stressed out. I was stressed out to the extent that I suffered acne eruptions of extreme volcanic proportions. I probably exaggerate, but not by much. I was stared at by pretty teenage girls; I couldn't decide if their expressions were of horror or of sympathy. Job interviews went badly. I wondered if it was my lack of saleable skills. Or was it the acne? Meanwhile, I was living in Philadelphia with Aunt Mary (father's sister), her husband Dan, and Mary's tiny terrier, a high strung, permanently quivering, yelping bundle of ill-will and evil temper. You know the cliché about biting the hand that feeds? This dog embraced it literally.

Aunt Mary and I got along well. We both had Limerick in our blood. She was kind and had a jolly laugh. I gladly relieved her of dish-washing chores. But "Uncle" Dan! He was jolly enough in his cups (I used to wish he'd stay there permanently) but out of them, well, I think back to Aunt Mary's evil terrier, and there minus the yelping was Uncle Dan. Actually, he wasn't evil, just mean spirited. There was the question of money or lack thereof. No job meant no income and no money meant no way to go job hunting; a truly vicious cycle. Dan came to the rescue. Every week he doled out a few dollars, car fare money he called it. I thanked him. At least now I had a steady tax-free income; just enough to keep me above the poverty line.

I needed more money if only to finance my job-hunting travels. "Rob a bank," I thought. Out of the question; I'd never been in a bank, not even in Limerick, where I accorded banks the same reverence I did Catholic—and only Catholic—churches. I was often tempted to bless myself when I passed a bank, and when a school friend got a bank job—as manager, teller, floor sweeper, it didn't matter—I wondered if

I should address him as "Father." So bank robbing was out. I needed a ready source of cash, a gold mine, a silver mine, anything of value. And I found one—a copper mine deep in the dim, dog-smelly basement of my new home in Philly, as I, a greenhorn, daringly called it. You see, the dog was house broken, but she had failed to absorb a fundamental fact: The basement was part of the house. Conclusion: She was not basement broken, so that a musty, dusty, dried dog-dropping odor hovered in the basement. Sometimes it hovered up the stairs and into the kitchen. As a recently arrived immigrant, I had no objection to starting at the bottom, and so I became a part-time cellar-dweller, basement cleaner, pooper-scooper. "It's a start," I told myself, "No place to go but up."

About to take parachute jump

And that was where I unearthed the copper mine—four five-gallon copper cans stashed in a corner. I attempted to move one—too heavy. I pried ff a tight lid and saw my trove; not gold, not silver, not diamonds, not rubies, not pearls, but pennies. There were thousands and thousands of them - legal tender, hard currency, and the coin of the realm. This trove was, I learned later, the detritus from a "gold mine;" the bar owned by Mary & Dan. They were so wealthy they didn't have to count their pennies. Welcome to America.

How would I turn my sow's ear into a silk purse? Weighted by a pocketful of pennies, I made a discreet foray to a nearby bank where a kindly older lady (she was enamored of my accent) explained the fine art of wrapping pennies and gave me a bundle of wrappers. I was on my way. In one masterly stroke, I mastered the American Way: I became thief and capitalist at the same time.

One day two nuns appeared at the door begging money and ended up telling me about a job in The Crown Can Company. I wondered if they were really St. Jude in drag. I spent a few months making cans; not putting anything in them; and eventually had to part company from Uncle Dan. We were just not getting along. I moved to Woodside, New York, to Auntie Nan who made me go to Mass every week and checked my breath regularly to see if I'd been drinking. Funny thing is I never touched the stuff. No dancing in the New York ballrooms for me—just work, on the Pennsylvania Railroad. It was a tough job repairing freight cars, and then I was given a night shift keeping the fires burning. This was slightly easier, as I could read a book and stoke the fire at the same time. Thus, I was free during the day and walked all over New York City. I just took the subway, picked a stop at random, and walked. One day on Wall Street I turned a corner and there they were—recruitment booths for the Army, Navy, Air force, and Marines.

Barely a year later, January 25, 1951, I fell down a rabbit hole and became an even stranger stranger in an even stranger land. I enlisted in the U.S. Army. One minute I was a civilian —good job and good pay, beginning to feel I belonged. The next I became, I knew not what, but the Army would tell me that. In fact, the Army would tell me everything. The Army would tell me all I needed to know, do, and be for the next three years. For I was now one of many mere cogs in the mightiest military machine the world had ever known. My only remaining iota of uniqueness was my one-of-a-kind Army Serial Number: RA12334392. The "RA" told those in the know that I was an enlistee, not a draftee. So, R.A. 12334392 was who I became and indeed remained forever after, a fact that today I find both comforting and meaningless.

As a new recruit, I was naïve and lost, but not alone. I was now one of a semi-organized mob, confused and a bit nervous, all of us just fallen into the upside-down, regimented Army world. Take, for example, the rank of Private. Private: there was no privacy. I'd soon endure communal sleeping, eating, even latrine visits. Gone was all semblance of personhood. I was pure Government Issue—a true G.I. I had a G.I. haircut, wore a G.I. uniform, and ate G.I. food, every waking moment I was a G.I. and I was sure that the Army was working on my sleeping, dreaming moments, and my thoughts too.

It was a cold, dreary dusk when we arrived at Fort Devens, Massachusetts. Not far from Boston, Devens was a huge staging camp for still semi-civilized recruits about to be fully de-civilized. For some, the transformation was already underway—bands of men in ill-fitting, greenish fatigues straggle-marched under the command of irritated, yelling NCOs: NO TALKING – STAY IN LINE – KEEP STEP – LEFT RIGHT – LEFT RIGHT – SHUT UP, SOLDIER. All these colored by choice Army adjectives—my first lesson in Army linguistics.

Once off the bus, the ubiquitous NCO hurried us to join other groups of equally tired, cold, and hungry souls. "Wait here. Don't move," he orders. "I'll be back." Off he went. I realized later, that I had just been introduced to a basic Army philosophy: Hurry up and wait - a very useful lesson. So we waited and waited and we huddled together against the nervous uncertainty and the cold, waiting for the Army, or at least our NCO, to order us to "hurry up and wait." "You are my tired, my cold, my huddled masses yearning to serve," says the Army. "Oh! And you're hungry too? No problem."

As if from a genie's bottle our NCO returned. I was growing fond of him now. He semi-organized us into ranks and files and jogged us to a large, gloomy, claptrap of a building. A lighted sign identified it: MESS HALL. "Get in line and wait," our NCO yelled. And we obeyed, of course. The line was long and snaky, so long and snaky that it might devour its own tail. Again we waited and waited, while I mulled over my three Army lessons so far. Lesson 1: You will hear many choice words. Lesson 2: You will hurry up and wait. Lesson 3: You will stand in many lines.

Inside the dining-hall all was clatter and clamor: tin on tin; boots on boards, voices raised above raised voices, buzzing bright lights. A cacophony of white noise—Satan's symphony in V (for very) sharp, arranged, orchestrated and conducted by the U.S. Army. It was a masterpiece. I passed before a long counter of steam tables, looked at vats of food unidentified and possibly unidentifiable. There were only "ish" colors in stock—whitish, greenish, pinkish, brownish, or is that blackish? I didn't know, but it was definitely "ish." My mother often told me, "When in doubt, say a prayer." So I whispered a little "Jesus, Mary, and

Joseph," plea, but the chow was still there; it did not disappear. In the end, hunger triumphed and tentatively I fed only to discover that it was, in fact, edible, and almost enjoyable. In the Army one never dines, only occasionally eats, more often feeds. And what does one feed on? On chow. And where does one feed? In the mess. Feed–Chow–Mess

Before I became a paratrooper, my main objective, I was sent to Advanced Infantry School, which entailed periods of field training and classroom work. During one of our college type courses a classmate, Rossi, announced that America was the most moral country in the world. Of course, I counteracted by declaring that it was the most immoral. It was 1951 and everyone was scared of Communism, Joe McCarthy was just getting started, and I was investigated. I was ordered to appear before three officers to discuss my Communist leanings, but after taking one good look at me they realized that this guy was no threat.

I subsequently spent three weeks in Fort Benning, Georgia, training to be a paratrooper. After my first ever airplane jump I was called over the PA system to report to the Orderly Room, where I was handed a piece of paper. It was a telegram from my brother stating: Mother died Saturday, Eamon. I had just experienced the most exciting event of my life up to that point, and now I was about to experience my saddest. Things were piling up on me. I couldn't cry for a long time, I just sat in the chapel and thought about Mam. Quiet, kind, never criticizing anyone, unlike Auntie Nan who criticized everyone; reading by the lamp, kneeling on the cold kitchen floor for the Rosary; sewing by the fire; skillfully turning shirt collars; hugging Dad when he came home from hospital; annoyed with him once when he had a little too much drink; never annoyed with us even on a rainy day; her feet, like mine, corns and bunions, the sides of her shoes cut open. Did it pain her on Sundays when she had to wear good ones to Mass? Then I had to forget. For the next year I was a paratrooper in Fort Bragg, North Carolina, with the 82nd Airborne Division until I volunteered for Korea. I just wanted to test myself really; I wanted to prove my manhood.

We spent the first month in Korea in reserve guarding POW's on the island of Koje – Koje Do in Korean. There had been a prisoner "disturbance" that summer where they had even held a Colonel hostage for a while. It was easy duty and mostly boring. Four hours in a sentry tower standing behind a 30 caliber heavy machine gun staring into an empty compound can be that way, especially at night; especially when it was freezing. Then we were put "on line", manning bunkers along the MLR – the Main Line of Resistance. We were issued parkas and "Mickey Mouse" boots. They were clumsy for walking in, but they were so well insulated that our feet would sweat on all but the coldest nights. There was not much action on our part: an occasional patrol, maybe a fire fight around Pork Chop Hill, an exposed, morbid mound of mud about which there was a movie made with Gregory Peck. Small arms were fired, mortars lobbed, grenades tossed, casualties inflicted, and screams heard. All of it was viciously noisy, but it didn't last long. No ground was given or taken. There was no movement on the 38th Parallel the whole ten months I was there with the 17th Infantry. I can't say I was afraid, but you had to develop a healthy fear, not only from the enemy, but from our own too. The whole place was riddled with minefields.

My most memorable two days were spent with Sergeant 1st Class Smith, a combat engineer, whose job it was to check these minefields. The first day I was ordered to report to him for duty and he informed me that we would be inspecting an anti-tank minefield. He showed me how to read maps of the minefields; how to find the base mines that lead to the other mines; and how to find the safe path, with the warning, "Nothing's safe out there." He talked with passion about booby traps and anti-tank and anti-personnel mines, which he referred to as 'little bastards.' But his efficiency and expertise made me yearn for his approval. At the end of the day he questioned me on what I had learnt and I told him what I knew about AP's (anti-personnel) and flares.

The anti-personnel mines consisted of two cylinders, one inside the other, buried so the top is level with the surface. A little dirt was thrown over it so it was camouflaged, difficult to see. It was awakened by stepping directly on it or by tripping a wire so fine you could search on hands and knees and not find it. Either method blows the inner can 10–12 feet into the air where it explodes into god-knows-how-many pieces of shrapnel, each one capable of killing or maiming. "Cost effective," said the Sergeant. The flare is almost identical, except it doesn't explode. Instead the inner can shoots maybe 100 feet in the air before it ignites into a brilliant white light that illuminates the area below as it floats down under a small, white parachute. It was not designed to kill. But it could.

I was prepared to tell him more: how front line troops scatter illicit AP mines and flares in front of their positions as protection, as warning, so they feel a bit more secure. I'd tell him how they kill the unwary GI who takes a misstep, perhaps an unarmed young man wearing a red-cross armband answering to the cry, "Medic. Medic." I'd tell him that we call them Bouncing Betty's. "What else?" He interrupted me before alighting into his truck. I wanted to shine my boots on the spot, anything to please him. "Always be prepared." I said. He nods. "Always tell someone you're going 'out there.' Always move slowly. Speed kills." I'm on a roll now. "Overconfidence kills." He started up the vehicle. "Kill one, it happens; kill two, it shouldn't." I paused expecting some friendly farewell. The gears crunched and he drove away. "Good job." He shouted back at me. Private 1st Class Browner was just praised by the most remarkable soldier I would ever meet.

The next day after a few hours sleep I'm told that Sergeant Smith wanted me again. A surge of elation swept through me, as I knew I had his approval. We are to inspect more minefields, but not the same as the previous day, as "it's never the same," I was told. We climbed up an access trench to reach the MLR. Sergeant Smith warned the Infantry C.O. that we were going "out there." We left the safety of the main trench and cautiously made our way down a hill. We moved step by careful step. The ground was rough and covered with the remains of the previous summer's growth. Dead leaves, broken twigs and bare shrubs slowed our descent. All of it provided cover for stray tripwires and for the mines. Even with the Sergeant leading, this was still a tension filled process. My neck was stiff. I paused to rotate my head when I noticed a vague, residual image to my left. It was a pair of boots, or more accurately a pair of soles, minus the boots, and beside them a long formation of bones, bleached white. I alerted the Sergeant. We had found a skeleton.

The boots and the bones were about twenty yards away from us, the boots precisely arranged, heels and toes together as if at attention, as if this unknown soldier had grown jaded of war and wanted to sleep it off. It was a lonely scene, but now he had company. While the

Sergeant went to get help, I sat and chatted with my new friend. I lit a Pall Mall and reached for a small bone, a finger perhaps, and it resisted. I pried it loose from the frozen ground and cleaned it with my bayonet. As I cleared some of the mud away I discovered bits of rotting fabric, some rusted with blood, and then something else. It was an arm band, tattered and dirty, but with the Medic's Red Cross, faded but clear. He was one of our own. A second trove turned out to be his wallet, which contained an army ID, his rank was Corporal; a driver's license from Minnesota, pictures of his family and girlfriend in front of a sturdy, red-bricked house, and a letter I did not read. The impersonal pile of bones was now a person.

I wondered how long it would be before Mom and Dad would learn that their son was no longer MIA, but KIA; that their hope was hopeless, their prayers wasted. How long before the phone call, "the Army regrets." I nod at my skeleton. "Corporal," I said, "You've created a heap of harm just because you didn't watch out for the bastard mines." But how was he to know. He'd never gone mining with Sergeant First Class Smith, Combat Engineer. The Sergeant returned with a ROK soldier carrying a folded stretcher. I helped him drag the stretcher back up the hill while the bones bounced and Sergeant Smith cleared the way.

I had always especially admired the medics because they were never afraid of danger, always ready to run when help was called for. I could imagine my medic, for he was mine then, heeding the screams for help and stumbling and crashing his way down the hill, no thought for mines. Did he hear the explosion? Did he die instantly? Or did he linger, fatally wounded, calling, "Medic, Medic," as if talking to himself? We dropped him at Battalion Headquarters and Sergeant Smith took me for dinner in the sergeant's dining room. As he drove away from me later, he looked back, "You're a strange one at times, a bit weird, but you're OK in my book." He smiled. "I hope you make rank." He waved and was gone and I never saw him again. I hope he was glad when I did make rank. Before I left Korea, I too was a Sergeant First Class.

As Sergeant First Class Browner, I watched one of my own men being killed by a friendly fire. It hit him in the head and ripped his eyes and brain out. Sergeant Smith had been right, deadly right – "You never know what's out there." The following week, July 27, 1953, the truce was signed and the war ended. For years I couldn't get this man out of my head until I finally visited his grave in Kentucky. I left a note, which was found by his aunt, and his wife later contacted me. I have since been to visit her and finally found a sense of peace.

Summer '53. It's over! SFC Browner with Korean, Kim Bok Dong

Some mornings on sentry duty I would gaze over the valley, at the hills all covered in icy white-blue frost, so silent, so peaceful, nothing was stirring. It was like a Christmas scene, not a killing field. And I would wonder, "Why don't we lay down arms and leave the trenches? Why don't we walk across the valley to meet in the rising mist? Share cigarettes? Swap souvenirs? Admire family photos? Maybe in the mystery of the mist we'd find a common language. Why don't we walk away together, disappear into the field of mists; go home or wherever our hearts take us, so that when the call to arms sounds over the battlefield, there's no one there to hear it?" I'm reminded now of a Vietnam era, pacifist fantasy: "Suppose they gave a war and nobody came?" Suppose.

When it all ended we took off our green fatigues and waved them in the air. A month later we were discharged and had to leave immediately. They offered a fair amount of money for us to re enlist, but I wasn't interested. In the meantime I fell in love. I didn't meet Uncle Dan's niece, Isabel, when I first visited her home in New Rochelle, but had heard that all she did is sit and read. She was, however, one of the many young women who wrote to me in Korea. I found her letter the most interesting and sent her a reply. That began the whole thing.

As soon as I returned from war I went to visit her in Milwaukee where she was attending the Marquette School, and we hit it off immediately. We were married for twenty-two years, had three daughters, and then things began to go awry, as they do in relationships. Nothing major, just little things showed up and we decided to end it gracefully. Even the divorce lawyer was surprised at how amicable the separation was. We still get along and I haven't had the slightest notion of remarrying. I was never concerned about going against the Catholic Church. I remember though being glad at the time that my father was dead.

My six siblings and I grew up in Limerick City where Dad was a reporter with the Limerick Leader and we spent five years in Cavan when he was managing editor of a bi-weekly newspaper called the Anglo-Celt. There he became involved in a very serious car accident when he and four other men went to a football match in Dundalk. The car they were traveling in lost control (we don't know if it was from fog or alcohol) and ran into a ditch. Dad was catapulted from the backseat through the windshield and sustained very serious injuries to his head. He was never, ever the same after that.

I remember going to visit him in the hospital with Mam and my brother, Connie, and his head was covered in bandages. We had to return to Limerick soon after where, after a few failed business attempts, he found work as a bookkeeper in O'Mara's bacon factory; the newspaper reporting now a thing of the past due to his deafness. It was tragic really, as he had a very interesting career prior to that as an Intelligence Officer for the old IRA, and he was the first man to shake hands with DeValera after his election in Ennis. On their honeymoon during the Civil War he and my mother had to lie on the floor of the tram in Dublin to avoid the bullets and they harbored a man on the run for the first few months of their marriage. Dad himself was a marked man after holding the bugler's case at Sean South's funeral and led his pursuers a merry dance around Limerick City when he realized he was being followed. One night he waited for them in a doorway and asked. "Have ye nothing better to do?"

My three brothers and I attended the local CBS—the Cruel Brothers School—where I was subjected to many beatings, and the deep-rooted belief that I was not good enough. When Isabel suggested that I apply for University here I thought she was crazy, but did so anyhow. In a way Frank McCourt and I led parallel lives for a while. Sons of Limerick, we both worked as telegram boys in our beloved city; came to America; joined the Army; fought in Korea; and upon discharge became accepted to American Academia. He got in on probation, if he flunked the first semester he was out. I lied. That's when McCourt and I parted ways. I showed them my Intermediate Certificate, which was all written in Irish anyhow, and told them it was equivalent to a High School Diploma. They let me in and I graduated three years later with a B.A. in English. I later completed my Masters and taught in a small University in Illinois before coming to Florida to take up a position with the University of Miami.

I retired from Miami-Dade College some years ago and now live alone in Miami, but am in constant contact with my three daughters and three grandsons. Carol is a sounding partner for Albright Global Consulting and was a member of President Clinton's Cabinet as the EPA Administrator; Michelle is a Vice-President with Roche Pharmaceuticals in San Francisco; and Stephanie is Dean of Faculty with Berea College in Kentucky. I now enjoy jogging, playing chess, listening to Wagner and writing letters to the Limerick Leader.

On a recent visit home I walked all over the great city of my birth. From my headquarters in Faranshone I headed in the direction of the Treaty Stone and crossed over Thomond Bridge. I gazed up at St. John's Castle – an ugly slum in my boyhood, now a museum rich in the lore of Limerick's history. I ventured into St. Mary's Cathedral and even then guilt nibbled; as a Catholic youth this eloquent historical house of worship was forbidden to me. Another day I took the O'Callaghan Strand route. The tide was full; the Shannon smiled at me; the swans ignored me. Regretfully I considered the low stone wall where once I carelessly leapt and ran. As a boy I learned to swim in the Shannon. On a day that remains golden in my memory, I swam across and back at full tide, a rite of passage that changed me from a mere boy to a big boy, maybe even to a little man.

At Mount Saint Lawrence Cemetery, amid the soothing silence of the dead, I pondered at my parents' headstone – Frances and Cornelius Browner; and at that of my grandparents – Elizabeth and Michael Browner. Ah! My name already engraved. It gave me a start and then a sense of peace. On Sarsfield Bridge I paused to look up river at Thomond Bridge, the Strand Barracks, the Castle, St. Mary's Tower, and The Custom House – a thousand years of history captured in one magnificent view. At the meeting of the streets – Sarsfield, O'Connell, and William – I stopped to look and listen. I saw and heard a city literally buzzing with prosperity. The busy inhabitants seem confident, even happy, in a way that was out of our ken fifty years ago.

On my last evening I strolled along Arthur's Quay. It was ten o'clock, and near the end of the endless, mystical, Irish dusk. I thought to myself – "what better spot." I know now that on an evening such as this my ashes will float upon the waters of the Shannon above the invisible Curraghgower Falls where long ago I caught slippery eels. And I will be home.

Assembled from handwritten notes by and telephone conversations with Michael Browner, Miami; January - June 2006

My immigrant family

Julia Malpeli (Doyle) 1951

I left my home in the parish of Clogh, County Kilkenny in 1951, and traveled to Cobh with my brother and sister, where we stayed overnight in a hotel. There were more tears shed from one's hometown to Cobh than on any other lap of the journey. It was a very sad time for all of us and as well as tears, many prayers were said too. But in between, we sang. We raised the roof of the car with "On Top of Old Smokey" and Joe Stafford's, "You Belong to Me," but our hearts were hardly in either. The next morning I took the tender out to the S.S. Washington, which was a converted war ship. Soon after settling in I met people from Chicago and Canada. They were so kind to me because I was so young. They took me under their wing and I ended up spending every night with them. We danced until the wee hours of the morning. I never got sick at all; I didn't have time. It was the first real vacation that any of us had ever had in our whole lives; our first taste of luxury. I was so disappointed when we docked in New York, as the crossing was like a fairy tale.

I was the youngest of fourteen children and my father, a miner in the Castlecomer coalmines, died when I was just two years of age. My mother passed away when I was fourteen and I think I then blocked out everything that happened up to that. I had spent three months in hospital recovering from peritonitis and at one stage my mother and I were both in the same room, as she had developed an infection after gall bladder surgery. There were no antibiotics. They got me out just in time the night she died and I never made it to her funeral. Instead I was sent to England to stay with one of my eight sisters. The Second World War was raging at the time and we often had to sleep in shelters at night. When the air raid siren would sound, I would run as fast as I could with my one-year old nephew, as we would only have minutes to reach safety.

I got a job in The Apple Blossom Tea Room on Kensington High Street. It was owned by two Scottish spinsters who were fashionable old dowagers, and very independently wealthy. Our clients were all of the shoppers and shopkeepers in this very exclusive upper-class area, who kept us supplied with Clarke's shoes, which were in big demand at the end of the War, and very hard to get. I rented a furnished room in a boarding house with one of the girls I worked with and all I was mad for was movies and dancing. We would go to the Hammersmith Palace and the Garryowen, where we would dance and drink orangeade. That's what I lived for.

My Aunt Jane lived here in America and she offered to sponsor just one of her nieces to come over. Two sisters and I stood on Trafalgar Square one day and tossed a coin. That is how I found myself on the other side of the Atlantic, while they headed for Australia.

The United Nations (UN) had just opened in New York in 1948 and as soon as I arrived I put my name down for the position of Guide. I thought it would be so interesting showing people around that imposing building. They told me they would call me if something came up. In the meantime, I took the job of Hostess in the coffee shop of the New Yorker Hotel down there by 34th Street and 8th Avenue. I was quite green, but the manager was very kind to me and showed me the ropes. He would take my side when the waitresses complained that I wasn't giving them enough customers. Then when I discovered that they made more money than I did, I was out of there.

I was living with my aunt at the time, weren't we all, and her daughter worked for A&P Supermarkets so I started there even though I was still hoping to hear from the UN. I had to work; I couldn't just sit around. I assisted in the deli section of one of their bigger branches on 86th Street. After six weeks I had to join the union, which was compulsory at the time, and wouldn't you know the UN called me sometime thereafter, but I had to decline. It was a pity really. I often regretted it, but I guess it wasn't meant to be. I stayed at A&P and worked all over the supermarket, except at the checkout. I was never into that. My supervisor encouraged me to go on for deli manager, but I wasn't interested; there would be too much aggravation. Instead, I transferred to a branch in Elmhurst, Queens where I was living at the time and there I stayed for three years until I got married.

Because I lived in Queens I didn't go dancing in Manhattan that much. Sometimes my cousin would come in from Inwood and we'd hang out in the Laurel Eye, which was in the German district. You knew the nationality of the guys from their diet. They would smell of liverwurst, knockwurst, bratwurst, and occasionally body odor. The men had a strange way of dancing. It didn't matter if it was a waltz, foxtrot or a two-step; they would hold you so tight you couldn't breathe. Most times I left them in the middle of the floor with the music still playing. It's funny how they never complained to management. The Irishmen would try and hold you tight too if they could, don't they do it today, although they wouldn't smell of bocasdio, maybe cigarettes, that was par for the course, which was alright because most of us smoked too. So, because I didn't mix too much with the Irish, I ended up marrying an Italian-American man and we had one son.

After we seperated I moved to Sacred Heart Parish in the Bronx and took on work with Grand Union supermarkets. One of my sisters, Theresa, had moved here by then, so it was great to have the company. I had also become acquainted with an older sister, Helen, out in New Jersey, whom I had never met until I came to America. I was born after she left home. It was like having my mother back all over again, and I was so happy to be near her. We got on great. She would tell me all these stories about home, as she could remember what somebody said in the kitchen when she was ten years old, unlike me. She told me about how my father was a trailblazer and the first one to go down into the mines to check for a gas leak. They would keep a canary down there and if the bird was still alive the news was good. The signal was that if the canary was dead, there must be a leak. What a horrendous way to make a living; he may have made a little bit extra for it, but could it have been worth it?

Her stories made me realize how much I missed not knowing him. She also told me about my uncle who had died in a cave-in. They would peal the bell so many times to indicate certain levels of injury; if there was no bell toll that meant the person was dead. She recalled how everyone in the village was wondering who was dead that day and then they discovered it was my mother's brother. She was heartbroken. I often think of them now when I hear those disaster stories of men lost in the Kentucky and Australian mines. My sister had to mind all of us little ones too, which was hard work, she said, and one of the reasons she left as soon as she could.

I became a member of The Bedford Park Shamrock Club. It's in St. Brendan's on Bainbridge now; although it started off on Decatur Avenue. I have remained a member for over thirty years. It is mainly a social club where people meet to chat, have tea and soda bread, and dance. We would be philanthropic if we had the money, but we do try to help out people in need and we run a lot of functions, but it's really just for socializing.

I also loved to shop and Fordham Road was just magnificent back then. It was completely different. There were Irish bars all over the place; I think McKeon's next door had a place there; and Schrafft's had a branch there too. There were ice-cream parlors where you could get the most delicious ice cream in a real glass with a silver handle and a long silver spoon from which to eat it with. There was the Colonial where they would give you a hot towel to wipe your hands, and in Jahn's on your birthday or other event they would make you a special treat called "The Kitchen Sink," which had everything in it. It was a very nicely decorated place, all nice wood, a bit like Rory Dolan's is today.

The stores were very exclusive back then and limousines would pull up outside Loehmann's and Alexander's to drop off the wealthy shoppers from Scarsdale and other rich neighborhoods. A lot of the Jewish people used to shop there for their holiday outfits. The fitting room in Loehman's was something else. There was one huge communal changing room with no privacy at all. And there'd be these ones next to you and you trying to fit something on and they'd be asking you, "What do you think, sweetie? Does this look good?" And you trying to do your own thing, you know. I remember this one time I was beside this big one who had stripped down to her panty hose and next thing someone picked up her pocket book and ran out the door. You'd want to have seen her run through the department store in nothing but her panty hose, no underwear underneath, no panties, nothing, and the rolls of fat wobbling on her like jelly on a platter. That was some sight, let me tell you. I got turned off straight away.

Eventually I had to leave Highbridge, as the neighborhood was changing so much. I was living in an all-White building, but I went on vacation one time and when I came back two big, six-foot, Black men were carrying their furniture into the apartment upstairs. My nephew advised me to leave and I did shortly after even though I had just rewired my home at my own expense. They burnt down that building later, as by then the tenants were all on welfare and had nothing better to do, I suppose.

On a Bronx rooftop

I moved on to Mosholu Parkway and by now I was working in home care, having been exposed to the chemical, polyvinyl chloride, in Grand Union. I became very ill with asthmatic like symptoms and was part of a class action suit. Unfortunately, I didn't have a very good lawyer, and didn't benefit very much from the experience and I had to quit my job. That's how I came to be a companion to New York's elderly.

One day I was taking the train downtown to work when a man approached me on the platform. We were on 203rd and the Concourse, which was quite good back then. I thought he wanted directions, but when he opened the copy of LIFE magazine that he was holding there was a switch knife hidden between the pages. He took my money and made me walk back up the steps of the station with him behind me so as I wouldn't raise any alarm. He wanted me to come all the way to Harlem with him, but luckily I convinced him that I wouldn't tell a soul and I managed to escape. So much for moving to a better neighborhood.

I always kept up my affinity with Ireland even though my family was spread all over England and Australia and I had my two sisters here, I never lost touch with the ones at home. It wasn't always that easy to get back because we couldn't afford it, but I always kept in touch. Nearly everyone is gone now, except for a sister in Ireland. That's the disadvantage of being the baby; you get to see a lot of death, and the disadvantage of being an immigrant is that you don't get to say goodbye. In fact, the only funerals I've been to were those of my two siblings here. Theresa, who lived here beside me in Woodlawn, just passed away at Easter, so that leaves me the only one here. They had a Month's Mind Mass for her in Ireland this week and sixty family members were present; with three generations represented, which is a great homage to her really. I have a wonderful relationship with all of my nieces and nephews, and they call me all of the time from all over the world. We all have great humor; that's what gets us by.

I am traveling to Ireland in September to attend a grandniece's wedding; which is being held in the K Club, the same place as The Ryder Cup. I am really looking forward to that. Also I have my lovely son, Michael, and his wife, Gale, up in New Rochelle and three adorable grandchildren, Marc, Erica, and Danielle. Who could ask for more than that? I also have to say that I met some wonderful people along the way who took me under their wing when times were tough and I thank them all for that. I often wonder what would have happened if the coin had flipped the other way that fateful day on Trafalgar Square and I had ended up in Australia, instead of my sisters.

Recorded and written at Aisling Irish Community Center, creative writing workshops, Yonkers, NY; November 2005 - May 2006

Eileen Moran 1951

I came to America by plane in June 1951. It was a TWA flight from Shannon airport, which was then called Rineanna. My mother, brother, sister and I took a taxi from Cork city, to the airport, and I had to walk out on the runway to take the movable stairway up to the aircraft. It took twelve hours to cross the Atlantic and our first stop was Newfoundland. That was the first time I had ever tasted coffee or orange juice and I didn't like either. Would you believe I got airsick? My mother had insisted that I wear ankle socks, as she said I should save my nylons for a job interview. I was only fifteen years of age and still did as I was told.

My parents had lived in America before, in fact, they had met and married here. My mother was attracted to my father because he wore spats, as did the doctor she worked for, so she presumed he had a lot of money. As a result of their being American citizens, I had an American passport which would expire on my sixteenth birthday, hence, my coming here so young. If I entered prior to that I could come in as a citizen too. We were always known as the Yanks and I suppose we were fairly comfortable. My parents had bought a house upon their return and we always had gas and electric light and running water, and a bathroom upstairs. We also had a sieve, which we used as a refrigerator, in the backyard.

The War years though were fairly uncertain with gas masks and ration books. Air raid drills were practiced regularly and all of the men were in civil defense. Rumors of invasion were rampant and there was a severe shortage of coal, oil and gas. The stove could only be used at certain times of the day and Inspectors would call to the house to enforce this law. There were regular black-outs and getting homework done before dark was a must. As a result, the Second World War was a great leveler in Irish society, as it did not discriminate and everybody was in the same boat.

I grew up on the Ballinlough Road in the parish of Our Lady of Lourdes. There was a grotto in the church grounds with statues of Our Lady and St. Bernadette, but the last time I went home St. Bernadette was gone. I guess she was dismissed by the Vatican during their last upheaval of saints. My father was a driver for Beamish Breweries and I marveled at how he could maneuver the large trucks through the narrow cobble stoned streets of the city, but my mother insisted that it was all the novenas she said for him. She was very progressive for her time. When I was very young I had a stutter and she sent me to elocution lessons with a Miss Lynch for half a crown a session. Later when I read My Left Foot, I discovered that Christy Brown also had the same teacher, the beautiful Miss Lynch with the army officer boyfriend who would call for her just as our class ended. He always told me I was a good little girl and one day he gave me a shilling. Ma wasn't pleased, however, that I spent so much time learning phonetics rather than poetry. She felt that for two and sixpence I should at least be able to recite "The boy stood on the burning deck" (the first line of "Casabianca").

Eileen (center) with school friends,
Mary Frances and Breda Sullivan, Cork City

Pa was more of a softie and would always take us for a walk on Sundays, maybe to feed the swans or watch a match with him. Once he took us to see the fever sheds, which were galvanized structures that had been used earlier in the century to house sick children with contagious diseases. Some English politician's wife had them opened when she saw how many children were dying, and though the intention was meant well, it was always regarded as being of a political nature. Thus, they were closed down in 1921. On our visit, they were on the grounds of the Cork Infirmary, they were being dismantled. Men were watching with tears in their eyes. Upon inquiring my father was told that it was the only place the Black and Tans wouldn't go near and they could always hide from them there during the War of Independence.

We loved these walks with Pa, my sister, brother and I and learnt so much from them, but it was really Ma that made sure that we survived somehow. When I contacted scarlet fever she made sure I got plenty of penicillin, which saved my life really, as four other girls in our town had died from the disease. She also insisted on a proper education. When I wasn't doing so well in Irish she transported me off to the Gaeltacht in Ballingeary, West Cork. She took me out of the National School after second class and sent me to the South Presentation Convent on Douglas Street, where I stayed until I completed the Intermediate Certificate in June 1951. A week later I left for America. She had always wanted to come back herself, but my father didn't, so she sent me instead.

My Aunt Julia worked in the cafeteria of the Chase National Bank on Pine Street, Lower Manhattan and she had asked a man who worked in the personnel office to help me get a job. He kindly paved the way through an interview and health check and eventually I was offered the position of page girl. I timidly asked my aunt on the way home what exactly that meant, what would I be doing, and she declared that I would be a messenger. Now the only messengers I had known up to this were the boys in Cork City who rode bicycles with big baskets in front and kept whistles in their mouths. When I expressed my anxiety at riding a large bicycle through a crowded Manhattan street, Julia insisted, "Don't be so dense." She explained that I would be indoors at all times carrying messages to the different departments in the twenty-two-story bank building. I had now heard two very familiar words—page and dense—in vastly different contexts than I had ever heard them before.

Orientation day was a wonderful experience and I loved everything about the place; everything I heard about the job. As my visits to the bank up to this had been during off peak periods, nothing had prepared me for the subway ride in a packed, crowded carriage during New York's business hours. I couldn't see the names of the stations we passed through, but fortunately fought my way off at my stop. Wall Street at the height of rush hour was indescribable. I had wandered through Patrick Street on a busy Saturday evening thinking it must be the busiest place in the world. But New York City was something else. It was awesome. And so was my first new job. I was kept busy all day transporting mail and files from floor to floor and gathering signatures for the different documents and figures for the heads of departments. I soon got to know everyone who worked there and they soon recognized me in my smart green blazer. Of course they all loved my accent and loved to tell me about their relatives and ancestors who were from Ireland. I can still vividly remember the elation of my first paycheck—twenty-eight dollars for the week.

I worked as a page girl for two years while attending school once a week, where I learned how to type. I was then promoted to the filing room and eventually to the change-of-address department. I can remember the change from manual to electric typewriters and one of my colleagues, an older woman, spent the day in the bathroom crying; she was that traumatized. The bosses were all very concerned and I heard two of them discuss the situation in the elevator. They felt they hadn't handled things properly and felt that they should have given her more time to get used to the idea. That was how they were back then.

The only drawback about Chase was that the pay wasn't that good. Every time I got promoted, I only raised my salary by two dollars. I was living with four girls from Kerry at the time who were working as waitresses and making piles of money. So as soon as I turned eighteen and could serve liquor, I joined them in the service industry. I started working at Schrafft's on 77th & Madison. It was an upscale restaurant like Rory Dolan's and there were branches all over the city. They were the first people to employ female managers, but they were very strict. We had to wear hairnets and have our nails inspected before every shift. I loved it there and made tons of tips.

Narrator in her pram (left); mother and sister

At first I stayed with my Aunt Bridie in Brooklyn, but she died three months after I arrived so then I got a room in a boarding house on 96th Street and Park Avenue, in the very Irish parish of St. Francis De Sales. The landlady, Mrs. Kelly, a widow from County Galway, was very strict, but kind. She was a go-getter and had rented rooms in her apartment after the Depression. She charged $8 a week for what was called a cold water railroad flat, as all the rooms had to be passed through by connecting doors, the kitchen being the first, then her bedroom and so on and so forth, just like the carriages on a train. Thus we had to pass through her quarters before we got to our own, and she always knew what time we came in at. If we had a date she'd make us take him up to meet her first so as she could give him the going over.

Paddy in Korea

When I got the job at Schrafft's this suited Mrs. Kelly too, as she didn't like us using the kitchen too much for cooking and as a result she liked renting to waitresses, as they could eat at work. Thus, we only used the kitchen table for drinking tea and sharing our new adventures at work and in the dancehalls. We had so much fun together. It was a great little place and I stayed there until the day I got married.

My original plan for coming to America had really been just to save to go home again and when I had $124 in my deposit account, a thrifty uncle, Denny, who lived on Long Island, asked to see my passbook and told me he'd match whatever money I had in it. So he doubled my $124 whispering, "Don't tell anybody." I thought I was made up! But despite all that, I never did go home in the end. My mother had other ideas for me. I wrote to her after six months asking if I could return now that I had my fortune and obviously I made a lot of spelling mistakes in the letter because I received her reply on Christmas Eve, which stated, "Stay put and get a dictionary."

It was the great friends I made here that helped me survive and the wonderful social life we had. We were always dancing and when we weren't we would buy a cake in Cushman's Bakery, there was one on every corner, and go visiting our girlfriends. I loved the Jaeger House on Lexington the best. When you walked down 86th Street you could see the big neon sign in the distance, as it beckoned us to its doors. Inside there was a restaurant/bar area, a bit like Rory Dolan's and upstairs was the ballroom. We not only went to the dances to meet guys, it was where we met our girlfriends too. It was where we met everyone. But we mainly went to dance. If the management caught you refusing too many fellows, they'd tick you off about it, as it was bad for their business. Ruthie Morrissey would be singing in her big crinoline skirt, with her skinny little legs, and you should have seen her shake those hips. All the men were crazy about her. Then there was the Tuxedo Ballroom where the fellows fancied themselves as dancers; they didn't want to dance at all, but swing you off your feet. If you saw them anywhere else you'd say, "There's the Tuxedo swing."

Our Four Boys

Gaelic Park was a great place for meeting men too. On a Sunday afternoon you'd go to the game and if you saw some nice guy on the field or when passing by the changing room you'd "accidentally on purpose" bump into him later at the dance. But there would be a lot of drinking there too. Sometimes the girls didn't like it because of that. For us back then it was strictly dancing, not so much drinking. The men would get a stamp on their hand to go to the Blue Room, which was across from the Tuxedo. The Jaeger House and City Center did have a separate bar area, so you always knew you'd get a drinker if you went there.

There were two very sleazy halls on Third Avenue when they still had the old EL there—the Leitrim House and Ireland's Thirty Two. If you went into either of those places you'd be taking your life in your hands. There were always fights there. Third Avenue was completely different then. It was full of dives. It changed completely when they got rid of the EL. There were a lot of tenements there too. It wasn't the best neighborhood either. If you were out late at night and a fight started it was scary. The subway in general was very safe, nothing ever happened to us, but there were certain areas you didn't want to go in to.

By the time the Red Mill came along I had babies so my dancing days were over. It was much better between men and women back then. We took the time to get to know one another before we got involved. We didn't have our hearts broken so much. The kids today are just one, two, and three. It must be terrible now. Imagine giving yourself to someone and then seeing him with someone else? The pain of that must be something desperate.

I met my husband in the Connemara Bar. Couples would sometimes gather there before the dance. I was with another boyfriend at the time, as women usually didn't go into a bar unless they were with someone. Next thing this very tanned gentleman sauntered in the door and I just assumed he was Greek or Italian, definitely not Irish. He was giving me the eye and next thing he came up to my boyfriend who flung his arms around him, crying, "Paddy how are you." It turned out that Paddy was a Galway man just returned from Korea where he had been a Sergeant with the Combat Engineers Unit. Hence the tan. He winked at me and whispered, "I guess you're going to have to get rid of this guy!" I did, but not for another six months. We got engaged when I was seventeen at Elizabeth Flaherty's wedding and were married within two years. I guess it was love at first sight! I had four sons and Elizabeth had four daughters and, as both men worked the same shift in Seman Brother's warehouse, people used to kid us that we should swap husbands to get a child of the other sex. Paddy and I now also have five grandchildren and one great grandchild.

I didn't go back to Ireland for about twenty years. We just couldn't afford it with tuition fees and that, as the boys all went to Catholic school. My father was by then dead and my mother was in fairly poor health. Here I was already a grandmother and doing so well on all of my progress reports in my new job as Ingredient Issue Clerk at Columbia Presbyterian Hospital when my mother greeted me with, "Where did you get that terrible outfit?"

There was a lot of joy raising our sons; seeing them graduate from high school and then two of them from college. We are very proud of our third son in his Court Officer's uniform and our youngest who was with the Coast Guard. He used to travel a lot and when they would near land, the Captain would call out, "Whose home town is this?" If it was New York, my son was allowed steer the ship into the harbor. That was a great thrill for us.

Now, Paddy and I are in the third phase of life. We are both retired with union pensions and enjoy morning walks along Orchard Beach, evening strolls in Woodlawn and Sunday dinners with our very extended family, including cherished daughters-in-law. The only regret I have about coming to America is that I was not prepared here for growing old. At home you'd have had to take care of a mother or a grandmother or an aunt in their later years and it would have given you an insight of what to expect. As I had not been in any real contact with the older generation, I had no idea what ageing entailed. I am learning very fast now, let me tell you.

I wonder if my mother ever missed having me around to mind her when she got sick. Would she have liked to have met my children, my husband? Did she regret sending me off that day, her little girl in ankle socks, on a journey from which I would never return? I often dream of Ireland, but I made my life in America and may God Bless Ma for that.

Recorded and written at Aisling Irish Community Center, creative writing workshops; November 2005 - May 2006

Our Wedding Day

Terry Connaughton, 1952

I flew from Shannon to New York in 1952. We had to stop in Gander on the way so it took about eight or nine hours at least. My brother was here before me and if it wasn't for that I probably wouldn't have been able to come at all. But back in the day the oldest brother came first, then the next, and then the next. My brother, Benny, came by boat in 1949. I came next even though I wasn't the next in line. Rory came after me and Albert came after him. When Benny came out, he sent his suit back to the next fellow, who was me, and I sent the suit back to the next brother and so on and so forth. That was how it was back in the day. I come from Athleague in County Roscommon; a small village with four pubs. That was the best way to describe the size of a village back then, by the amount of pubs in it.

I was born in 1933 to Peter and Dorothy Connaughton, and I was one of five children. My father ran a hackney business in the village and I think he had the first car ever in Athleague. He would take people on pilgrimages to Knock. He also repaired bicycles and I remember he had a sign outside the house for shoe repairs. He worked for a draper in Listowel for a number of years before he got married and was a member of the old IRA down there. A nun wrote a book one time in which she mentioned his name. She recalled how he had come to their house one night seeking refuge or a lift to a safer place and she had to refuse him. Her elderly parents were asleep at the time and she was afraid to endanger them. I was twelve years of age when he died and after that life became very tough for us. We hadn't a scrap of land and very few resources. I don't know how we survived at all.

There were happy times too at Athleague National School at the top of the hill and on the great fair day every year on the eleventh of July. We would wake up really early and the fair green would be packed with people and horses, the farmers erecting their pens. It was a huge boost to the village. I also attended the Christian Brothers in Roscommon and started my career as a barman/shop assistant in Roscommon town. From there I roved around County Galway in the towns of Mountbellew, Moylough and Ballinasloe. I even spent a year in England working in a distillery in London's West End.

Hurling was my first love though and I played at minor and senior level with Athleague, and I also lined out for the Roscommon senior team. I remember playing in Roscommon's 1952 Connaught Junior Hurling final win over Galway in John Murray's field in Athleague, their first time to win it in forty-six years. Shortly after that victory I left for America in my new suit and a pound in my pocket.

I liked New York straight away, it was very nice. I arrived in September so the weather was still warm. Because I played hurling, before I knew it I was playing here with Cork for the balance of that year. The following year, 1953, I transferred to the Clare hurling club and was with them for many years. Through the GAA you got to know people right off the bat, so that helped me to settle straight away. Also I stayed with my brother in an apartment in Inwood and, eventually, when my two other brothers arrived, we shared the place between us, so I didn't ever really feel homesick. If you gave the couch a wallop the dust would rise to the ceiling.

My first job was in construction with a man from Limerick, called McGlynn, and that lasted two weeks. Then I got a job with my brother out in a Grand Union warehouse, the supermarket people, out in New Jersey. I was working there for six or eight months and there was a strike vote with the employees and I remember getting a notice at the apartment, "You show up for work tomorrow or you'll be fired." So nobody showed for work, and everybody got fired. Then I went working in another warehouse in Merchant's Refrigeration with a man by the name of Paddy Sullivan who was president of a local union downtown. He had a lot of Irish guys working for him.

I was only fourteen months here when I volunteered for the draft. That means you're going to be called up anyhow so if you volunteer you get called sooner. I did my basic training out in Fort Dix, New Jersey, and then I was stationed in Germany for a year and a half. In Fort Dix at basic training, there were maybe three hundred troops in the one battalion and out of that three hundred; there might have been less than ten Irish born. The Americans then had an occupation force stationed in

Germany since some time after the Second World War. There were a lot of soldiers and troops in Germany then, in several different cities.

I was stationed in Bamberg, in Swiedford, and we had great fun in Germany. It was a lovely country with a great social life when we were there anyway. We were out every night, just about, if we had the money. Well really the pay scale wasn't very high and in my case, in those days you could get what's called a Class Two Allotment which meant that one hundred dollars we'll say of your salary was taken out and they would send another hundred along with it home to your mother. That was great for my mother. Two years later my brother, Rory, was able to do the same thing, so, for four years, she was getting all that money, and at that time it was a good bit. Of course, I was suffering because I was short in my salary, but I still had plenty.

U.S. Army 1954

You made your own fun anyhow. I got to go home to Ireland three or four times in the eighteen months. Korea actually had finished up in June of 1953, but anyone who signed up for the service in the few months after that were still considered a Korean vet and were eligible for any benefits that came from that war. Not that it amounted to that much, but I was still entitled to them all the same.

I came back a little early before discharge and I was sent to Fort Reilly, Kansas. There were six of us from New York. One fellow was probably what you would call an entrepreneur. He bought a car and charged us all a certain amount of money to accompany him home, which turned out to be cheaper than if we had to take a train or a bus. Anyhow we only got fifty miles when the car was run off the road in the snow, so that was the end of that. We'd already paid him so there was nothing we could do about it. In the end we had to take public transport back to New York.

I arrived back two years to the day from when I had set out. The law back then was that you were able to hold your superiority in any job you had held when you'd been drafted into the army. That was a strict law. They were obligated to take you back into your job at the same seniority. So I went back to the warehouse until I took the test for the Police Department. And maybe some six months later, I became a member of the NYPD, where I stayed for twenty years. I was stationed in Times Square for probably about twelve of those years. I loved the job. It was probably the first time in my life, especially in the early days that I actually looked forward to going to work, but that did wear off eventually.

Athleague, next stop America

It wasn't really dangerous, because Times Square back then was quite safe. There were always so many on the street. A lot of small things would happen and of course you could have a crowd of three hundred gather in five minutes when something did happen. There were always preachers on the street that time, and there was one lady called Nellie who preached the Gospel there on the corner of Broadway. The rule at the time was that they had to finish at eleven o'clock. But Nellie would never finish up until you forced her. Every single night we'd have to move Nellie and every night she'd say, "When you live by the gun, you'll die by the gun." I'm sure I had to tell Nellie to go fifty times, and that was Nellie's answer every night. We used to get a kick out of her.

After twelve years I got into the taxi squad, which was a plainclothes assignment, which was very nice. It basically was enforcing the taxi regulations. Back then we had the gypsy cabs, and they're still around today, but not in the same way. Gypsy cabs by law were not supposed to stop for people unless they had an appointment. You weren't supposed to hail down a gypsy cab. But sure they were stopping for people all over the city left, right, and center, with lights in their windows and taxi signs and what have you. So we would be enforcing the law on them. Then the medallion cabs that could pick up on the street were known to play games too—overcharging, refusing to take people, etc. That was the assignment anyhow, which was a nice job as police work goes. Then in 1974 or 1975 there were police officers laid off because of the financial situation of the city. I know there was somewhere over 3,000 officers laid off, which was a huge decision for any city to make. So the cozy taxi job was no longer in existence, and I was suddenly transferred back on to the beat, which didn't go over very well with me. I was sent down to 19th Street on the East Side, which was a nice area, and after about a year I was sent down to Police Headquarters to the Criminal Liaison Department where I retired out of. It didn't take me long to get through twenty years. I never regretted joining the force and its one job I'd encourage any young person to go into.

When we arrived over first, the older Irish people who were already established here, told us over and over again to get a job in the New York Telephone Company, in Con Edison, in the Police Force, or the Fire Department. They were the four jobs they always encouraged us to try for. I'd say it's a different story for the young Irish coming over today. Of course, they're much more educated now so they're probably going for different things. But I have to say, we may not have been as educated, I never went to school a day beyond twelve years of age and yet, nine years later, I was able to sit for the test for the Police Department, and the GED before that in the army. You needed a high school diploma and they made you sit for the equivalency in the army. We may not have been highly educated, but we were smart and I attribute that to the marvelous national school system in Ireland.

The other thing that helped me to get on the police force so fast was that after six months in the army in those days you could get your citizenship. So I became an American citizen in the embassy in Frankfurt, with a Polish guy and an Irish-American as my sponsors. I think if you signed up voluntarily you got the citizenship quicker than if you'd been drafted. So I was an American citizen in less than two years after landing here. That helped me get into the police force faster too.

From the time I was born, I've been deeply immersed in the GAA. It was a great outlet for anybody, and a great bonding thing. You were constantly having fun with other players that you played with and against. I wasn't a week in New York when I was training in Inwood Park. Back in those days there were goalposts erected by the Parks Department, not like the ones they have today in Van Cortlandt. On any given evening down there could be anything between thirty and forty Irish lads kicking ball and playing hurling. And that's just in Inwood alone. Sunday then Gaelic Park was automatic, after mass in Good Shepherd. And the strange thing about those days is that every man wore a white shirt on Sunday, even in the height of summer. If you actually ever saw any picture of spectators in Gaelic Park in those days, you'd see a sea of white shirts. It wasn't just the odd one, it was everyone.

I played Senior Hurling with the Clare club here for twenty-three years, during which time we won three championships. In 1957 I togged out for the New York All-Star Hurling team against Wexford, the reigning All-Ireland champions. In 1973 I toured the South Pacific with a New York All-Star Hurling and Football team playing games in Los Angeles, San Francisco, Auckland, Melbourne, Sydney and Camberra. In addition, I played Junior Football with Good Shepherd here and Senior Football with Roscommon. So I was kept busy, you could say.

Then there was the dancing. Friday night was always City Center; then you had the Jaeger House and the Tuxedo Ballroom. The Caravan came later on; that was in the Bronx, and that came later on. It was great fun, totally different than now. There was no music in pubs then, you just went to the pub for a drink. There was a bar in City Center, and of course it was a very busy one. And there was always an Irish bar near these places where you went for a drink first, that was automatic. But the women didn't go unless a man took them. The women never went into the bar alone or with each other. There was none of that; none of that. Across the street from the Jaeger House was a bar named the Carlow East, and that was automatic before the dance. You had Ruthie Morrissey singing, and Mickey Carton, and there was a fellow in City Center called Clint Miller, who was a great Country and Western singer. He had a huge following and that ballroom was probably the biggest of them all. It was the most popular too. It's a ballet place now, I think. There was no ballet back in those days, I'll tell you!

I met my wife, Ann Tuite, in Gaelic Park. She's from Oldcastle, County Meath, and during the course of one of our first conversations we discovered that every one of her siblings, and there were eleven of them, went to school to my aunt and uncle who were schoolteachers in Ballinacree near Oldcastle. That was an amazing coincidence. She was working in Emigrant Savings Bank in a branch down on 42nd Street, which was basically in the area where I was working also. So I would go in now and then to say hello, and that was the start of our romance. Even though there was a dance in Gaelic Park every Sunday night, it's funny that it was at the actual games that I met Ann. We are now the very proud parents of five children and seven grandchildren, and successfully run the Riverdale Steakhouse here together.

Inwood, early 60's – L to R: Terry and wife, Anne; brother, Rory and his wife, Carol, Brian Smith (Cavan) and John Cunningham (Roscommon)

I was vice-president of the New York GAA in 1971, 72, and 73, and then I was president in 1974, and again in 1988 and 1989. I beat Oliver O'Donnell in one of those elections. It was a busy enough job, especially in the fall or the winter because every club had a dinner dance and every club expected you to go to their function, otherwise you'd be the bad guy. Another activity I was instrumental in introducing into New York was Ladies Gaelic Football. I placed an ad in the paper in 1991, in the month of October, and the following season we started off with seven teams. I was President of the organization for four years and then I guess to keep me happy they made me Honorary Life President, a title of which I am very proud.

I always kept up the ties with Ireland. I even moved back there one time. When I retired from the Police Department, I packed up bag and baggage and moved my wife and five children back to Cloonbrackna Avenue in Roscommon town. It was a big change. Well, big is not the word I would use, huge is more like it. Ann and the children went over six months before me and they loved it. By the time I arrived they were well settled into school and everything, but sad to say after only three days I made the announcement, "I don't think I'll be able to stay here." And they wanted to stay. But I found it a huge change in life altogether.

We returned to New York a year later, the day Elvis Presley died, and that was that. We moved back to Inwood again. That was a big Irish neighborhood then, like Woodlawn is today. I got a job as night manager in Rosie O'Grady's when they were on 52nd Street before they moved up to 51st Street and Seventh where they are today. I was also down in their place on Murray Street. I probably worked for them for a year and a half at least. Then this accountant gentleman that I knew told me that the two brothers who owned The Riverdale Steakhouse had made an agreement that after a year if they didn't agree they'd sell the place, but they wouldn't sell it to each other. It was probably an unusual arrangement, but that was their decision anyhow and obviously they didn't agree, as they were ready to sell. So I pursued that and with a little help here and a little scraping there I managed to pull it off. That was in March of 1979, and I'll be here now twenty-seven years this March. It's a long way from my first bartending job back in Roscommon all those years ago.

I've been to every All-Ireland for the last twenty-five years and often visit Ireland once or twice a year besides that. Sometimes I went three or four times a year. The Ireland today is so different that you would think you were in another country almost. The economy is so good, it's fantastic. I'm delighted to see it. But unfortunately, as far as the GAA in New York is concerned, it's hurting us big time. We're suffering from reverse immigration. One time we had nine hurling teams here and we lost three of them in one year. The GAA in Ireland is improving in leaps and bounds. It's an extremely popular sport now over there at the moment with huge attendances, despite the games being broadcast on television, they're still getting crowds. You'll still have people go to see the game live on a cold day when they could as easily watch it at home. It's great. And of course, the new Croke Park is beautiful, no doubt about it. Everybody is extremely proud of it. The museum there is really something that everyone should go and see. You can click into All-Irelands back twenty, thirty, forty years and watch part of the game.

I've been to great All-Irelands. I was at the game in 1982 when Offaly did Kerry out of the five in a row. That was fantastic. I was with my brother, Albert, and it was just about almost over when he said to me that we should leave to beat a bit of the crowd. We were down near the bottom of the steps when I said, "The ball is coming down here one more time for Offaly. Let's just wait until this finishes out." Next thing we saw the ball go in. We saw the goal, to my delight, I might add, to my delight.

I've been in the bar business now so long and I love it. I only live a couple of yards away so it's handy. I can come back and forth; it's very convenient. The place almost runs itself. All the staff is here so long and everyone knows exactly what to do. Rosie was only saying to me the other day that she's here sixteen years now. Jimmy is here a long time too. Then you have Philomena; she's probably here longer than either one of them. And Breda must be here five or six years. It looks good. They're all happy. Well, they must be anyhow or they wouldn't still be here.

Well, that's it now. I've remembered things today that I haven't thought about in a long time. I'll be thinking of them again. I think it's something people will be interested in hearing about. There's hardly anyone coming over at all now and that's a pity. I'm here since I was nineteen years of age, and I've never regretted it. I've never regretted a day of it. I'm still very close to Athleague though. That's where I'm from and your home is your home no matter what.

Interviewed at The Riverdale Steakhouse,
Bronx, New York; January 14, 2006

Blowing the whistle to officially start
the 1968 St. Patrick's Day parade

Theresa McNamara, 1952

I came to New York in September 1952, on the SS Georgic with my two children and my mother in law, Mary McNamara. My son, PJ, was two and half and my daughter, Maureen, was only sixteen months old. My husband, Hugh, had left six months before us and we were coming out to join him. A neighbor of ours in Dromahair, County Leitrim, drove us to Cobh and I thought it was the greatest thing in the world to be going to America.

I didn't have much time for the entertainment on the boat because PJ became very ill and spent most of his time in the sick bay. There were a lot of American soldiers on their way back from duty in Germany and many of them were sick too. They must have caught some bug and passed it on to PJ. Maureen was sick too, but not anything like PJ. It was harder to watch the old lady sometimes than it was to watch the children, as she loved to walk out on deck along by the railings and I was afraid that she'd fall overboard. I was also afraid that she would become ill too. She was seventy-six years of age and it wouldn't do to lose her at that stage.

At night we would feed the children first and then the young mothers would take turns babysitting while the others had dinner. At our table was a lady from Cavan who was traveling to New York to attend her son's Ordination. She ended up staying here for a few years and we met up a few times, but when she returned to Ireland, we lost touch. Sometimes I tried going to a show, but more often than not I would be called down to the hospital room again to see to PJ.

I will never forget sailing up the Hudson River and seeing Manhattan for the first time. Hugh and all of his sisters and brothers were standing on the pier waiting for their mother. That is the reason she came, because all of her family were here, except for one son, Frank. She hadn't seen some of them in donkey's years. She also wanted to meet the grandchildren that she had never met. I was so delighted to see New

York that day, as I had been subjected to so much hardship on that boat.

We moved into an apartment on 327 Beekman Avenue, off 141st Street, in St. Luke's parish. I thought everything was just great after the scourging I had on the boat. I loved the apartment at first and couldn't believe we had our own phone. I also loved going to the Laundromat, as I'd never seen a washing machine before. Then an old man who worked with Hugh on the railroad gave him an old machine and I couldn't believe I had one to myself. I tried to describe it to my father when I called him at a neighbor's house one night; and he said "Well that's a new one on me."

Everyone in the building was Irish, except the Super, and people that time left their doors open so you always had company. Of course it also meant that you had no privacy and everyone knew your business. Despite all the excitement of getting familiar with a new place, I was lonely at first, as I was left at home with the children and couldn't look for a job, nor did I take part in any of the New York socializing at the time. I thought to myself, here I am over here all by myself and I only twenty-four years of age. None of my family was here, except for a few cousins whom I didn't know very well. My mother at home was dead lonely for the children, and the day I left my father had said, "I'll probably never see you again." I hadn't realized what I was letting myself in for.

I would take the kids out for walks and go over to my sister-in-law who had a boarding house on 140th Street. She had fourteen lodgers and I would help her make sandwiches for their lunches while the children played out back. I also loved to go shopping on Brook Avenue, but I was very nervous going downtown on the subway unless someone was with me. All of the stops had to be written down for me. One day I lost the slip of paper and got very anxious altogether when I thought I was lost.

Hugh was a very quiet man. He loved it here, because his whole family was here, but he was the type that would settle down anywhere. He was with the telephone company at first, but he left that and went on the railroad out in New Jersey. He played the accordion with a man named Mike McKenna and they would go to all the gatherings, but they never played at dances or anything. He used to enjoy it. We didn't go to too many dances until the kids grew up, then we would go to see his three nieces, The McNamara Entertainers, who played Irish traditional music.

They made several records and one of them, Margaret, owned a school of Irish dancing.

I only went to Gaelic Park once in a blue moon. Hugh went every Sunday religiously and he would bring the kids, but one time PJ got hit with a ball on the side of the head and after that I would keep them at home with me. We also vacationed in the Catskill Mountains several times. Another place we loved to go was Pinebush, upstate New York, where we stayed with Mike White, a cousin of my father's. Recently I spent one whole day up there with my son, Hughie, trying to find the place where we stayed. Do you think we could find it? No way. I was so disappointed.

The real reason we came to America was to save to build a house back in Ireland. Hugh had a small farm there, but the house was in very bad condition, and he the idea that we could build a new one. We thought it would be easy; that we could just come to America for a year or two and that would be it. But, boy it didn't turn out that way.

We did return once, in 1959, with the intention of staying, and I had a job getting used to it again. You never can get in on the habit of home after leaving it. We settled outside Dromahair and, instead of rebuilding the old house, we bought a farm with a two-story house on it. My mother was delighted to have us back and would cycle down to see us every day. Hugh loved it and got in on going to the fairs again, but then he developed sciatica and he was nearly crippled with it. His family out here in New York advised him to come back to the hot weather, which we did, but it didn't do him a bit of good. Even though I had found it hard to settle, I still didn't want to return to New York, but Hugh did and the children did. They couldn't get used to the schooling in Ireland. My mother-in-law had gone back to Ireland before us with her daughter and son-in-law and she was supposed to come back to New York with them, but she wasn't feeling that good, and then she was supposed to return to New York with us but she wasn't able. She died around 1964.

We left Ireland again in 1962, this time on a plane from Shannon. We were so excited, because we'd never have flown before. I thought I'd never get on that plane. Before we landed in New York I remember seeing all the lights of the city and my son, Hughie, who'd been born when we were at home and was still very young, exclaimed, "Do you think it might be Christmas over here?"

We came back to St. Luke's parish and the children all attended Catholic school there. I went to work downtown serving the lunches in an office cafeteria. It was so funny at first because when they'd ask for something and I wouldn't know from the dog what they were looking for. One day this man asked for sherbet and I looked all over hoping I'd see something with the name on it, but I hadn't a clue what it was. In the end he asked me if I was making it. There was one very nice customer who would come in and he would always help me find things. I eventually got used to it, but I couldn't believe that there were so many different types of food compared to what we were used to in Ireland. I would say to Hugh, "If you're waiting on me to make our fortune here, you'll be waiting forever."

We didn't go back to Ireland again for a long time, as we couldn't afford it, and nobody ever came over to see us. I wanted in the worst way to bring my father out, as he'd been here too for many years and he'd always be asking me about different places. His name was Michael McHugh, and he had lived in Brooklyn, and worked on the building of St. Patrick's Cathedral and then was involved in the construction of a railway out in New Jersey. He would like to have stayed in America but he returned to Ireland because of the Depression and met my mother in Mullaghmore, County Sligo. They settled in Leitrim.

I was born on the 4th of July, 1927, in the parish of Killenummery, townland of Tullynascreena, in the village of Dromahair. Of course nobody back in Ireland passed any remarks about my birthday when I was growing up, and then when I came to America there was a big fuss made out of it. I had three brothers. One died at infancy, the other at six years, and then the third lived right into his seventies. I had six sisters and none of them immigrated. I was the only one. We were probably a bit better off than most at the time because my father bought a farm when he went home and he rented another one up in Sligo where he kept cattle. They called him the Yankee. He had a slight accent and we used to copy him.

His sister, Ann, stayed in America. She lived in Brooklyn and fostered fourteen children. I went to see her when I came out. He had another sister back in Ballinagar who lived with their mother and they died five weeks apart. I remember getting into the car to go to my grandmother's funeral and we were so excited to be going in a car. Then five weeks later we heard that Aunt Ellen had died and all we could think of was that we'd be going in the car again. I remember that well.

I loved my maternal grandmother. Only one of us would be let go visit her at a time, as we had to sleep in the same bed as her. Then she'd make us our breakfast and get us ready for Mass. We'd have to walk two miles up the road to the church, but we loved all that because it was a novelty to be away from home for a while and made a fuss of. She lived in the nearby village of Drumkeerin. Rose Cunningham is also from there, from the Black Road. I'll always remember her and her sisters; they were such a good-looking family. I met her here in the Aisling Center one day and she could not know how I remembered her. Because I'm seventy-nine now, you know, and she must be nearly ninety.

Theresa shortly after arriving in NY

I went to the local National School in Tullynascreena where our teacher's name was Miss McMurrough. She was nice. She was older and would get tired a lot so we would be delighted when she needed a rest. Then at lunchtime she and the Master would go into his room and lock the door and we knew well what they were doing. Courting of course. One day this lad, oh he was a blackguard of a buck, went in and knocked on the door and then ran away. Oh! And of course we all got slapped for it. The Master was a very thick man; he would slap you all the time depending on what humor he was in. Oh! I was glad to get out of it when I was fourteen. I watched these neighbor's kids for a few years and then got married when I was twenty. We also had to work on the farm at home and I hated it. That's one of the reasons I was delighted to come to America, to get away from the farm work.

I met Hugh at the sports day in Dromahair. He was also from

Drumkeerin in the parish of Creevelea. A friend of mine introduced me to him and he bought a bag of oranges from one of the stalls and put it on my bike. He asked to walk me home, but I only let him leave me as far as the Five Roads – a great meeting place in our time where the five roads from Tullynascreena, Killagvoggy, Dromahair, Ballinagar and Drumconnor converged. I had a date with another lad that night and I didn't want him to see me. Hugh then asked me to meet him that night as well and I didn't know what to do with the two of them. I decided on Hugh anyhow and wore a scarf down the road that night so as the other lad wouldn't recognize me. I wanted my sister to go up and meet him and tell I wasn't coming, but she wouldn't. I let him down anyhow and took Hugh and never regretted it. The following week I was out turning a cow and didn't she run off on me and I fell and broke my ankle trying to catch her. The other lad said it was because I couldn't have luck after letting him down. But Hugh would come all the way up to Manorhamilton to visit me in the hospital and I knew he was sound after that.

Theresa and Hugh on their 40th Wedding Anniversary

We had one of the biggest weddings around that part of the county in a while, because both my sister and I got married on the same day. The ceremony was in Killanummery Church and we had the reception in the Abbey Hotel in Dromahair because there were too many people and we wouldn't have been able to put them up in the house. I remember for the breakfast we had chicken and ham and that was a big thing that time. I made my own wedding cake and I brought one of the tiers out here with me. We ate it that first Sunday in the Bronx at a party given in our honor.

My wedding dress was blue and I wore a navy blue coat that I'll remember to my dying day. I bought it in Sligo and I just loved it. I had a hat and gloves too and it was the first time that I had the whole lot together. My sister wore royal blue and someone teased her because it was the color of the army at the time. She married a Mayo man; he was a contractor from Ballina. We celebrated our 50th wedding anniversary in 1997, but, unfortunately my brother-in-law didn't make it, as he'd only died a few years previously from cancer. Hugh and I celebrated ours with a mass down in St. Patrick's Cathedral and a party afterwards in Rory Dolan's.

Our three children have all done great. When she graduated from high school, my daughter, Maureen went to work in a bank downtown. She eventually went back to school to study physiotherapy and now lives in Dublin, where she has her own practice. She went back when people over there told her there were a lot of opportunities in that field. I never thought she'd settle there, but she absolutely loves it and is doing extremely well. Her son, Eugene, is attending Trinity College and her daughter, Linda, will be starting there in September. Her other son, Michael, remained in New York. PJ started off his career in Gristede's, the grocery people downtown. Then he was a Manager with A&P supermarkets for years before going into the bar business, and now he has his own Deli here in the Bronx. Hughie is a contractor and has his own construction business, so they're all doing very well. They've all been so good to me, my children, absolutely marvelous—and my grandchildren too. My granddaughter, Siobhan, is getting married on the 22nd of July and I can't wait for her wedding in Pearl River. She's taken me shopping a few times for a dress, but in the end I'm wearing one I've had all along. She is such a wonderful girl; I hope she is lucky in her marriage.

I think Ireland is changed too much, I can't believe it. People don't have as much time for you anymore. They don't even turn off the television when a visitor arrives. My mother used to tell me not to mind them. She died when she was seventy-nine, but I couldn't go home for her funeral. Hughie was at summer camp at the time down south in some Christian Brothers college and he got very sick. He was sick for months, ended up in hospital and all, and I couldn't go to the funeral. I did make it to my father's and people thought it was because I preferred him, but that was not the case, it was just circumstances.

I go back all the time now and stay with Maureen. Last year I spent five months with her and went around visiting them all. Thank God I got to see my sister in Sligo, as she died only a few months ago. I'm glad I came to America, and even gladder now, as I don't think I could live in Ireland again. Maureen thought I'd go home and stay with her, but I prefer it in New York.

Hugh died in 2001 after a long struggle with Alzheimer's. Oh! My God! What a disease that is. I now live here on Bronx River Road in a one-bedroom apartment close to my two sons and my grandchildren. Next year will be the big 80, so I hope I make it. I'm finding it very hard to get around now and don't go many places unless Siobhan comes down and takes me shopping or I come up to the Aisling Center. That's been a great outlet for me and we have a lot of fun and Thank God I'm still in fairly good health. It's been a long road though since that day we sailed up the Hudson and I looked down on to the pier and saw Hugh's smiling face waiting there for me.

Interviewed at Aisling Irish Community Center,
Yonkers, NY; June 19, 2006

Mike Cremins, 1953

I came September 25th, 1953, on the Italia, the home lines, from Southampton. I was working in London at the time in construction; before that I had been in Glasgow and in Edinburgh in the paper mills. One summer we were living in a camp away out in Glendevon, a beautiful place, out in the mountains, but we had to leave after five months, before the snow came down and the frost. Eventually, I figured out that America would be a better country and that I couldn't always be packing my satchel every second year. I had a brother and a sister here already, and my father's people were in Boston and my mother's in Connecticut. I was all set.

I grew up in Ballinskelligs in County Kerry in the Parish of Prior. Baile na Sceilge was a beautiful place located on the magnificent Skellig Ring between Waterville and Valentia Island. We spoke plenty of Gaelic in our time and ate plenty of fish, fresh and salted. However, it's changed so much now, too many houses; there is nothing but houses everywhere. You won't see a green field soon if they keep going. It's a beautiful area still and great for the tourists. In the parish of Prior you have three churches, ours is St. Michael's and the next Church is the Glen, which is St. Finan's and then in Portmagee there's St. Patrick's. In our day, the three churches would be kept going, now they only have the one priest and they take turns having Mass. They swap around and the priest has to move from one church to the other. The bishop said to me he's lucky to have one, and that it's not that there's not enough priests; it's that there are too many churches. But I had an argument with him over that. Some of the people in the really rural areas were too far scattered around and couldn't travel twenty or thirty miles to Cahirciveen, or Waterville or even Kenmare, so they had to build all those churches.

St. Michael's was the capital. It was to there that the parishioners from the Glen and Portmagee used come to be confirmed. We used to be delighted as kids. Our house was nearest to the Church on the main

Cahirciveen Ballinskelligs road and it was a stop off place for everyone. They'd leave their horses and traps in our yard and the women would bring their daughters in to see my aunt who was a dressmaker and she'd put the finishing touches to the outfits. Then they'd come back again after the ceremony and tea would be made and some of them wouldn't go home until five o'clock in the evening. And of course we kids would get a few pennies and we'd be delighted. That was a lot that time. It was the same for funerals or other important occasions. The burying ground was back in Ballinaskelligs west. There used to a monastery off the coast there on Skellig Michael but, it was shelled by the Vikings. They arrested the monks and the last one died of starvation on the boat.

There was a great Gaeltacht there in my time and they came from all over to learn Irish. Everyone made a penny out of it, keeping children in their houses, but there's not so much of it now, as the insurance is too high. A few of them might come, but they stay in a bit of a hostel. It's become too expensive for the local people to keep them, as everyone has to be insured. What a shame. I loved growing up there on a small farm and it broke my heart the day I left it on the 29th of September, 1949, the day I went to Scotland.

I had a great time on the boat coming to America. It was full of Germans who got on at Le Havre, which was our first port of call and that was it then until Halifax. We were all day there and couldn't go ashore because we weren't American citizens. It was a beautiful day and the crew was out fishing for mackerel. The Germans were very friendly and their beer was only ten cents a glass. There were five of us at the breakfast table, two German couples and me. And I don't know what was wrong with the women, whether it was jealousy over their dress or their make-up or what, but every morning they came down to breakfast fighting. They'd be shouting away at one another in German and the two men never said a word. There were also a few English and Scottish passengers and the rest were French.

There were only three of us Irish, myself and two girls; one from Tipperary and one from Kerry. I was lucky; I had two lassies with me. One of them was engaged to a lad from Donegal, I think O'Donnell was his name, Pat, and he was to meet her at the boat. And he did. He met her alright, but they went their separate ways after. He married someone else and she married eventually, a long time after. She used write to me every Christmas and then all of a sudden for two years running there was no Christmas card and when I contacted her sister, she told me she'd died.

I came to Broadway at 92nd Street and I stayed there with my aunt and sisters in St. Gregory the Great parish. I didn't like New York at first. I couldn't get over the subway, how old-fashioned it was in comparison to the London underground. The seats were made of straw and it would stick up your backside; and we were all packed in like cattle and the people were much rougher back then, although they were more refined than they are now, I suppose. You'd get a seat alright on Canal Street and if you didn't that time you'd surely get one around 145th Street, as all the Jewish people would be getting off there. They all lived down near Yankee Stadium that time, on the Concourse, and around Jerome Avenue. Or else if you started coughing you'd surely move them then. This guy told me that trick, start coughing behind your newspaper, he told me, and they'll jump up straight away. They were all scared of getting tuberculosis.

Ticket to Gaelic Park

Of course the main thing was to go to Gaelic Park the first Sunday I landed. It was always a place you'd meet somebody, a great place for finding a job, a real hiring hall. There'd be about four thousand people there every week. They had seats inside and there was a big stand at the back of the goal. Then we'd have the day of the big Feis, the United Irish Councils Feis was held in Fordham University in the morning, and the finals of the games would be played in Gaelic Park the same evening and could go on till nightfall. That was one of the most important occasions of the year, and then of course there was the Cardinal Cushing day. He was from Boston and John Kerry O'Donnell would give him the field that day and it would be crowded. Then we would go up to Boston for his field day up there. Every county had a field day back then, and that drew an awful lot of people because they'd get a cut out of the gate.

There was immense rivalry between Kerry and Cork at the time and some pretty vicious battles between these two teams, but Kerry always seemed to get the better of them some way or another. If they were playing you were sure of a huge crowd.

Then of course there was a slump in the seventies and there was no immigration at all for a long time. They all blamed Bobby Kennedy for that but he played no hand, act or part of it. What happened was the Irish weren't filling their quota at all, at all, and so they gave the surplus to the South American countries whose quota was low, and eventually Ireland lost out altogether. The games were bad in the park during that time and they didn't pick up again for another ten years and now of course it's gone back to that again.

John Kerry O'Donnell, who leased Gaelic Park, used to say, "I'm ninety percent Kerry and I'm ten percent mule." They were his words. He fell out with a lot of people, but I found John Kerry to be a very, very, very good man. He helped a lot of causes here. Any kind of a charity at all, when he was approached he'd give the hall free without fear or favor. He was very outspoken, a very, very, straight man. As good as you would meet. But I would say at times you would have to keep on the right side of him.

One time they were picking the New York team to go back and play in Ireland. Normally they would go through all the counties here to pick the team. Paddy Hughes, from Leitrim, was one of the selectors. He was an old man who smoked a pipe. One day he pulled on the pipe and said; "I'll pick the team to go back to Ireland—there'll be fourteen Kerry men and my son, Jack" I don't know if he got his way or not. His son got on the team all right, but I don't know about fourteen Kerry men; there would have been nine all right. That was the mid-sixties. There were some great players back then. Des Foley from Dublin was the best man to ever field a ball from the air besides Mick O'Connell. Kerry still has a good team. I still have great hopes for them, but Tyrone was the better team last year.

I saw two women fighting one day in the Park. It was a fine afternoon in May and Offaly and Mayo were playing. And honest to God the two women wouldn't stop. The Offaly woman would shout, "C'mon Offaly, show them your beef," and the Mayo woman would shake her umbrella. "Where would you find beef in the Bog of Allen?" My God! I thought she was going to hit her until the Offaly woman stomped off shouting, "Remember one thing, we were never afraid of the west." Oh! There'd be more fun down there. It was a great place. As for Darby's goal, when Offaly beat Kerry in 1982, it broke my heart, although I admired him for it. But they never expected it. They thought he'd get a point, but when he went for that goal, I'll tell you I sweated bullets. I was watching it abroad in the Concourse. It was a big thing. Offaly will never forget it, and neither will Kerry.

Mother's Day used to be a big day that time. Gaelic Park would be packed as usual. You wore a red rose if your mother was dead and a white one if she was alive and everyone wore one or the other. Now nobody can go anywhere if it's Mother's Day because they're all going out for fancy dinners. We had our dinner that time too, but we went home and ate it. The women cooked it themselves. There was no such thing as calling out for the Chinaman to bring it around. The majority of the Irish girls that time did housework downtown, on Fifth Avenue and on Lexington, and they all learned to be great housekeepers. They all had their own living quarters; their own apartments and they might have Sundays off. There was no such thing as a girl bartending; that was another thing. A few of them went into the telephone company and an amount worked at that big restaurant, Schrafft's and they all came out of those places with new experience in the line of cooking, and it never did them a bit of harm altogether. Do you think a girl nowadays would work in housekeeping? Not at all. That would be an insult. The majority of the Irishmen back then worked long shore on the docks. That started to fall away after World War II. The Unions were strong then too. Merchant's had a warehouse on 17th Street and 10th Avenue and seventy percent of the Irish footballers worked there at one time or another. The Cork team was even known as the Warehouse Team, as the President of the Local 818 Union, Paddy Sullivan, was from Cork and he picked all the best players by promising them a job. The telephone company hired a lot too. I could have been with them; I got the form, but I didn't go with them. I often regretted that. You would have had to suffer it out a bit, with a mop and a pail, but after a while you could have worked your way up and have made anything up to $70 a week.

I had various jobs. I started off working with the Grand Central railroad, but I knew it was only temporary. They'd be very, very busy coming up to Christmas from about October to New Year's Eve. Then I got laid off and the snow was on the ground. There was a great priest too, Father O'Donnell, at that time who helped people get work. But it was through a man from County Galway, Martin Donoghue, that I got my next job. He brought me down to the Henry Hudson Hotel there on 59th Street, off Columbus Avenue. The Manager, a man called Fox, offered me a job running the elevator for $35 a week. I stayed there for about six months and then I joined the warehouses down on Twelfth Street—a rough job and I had an Irish boss and then I was laid off there. So it wasn't always that easy.

Then in April 1955, on Good Friday, I got a job in Merchants Refrigeration. I stayed there until I retired, close to thirty-seven years later. I operated a forklift and did manual labor for about a year down on North Moore Street just below Canal, handling fish, all kinds of fish, and dates and figs from the Middle East, Iraq, and Iran. They even came in from Iran in the Eighties after the hostages being released, but they were too expensive then, the tariffs were too high so people stopped buying them. I wonder are they coming now?

The dancehalls were great. That's another change. Now you haven't a dance hall at all. You had the Peter Stuyvesant on 59th Street, and of course you had the Caravan, and the Jaeger House, that was the main one. Then of course you had two cabarets that hardly ever closed. You left the dance at one and then went down to Kennedy's and the place would be full of smoke, you'd hardly see the person next to you, and then there was the All Ireland bar on Third Avenue. There was great music there. Of course the girls wouldn't be satisfied unless you brought them to Pickford's. Oh! They wouldn't go home until they had their ham and eggs in the morning. We wouldn't go home until five o'clock, change our clothes and then out to work or to Mass. That was another thing. Nobody missed Mass and it wasn't that you thought that you should go, but you went because it was the proper thing. But now that's all gone. Every church was packed. You'd have to stand, but not anymore.

I met my wife in the Catskill Mountains. Everyone went there at the weekends and we did the same thing up there as we did down here. Dancing, swimming, singing, but I'd say there was more singing done at the bar than there was around the swimming pool. Sure they were great times, the food and all was lovely. We lived on Walton Avenue when we got married about three blocks west of the Concourse, where my first child was born. Then we moved on to University Avenue. My children went to school to St. Nicholas of Tolentine and then my two girls went to St. Simon Stock at 180th and St. Andrew's Avenue, and my youngster went to grade school here in Yonkers. Two of them went to College and my eldest girl got a job in Metropolitan Life the day after she finished high school. She's there now twenty years. She came out great.

The most exciting night ever in my life was when President Kennedy was elected. There was a Cavan man living across the hall from us on the Concourse. We were up all night. We couldn't sleep. We'd go from apartment to apartment according as the votes were counted. We'd have a beer and a shot and the women would chat over the coffee. When we got up the next morning at six o'clock, Nixon still hadn't conceded even though he'd lost Illinois. He didn't concede until four o'clock the next afternoon. The boss at work, a Dutchman, was a Nixon man, and he was mad. He started to fume altogether when a young messenger boy swung by on his bicycle and we told him the news that Nixon had conceded. He whistled, "That bum should be gone long ago."

They were great years, the Kennedy years, and it wasn't just because he was Irish. I went for his policy. He was too far ahead of his time. He brought a lot of things along too soon, like Civil Rights and things like that. A lot of the Irish didn't like him because they were McCarthy men, radicals, against the Communists, and McCarthy having an Irish name and being a Catholic and all that. An awful lot of the Irish turned Republican because of him. In the present day, the Democrat party in my books is going too much to the left, and that's what's ruining them, the abortion thing and the gay marriage thing. They have to get rid of some of those ideas and they've a long way to go yet. But on the other hand, the other ones are gone so far to the right, a way, way off to the right. I'm still a Democrat to the backbone, but it wouldn't be any harm if they got their act together.

Besides that of President Kennedy another great election that I remember is Fianna Fail's first victory in 1932. There were bonfires blazing all over the Ballinskelligs Portmagee headland. Eamon DeValera had formed the party in 1926 and ours was a real DeValera house. When we came from school we were given sods of turf and told to go up to this field high above the house where the rest of the parish was gathered and we got the bonfires going. Then they all assembled at Garry's cross with pikes topped with sods of turf, which they covered in paraffin oil and set alight as they marched down to the village. Someone was playing an accordion. You could see the torches and hear the music for miles. And of course the next day in school the children were fighting; as if the Civil War was going on, and you'd get a thumping if you disagreed with someone.

DeValera was a great statesman, but I don't know if he was a good president. I turned against him because of the executions during the Civil War. I admired Michael Collins very much. It was Fine Gael and the blueshirts who stole Collins' great name away from him. But I guess he wasn't clever enough for Lloyd George who was a "wizard" altogether. George said to him, "Me and you will talk over here, a Celt to a Celt." But it was only a ploy to get him away from the others. He was cutting his throat at the same time.

I was here seven years before I got back. I would have gone home for good anytime within the first ten years, but after that I wouldn't have bothered at all. My father died in June 1959, but I wasn't able to go back because I had a job and a young family. Before my mother died in 1960, I went back for six weeks. She died the week after I left to come back here. The Kerryman's Association ran a charter and it was the first of its kind from New York to Dublin. I was lucky to get leave off the job because my foreman who was from Westmeath hadn't been in Ireland since 1927 and of course they had to let him go. Luckily they let me go too. He hadn't seen his mother in over thirty years and the only way he would know her was that she was to tie a white handkerchief around her wrist. I'll always remember walking across the tarmac in Dublin airport that day and seeing this little old lady all dressed in black waving the white hankie at a son she would hardly recognize. That's the price of immigration.

Interviewed at The Riverdale Steakhouse,
Bronx, New York; January 29, 2006

Gaelic Park, October 1, 2006
Spectators at 2006 NY Senior Football Final
Kerry beat Leitrim 14 points to 1.10

Chris Butler, 1955

I left my home in County Offaly in 1955 to board the S.S. America, which was the fastest ship in the world at the time until the S.S. United States came along. I had the option to fly or sail, but my mother's relatives had come by boat, so that was how I would come too. I had two uncles and an aunt from my mother's side over here, but nobody from my father's, which was unusual at the time. I came from a family of six boys and I was the one picked to go. It wasn't really necessary for me to leave home, as I was working in a hardware store at the time, D. Williams in Tullamore, and by then there were only four of us brothers left – one having died at infancy and the other when he was seven years old. The eldest son was working at home and the next had been called to the guards, so it wasn't that I had to go in order to pursue a better way of life, but my mother had it in her head that I would be the bridge between her two families on each side of the Atlantic. Somehow or other it fell to me, Christy Butler, that's what they called me at home, and off I went to America.

My clearest memory of the trip is being offered these exotic cocktails at the Captain's dinner every night and not trying one of them. I left Ireland as a pioneer. Needless to say I didn't remain that way, but I didn't taste my first beer until I was stationed in Germany with the U.S. Army a few years later. My first impression of New York was mesmerizing. I thought it was massive; a terrific place altogether. I'll never forget it, it was the 3rd of July and ninety-six degrees when we landed, and I dressed in a dark, heavy suit. The next day was Independence Day and my cousin, Frances, took me out to Rockaway Beach where I got massive sunburn, which kept me sick in bed for a week. I got blood poisoning and everything. I remind her of that to this day. We have a great laugh over it. And listen to this, her father was Frank (Francis) Callan from Dunleer in County Louth, her mother was called Frances and then they christened the daughter Frances too. There must have been some confusion in that house when the mail came!

They lived in Mount Vernon at the time and shortly afterwards they moved to White Plains, and I went with them, where I got a room in a Boarding House on Mamaroneck Avenue. My first job was in a local supermarket, the First National, where I was moved around from check-out to filling shelves to packing groceries and all that kind of thing. It was a different world back then, of course, and we had to have good addition, subtraction and multiplication skills, as there were no computers, cash registers or calculators. Everything had to be totted up on paper or even in your head. Then my aunt decided that I should work in the New York Telephone Company. It was the only one then; there weren't all the different telephone companies you have today. She took me downtown to West Street where she knew someone, she may have slipped them a bottle or something, who knows, but I was hired anyhow and started the following Monday morning at the branch in White Plains. The boss wasn't a very nice guy and the first thing he asked me to do was to take a broom and sweep the street around the building. Well, I wasn't very pleased, and I guess I took an attitude, you know, Irish pride and all that. Did he think I came all this way to sweep the streets, after all weren't they paved with gold? We didn't get off to a good start, but I did stay for a while until I got in with the Irish crowd, found my feet, and headed off in a different direction. I don't know if my aunt ever forgave me for it, as it was considered a great job back then. I might have made the wrong decision at the time, but I can't look back now.

Anyhow, I had started going to the dances and playing hurling in Gaelic Park and meeting loads of the Irish down here. There weren't that many up in White Plains, so this was a great breakthrough for me. I met a fellow, Pat McEvoy from Cavan, who worked for TWA, and one night he asked me did I ever want to go home again? Of course, I did. So he suggested I go working for the airlines. He told me that Eastern Airlines were hiring at the time so I applied and got a job in their reservations office in Manhattan. I moved in with Pat in his two-bedroom apartment somewhere in the area of Eagle Avenue and 149th Street. We danced in The Star of Munster, City Center, the Jaeger House, and the Tara ballroom, which was around 149th Street and Third Avenue. There wouldn't be any resemblance of ballrooms like that around today. In fact, The Shamrock Club down there in St. Brendan's, would have similar sort of dances, like the waltz, foxtrot, quickstep, which was all we did back then. However, my six-month stint in America was almost coming to an end, and it was time to register for the Draft. I went down to the Selective Services office, got my draft card, and within the next six months I was sent to Fort Knox in Kentucky for eight to ten weeks basic training, and then up to Fort Dix in New Jersey to be prepped for overseas before being shipped out to Germany. Nearly a year to the day of arriving in America, when I think about it, I was gone again.

In the meantime, I had met the girl who was to become my future wife—Lily Philbin from Belmullet in County Mayo. She was staying with her aunt on the Concourse, a Mrs. McIntyre, and was working in Duvernoy Bakeries in Mount Vernon. The night I met her I left the apartment to take the subway downtown to one of the dances in Manhattan. I stood for ages on the platform of the Lexington line there on 149th Street and still no sign of the train coming. I had bought my token and all, which was only about five or ten cents at the time, when I suddenly said to myself, what am I doing waiting here like this when there's a dancehall only up the street. So I walked back up the stairs, out through the turnstile and headed for the Tara and that was the night I met Lily. We were going out for a few months when I got my orders to go to Germany.

It never dawned on me not to do it, not to sign up nor to fail any of the tests, as the rumor was that if you didn't do well you'd get early discharge. I did think about it at times, as I found basic training very rough. I didn't like it at all, but I always remembered what was said to me before I left home and that was, "No matter where you are, Christy, always do your best." So I did my best. And what came out of it was that I always had easy service and spent the whole sixteen months in Germany. The irony was that a lot of the guys, who had deliberately failed tests and all that, were sent on infantry duty to Korea. Even though the war was over, that was still a terrible job altogether. I, meanwhile, got home two or three times to Ireland and I did a bit of touring around Europe with a few of the boys. We visited places like Paris, Vienna, Luxembourg, and several parts of Germany itself. In the meantime, I was still writing to Lily. In fact, we have a big bag of letters at home that we wrote to each other during that time. Of course, we never look at them now, maybe one day somebody will.

Lily reluctantly gave me her home address in Mayo before one of my trips to Ireland. One day, my brother, Michael, drove me and my parents from Birr to Belmullet to see my future in-laws, which was what I had in my head at the time. It was probably very presumptuous of me, but that was the way I was thinking anyhow. We got to Ballina and it was pouring rain. We thought we were in Belmullet and settled my parents into a hotel for a cup of tea, only to discover that it was a further thirty-eight miles to Knocknalower, so Michael and I set off again, leaving my mother and father behind, as the journey was proving too much for them, and we reached the Philbin homestead by evening. We met her mother, father and three sisters, the other three were out here, stayed the night and had a lovely visit altogether, and before I left I told them I'd be back.

Chris & Lily, New York, 1960

In 1958 I found myself in New York again, only to discover that Eastern Airlines was on strike and I was out of work. Luckily, Aer Lingus had just opened their office in Manhattan, so I applied and got hired almost immediately, and there I stayed for thirty-seven years. I started out in the mailroom, and then moved on to reservations and sales. We would often take off on what was called a sales blitz when we would visit the various travel agents all over the country and the main Aer Lingus offices in the United States. Somehow I had got the traveling bug into my head and it was a great job altogether for that.

In the meantime, I married Lily. The wedding took place on the 30th of April, 1960, in Our Lady of Refuge Church on 196th Street off the Grand Concourse. We had our reception in Alex & Henry's on 161st Street and lo and behold for our honeymoon I took her to Ireland for her first trip back in the five years she had been here. So she'd left home single and went back a married woman.

That was our first trip of many. Because of my position with Aer Lingus we were able to get home twice or three times a year. As the old saying goes, we were always going home. We visited Russia during the Soviet Union time and have practically been around the world twice, out by the Pacific and back through the Atlantic, visiting my cousins in Melbourne several times. We weren't blessed with children, through no fault of our own, which was a terrible pity. We also had a few disappointments with adoptions, both here and in Ireland, the red tape got to us and in the end we gave up. Maybe we shouldn't have, that has always been a huge regret, but let's put it this way, we've never blamed one another. We've had a very happy marriage, it will be forty-six years in April, and we're still enjoying a very happy life together. But I guess the reason we could travel so much was because we were childless. God works in mysterious ways.

I grew up outside the town of Birr in County Offaly, in the Parish of Eglish/ Drumcullen, but we always went to church in the town and I went to school to the Presentation Brothers in Birr where we were called the country boys. The brothers were the bad boys, however, and we were often badly beaten by them. I was terrified of school and would be shivering walking in the road every morning, but they did give us a good education, and I suppose when you think of all we've heard in recent years, we were lucky to get off with just a beating.

I played a lot of hurling in my day, all the boys did. I have seven school medals, and didn't I lose every one of them? I would love to get replicas some day, if that was possible. One year I had the choice of playing minor hurling with either Birr or Drumcullen and I chose Birr. Would you believe it, Drumcullen won the championship that year? I missed all that terribly when I came to America. I arrived in New York with three hurling sticks tied together and started off straight away playing for Offaly in Gaelic Park.

I also missed the social life at first, the dances in the Marian Hall and the Oxmantown Hall in Birr and heading off in a car to Ferbane, Kilcormac, Tullamore, Roscrea, Thurles, we'd go anywhere to dance. That was the great showband era and we would drive miles just to see Mick Delahunty or the Clipper Carlton. I always loved Irish music and song and was a member of the Gaelic League. We used to run ceilis in the Town Hall in Birr every Tuesday night and I was also involved in the annual feis. Oh! Yes I missed home a lot at first and my family especially. I just missed the little things they'd be doing every day. It was a very innocent world back then compared to what it is now. It was just the lack of contact that you'd miss more than anything.

I missed my father most of all, I missed my mother too, I don't like to make distinctions, but talk about a man, my father was just a great man. He had a garden that was second to none, flowers like you never saw and vegetables for our own table every day. In a way we were better off than the townspeople in that respect, as we hadn't to buy any produce at all. I used to love helping him with the barley and the potatoes; I just loved working with him out on the small farm. He never drank, so we never suffered in that respect, I never saw alcohol in our home. Yes, I missed my father an awful lot, but I was lucky that I got home more than others.

I have tried to keep up the old Irish traditions, to keep the culture alive in this country. I have been a member of the County Offaly Association since the very beginning and have been with the Ancient Order of Hibernians since 1970 or thereabouts, a good thirty years anyhow. Founded in New York in 1836, the AOH is the oldest Catholic lay organization in America. My brother-in-law encouraged me to join the Bronx County, Division 9, and I have been the President of this section for almost twelve years now. We are a fraternal organization and we support various charities, but our numbers are dwindling due to reverse immigration to Ireland and also the younger generation are not as interested in joining societies as we were back in our day.

We are still sticking together, however, and still hold monthly meetings. We used to meet in St. Philip Neri's parish there on the Concourse and when their church burned down; we ran a dance and donated the proceeds towards its repair. We support a lot of Irish causes especially that of immigration reform and are ardently in favor of the newly formed Irish Lobby for Immigration Reform (ILIR) in their lobbying for the Kennedy/McCain immigration reform bill. We run a dance every year up in Rory Dolan's, and last year I was the Bronx County Aide to the Grand Marshall of the St. Patrick's Day parade, Denis Kelleher. That was a tremendous honor altogether.

When I left Aer Lingus in 1994, I didn't miss the job, but I missed the people, and I knew I wanted to get involved in something. A friend of mine who was an ex-captain in the Air Force told me that I was eligible for a medical card from the Veteran's Hospital in the Bronx and that I should go along with my discharge papers and apply. When I was down there I saw a sign that the Chaplain needed a helper and I went to see him and he took me on straight away. I've been there since giving out Communion and talking to the patients. God works in strange ways though, as I had to have a medical examination in order to become a volunteer and they discovered that I had prostate cancer. That was a terrible shock both for me and my wife, but, thank God, they caught it in time and I made a complete recovery. However, if I had not seen that sign that day and had not decided to become a volunteer, things might have turned out different. As well as that I like to sing and one day I sang Our Lady of Knock at a Memorial Mass in the hospital. The priest who co-celebrated the mass was a member of the Mendelssohn Glee Club of New York City. He asked me to join them and I did. We are the oldest male chorus in the United States and I don't mean age wise, and we are at present rehearsing for a concert in April. We sang at the St. Patrick's Day party of the East 73rd Senior Citizens group last week, so even though I had no formal training the old voice is getting plenty of practice now.

Lily and I love to dance

The changes in Ireland are massive. There is so much money there now; it boasts one of the best economies in the world. It has a more open society too, which will bring its own problems in time, but they're part of Europe now and they have to accept that. We sometimes think about going back to live there and my big regret is that I didn't buy property there back when I should have. Somehow, I think if we'd had children, we would have done so, but it's no use regretting, as a lot our counterparts are gone already and we are both lucky to be alive and to enjoy great heath. My brother, John, a Police Superintendent in Cork, died at the age of forty-five and another brother, Joe, at fifty-two, both with heart problems. His family lives in Newbridge, County Kildare, where he was in the grocery business. My oldest brother, Michael, is the only one left at home, in County Wicklow. Then Lily's sister, Maureen, was killed by a car many years ago in Brooklyn along with her six-year old son who was on the back of her bicycle. She left three young children, and a husband who worked long hours on the buses. So we spent a lot of time with them, as there were we without children and them without a mother. God is strange sometimes.

I still follow Offaly in the hurling and football and Manchester United in the soccer up the road there in The Heritage bar. I was in Croke Park the day Offaly beat Kerry in 1982, right there on the sideline in front of the Hogan Stand. That's where the seats from the States were always sold. They were two great teams, but Offaly deserved to win. There was no push in the back, Darby's goal was nothing but authentic. When Mick O'Dwyer was asked did he think it was a shame that Kerry never won the five-in-a-row, he replied, "Wouldn't it have been a worse shame if Matt O'Connor had never won an All-Ireland medal?" That puts it all in perspective.

Birr was always a great hurling town. During the forties there were three All-Ireland semi-finals played there in St. Brendan's Park and Galway lost all three. The famous Christy Ring played there for Cork in one of them, and the first ever All-Ireland hurling final was played in Birr between Galway and Tipperary in 1887. Thurles for Tipperary beat Meelick who played for Galway. That time the county champions represented the county itself in the All-Ireland series. Then, of course, there was the 100th Anniversary of the GAA football final in Thurles in 1984 between Offaly and Cork, when poor Offaly lost. I was at that too. I have always kept up the old traditions of home; I have always kept them alive.

I don't think we'll ever see a united Ireland in our time. I always thought we would, but people will have to make too many changes, and I can't see that happening. Wasn't that a ridiculous thing that happened in Dublin the other day? They should never have let the Unionists march, as it is obvious now that they are not willing to give up their power. Stormont would still be there except for the Civil Rights Movement of 1969. For the size of Ireland it has an awful lot of history, which is a sad thing in a way.

The war in Iraq was a bad mistake, it is an absolute disaster. There was no planning for what would happen after the fact. I think they really believed that they would be welcomed with open arms full of flowers, but they weren't experienced with these insurgents. It is a different world over there, with a different culture and different society. Iraq is one of the most ancient civilizations in the world, going right back to biblical times. When World War II ended when we were kids, I thought there'd never be another one. Now, there are more wars than ever before. The world is a very unsettled place indeed. But we'll keep on trucking. It's been a good life, you could say. Yes, you can say, Christy Butler had a good life.

Interviewed at Aisling Irish Community Center,
Yonkers, New York; March 13, 2006

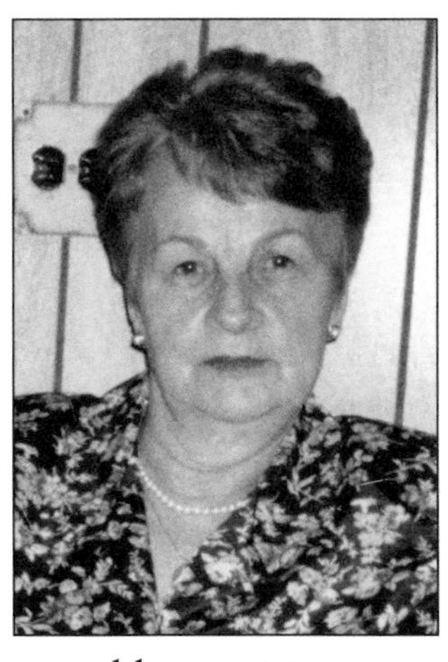

Anne O'Connor, 1955

I traveled to the U.S.A. on the Queen Elizabeth in May 1955. I was booked to travel on the Britannic, but due to a strike in Liverpool we were sent on to Southampton to board the QE. It was somewhat disappointing, as we were four friends traveling together and we were separated into all different areas of the boat, and it was so large we seldom got to see one another. I had to share with a girl who didn't speak English and all she could say was, "Up there," while pointing at the top bunk. A couple of us were very seasick, but I was lucky enough to escape. There was one lad from Cavan who as well as being seasick, was heartsick too. In fact, he was heartbroken. I met him a couple of months later in Gaelic Park and he told me that he was going home. He was the nicest young fellow, but he said he couldn't stick it any longer; he was just too lonesome. He was not adjusting at all. It was a shame. I came to America for a better way of life than I had in County Clare and what impressed me most about New York were the tall buildings, the stores, and the beautiful weather.

My first job was in Ridgefield, Connecticut, in a big house owned by a wealthy widow. She was fabulously rich. It was only a summer job to start and I have very mixed feelings about the whole thing, as I was very homesick at first. I was a kitchen maid, working for the cook, and I worked with a lot of young girls, but I found that the older Irish women were not that nice to the new ones coming over. I think they resented the fact that we were younger and making more money than they did when they started. There was this one from Kerry and she wasn't a bit nice, and another one from Cavan, and she was another one.

It was the foreigners who made me feel the most welcome. They were the nicest. Lisa from Sweden and Olga from Norway were so kind to me. Olga cooked for the help and knowing I was lonely and that I didn't eat everything, she would cook me special meals. And talk about religious, they weren't Catholic, but they would take me around to all these shrines and grottos here and there in the area on their day off. Then the chauffeur would take us out on a Thursday. It was part of his job to drive us around and we had a great time. The widow allowed him to do this for us. Even though we hardly ever saw her, she'd only meet with the cook to discuss plans for the day; she was very good to us in her own way, but there'd be no communication between the woman of the house and the maids. We'd also go around visiting the other girls in the other big houses in the evening time. So I got on grand in the end and after three months I moved into New York.

I worked then as a chambermaid with J.P. Morgan, the financier himself, way out on Long Island, out on his estate in Northport, and that was isolation. We had to take a taxi every Sunday to Mass. We never saw him at all, as he took off for business in the city every day, and the mistress took off with her dogs every morning and stayed on her boat for the day; so we hardly ever saw her either. She just wanted us to keep out of her way. Their children were all grown up and had left. Then I moved into the city and worked for the Saks family in their home on Park Avenue. The old lady was widowed at that time and it was her family who ran the store. We got the jobs through agencies or through our friends.

I was homesick really for three years and had to go home to Clare for a holiday to get it out of my system. I was born and raised in Feakle in the Townland of Curragh. The village consisted of sixteen houses and we lived on a small farm. I am the fifth of eight children and my mother was the boss; she made all of the major decisions in the house. When I returned there were these auld lads back then who lived up in the mountains and they all wanted to marry me. Before that they wouldn't even have looked at me, but they thought because I was home from America that I had loads of money. I couldn't wait to get back here. I gave my mother and father a good time and was glad to come home to New York.

I met my husband, Jeremiah, in the Jaeger House. He was a Kerryman who worked in the warehouses that time, and loved to play the accordion. We moved to the parish of St. Simon Stock and between there and St. Brendan's we raised our four children. We did move back to Ireland one time, where my youngest child was born, but

Jerry didn't get his health there and the doctor advised him to return. All of my children have a very strong attachment to Ireland; in fact, my daughter is married to an Irishman. They would all go down to the Archway bar on Jerome Avenue and meet the sons and daughters of Irishmen and women, repeating the pattern all over again. Losing Jerry brought sadness into my life, but my nine grandchildren provide all of the happiness I need right now.

Written and recorded at Aisling Irish Community Center creative writing workshops, Yonkers, NY; November 2005 - May 2006

Jimmy and Ann Chambers, 1956 and 1959

Jimmy: I came in November 1956 on the Franconia. I think it was her last voyage or her second to last, I don't know, but she turned over shortly after that anyhow. I was traveling with two little girls from home, they were only sixteen or seventeen, and they were in one cabin and I was in another. When I got up the first morning and went out on deck, I saw all these people heaving over the side of the ship. They were all getting sick, every one of them, every single one of them, I tell you. The guy who was in the cabin with me said, "Jimmy, don't go out, don't go out." But I went out anyhow and had breakfast and not a bother on me. There was this old woman there, she was about seventy and we were the only two down for breakfast every morning.

One night the ship nearly turned over and I never heard a word. I slept through the whole thing. Never heard them calling people to get out; never heard them lifting the lifeboats down; I heard nothing. I don't know what went wrong, whether it was bad weather or not, it was the winter time. The next day the old lady and I were the only ones up on top again, and she said to me, "can you play shuffleboard?' I said I don't know if I can or not, but sure I'll try it anyhow. The two of us spent the whole day on the shuffleboard and not another sinner around. It was great craic.

My two little companions spent the whole time in their room, as they were too young to go out, but they'd come down to the ballroom to check on me and then they'd come up to the cabin to make sure I was in bed. Instead of me looking after them, it was the other way around. We laugh about it all the time now. I played cards every night and went dancing. It was a beautiful experience. There was nothing like sitting out there on the deck with the waves lapping up against the side of the ship. I used to go down to the gym every day with a few of the lads and of course we'd never seen a gym before and we leapt up on these machines and nearly made bits of them. On the third or fourth morning when I arrived down I met the Captain with his arm across the door and he wouldn't let me in. He said I'd all the machines broken. Well, I thought, surely there was more than me?

Another day then I was out on the deck eating a sandwich and drinking a bottle of soda. There was a man a little bit up from me and every now and then he'd sprinkle this black dust into the water and some of it would blow up in my direction and stick to the sandwich. I took no notice of him at all. Sure I thought it was only caraway seeds or that and I ate away. After a while he got up and shook out this pouch thing and exclaimed, "God be with her." He walked over near me rubbing his hands together. "That's it now. Mother is gone." I looked down at my piece of bread with the black things stuck to it and hurled it into the water before I ate what was left of Mammy!

I come from Cooraclare in County Clare, the second best parish in the world. We're not going to argue over which is the best, but I can tell you that's the second best. I lived out in the country, at the back of the mountain, in a place called Dromelihy. Cooraclare is a big state, you know, and there was hardly a spot in it that I didn't know. We looked out on to that mountain every day of our lives and I rolled down it many a time when I was a young lad of six or seven. Sugán City it's called there because of all the thatched cottages. Sugán means straw. A ghost town my wife calls it. It's on the West coast of Clare on the shores of the Atlantic. I've missed it every day of my life. I think about it all the time. Why wouldn't I?

Growing up in County Clare was just wonderful. There were eight of us on the farm, five girls, and three boys. My two brothers are dead now as are two sisters. I had two sisters in the nuns, two Mercy's. One was in Macroom, Sr. Anthony who is deceased and the other one, Sr. Rita, is in Thurles now. We call her the flying nun because she goes all over. She could be in Dublin one day and Armagh the other, because she's retired now. My other two sisters, Liz and Ann are both living in Ireland. The home place is mine, well the house is, and the farm is Sr. Rita's. We had a nice place there.

I came to America because all of my friends were either going to England or coming out here. And then my sister, Liz, was here. My brother was at home and he'd be for the farm, so I was kind of in the way. Although the first time I went back my father wanted me to take it but I wouldn't. That's the way it wound up. My other brother died in a car crash. He had lived here and he went home for good. He bought a farm of land—120 acres for five thousand pounds at that time, then he put thirty-five cattle in it and after him going back from here he sold the cattle to pay for the place. That's the way it was back then. It's completely different now. It's unbelievable. Unbelievable the way things have changed.

I think the prosperity in Ireland is great. I hope it keeps up. I hope things stay the same as they are now. I hope and I pray that nothing happens, because if something happens there, God only knows. I mean they have it great, they have it fantastic. Ireland is booming now and everybody is working. Sure when we were growing up we had nothing only the farm and we might make a few pounds for a few days work here and there, not even a few pounds, a few shillings, at the end of the week. I'd often stop on a morning, maybe a Friday morning or it could be a Saturday morning, any morning, and I'd go up to where my father had a few rows of bog and I'd cut the turf and head off into town and sell it. I'd sell it for a few bob and I'd tell nobody and that's how I'd get some money to spend at the weekend. I'd be away with it, away with it for the week even. I'd have plenty of money with nothing to worry about. And that could happen and no one would know about it, not a thing. I always had money somehow or other. I had a great time there. I had a great life in Ireland before I came out. I was well-known through the football. Cooraclare had a good team. In fact, I am now a lifetime member and vice-president of the Cooraclare football club.

We used go down to the strand all the time when we were young. One day this next door neighbor of ours was down there to load up some sand. People often used it for building that time. So he drove the horse and cart down to the edge of the water to where the waves were coming in and decided to take a dip in the ocean. He stripped off all his clothes and put them underneath the cart and next thing the horse took off and left him there stark naked on the strand. The horse went off out along the road with your man after it and everyone down along the road was trying to stop the horse and your man streaking after him and no-one could catch him. That's going back years ago. That's going back years before I came out here. I was very young at the time, but I still remember the waves coming in up to your man without a stitch on him and the horse bolting and taking off with his clothes in the cart.

God! I could tell you stories of home, believe me. We were wild that time. We would go on a court to people's houses, a ceili some people might call it. It's when you go visiting. About seven or eight of us would go calling anyhow and before we'd leave the house, we'd lock the door coming out unknown to the people and put a branch down the chimney and smoke them out of the kitchen and they couldn't escape because we'd have the door locked. And we'd be laughing outside listening to them all roaring abroad in the kitchen. It was all clean fun though. That time it was just great.

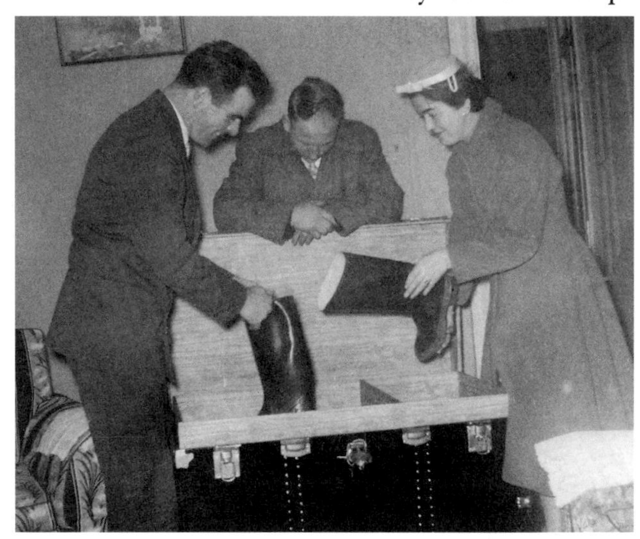

Jimmy packing the boots for America

Then we'd go into this other house where this man lived on his own, Johnsie, and his two nephews used visit him every night. When they'd be leaving at about eleven o'clock, we'd start throwing turf at the door just to frighten him like and next thing he'd come after us and we'd be laughing and he'd follow us down the road and we'd be still laughing, even though we were a bit afraid of him. Anyhow years after I came over here I met him one day after going back and he said, "Well, Bomber, did I miss you when you left." They used to call me Bomber that time. I don't know why, it wasn't after the Bomber Liston because I came before him. Maybe he was called after me? Anyhow Johnsie said he missed me because he'd no turf after I'd gone. The frigger used pile up the turf inside the door after we were done pelting it and he never had to go to the bog as long as we were around.

Oh! We used to have great times, and great friends too. I still have friends today that I had back then. Tommy Boland here, and Mike

Griffin, and there's Jimmy Gavin in Dublin; he works for Roadstone and lives in Clondalkin. He was my neighbor at home; in fact he drove me to the boat in Cobh the day I came to America. I emptied my pocket and gave him whatever change I had left; then he drove my woman back to Clare and he took her too! But I forgave him for it. He has a son an airline pilot, young Jimmy, a lovely fellow. He played for Dublin when they won the All-Ireland football final in 1995, and Clare beat Offaly in the hurling the same year and the two cups came down to Cooraclare. The two of them were in the town the same night. That was brilliant. I wasn't there unfortunately, but they sent me that framed photograph of the team. It's up on the wall. They framed it and had it sent over to me. They've never forgotten me. And I've never forgotten them either and where I came from. I even have a daughter called Clare.

Jimmy (kneeling in front) NY pier

When I saw New York for the first time, forget about it. We sailed up the Hudson River there and we could see these high-rises. This American pointed towards Manhattan and said, "You know you'll be walking in there some day." And he was right. I did walk into Manhattan many's the time. The streets looked so small from the boat. I came to live with my sister, Liz, down on 181st Street in St. Elizabeth's Parish. Her house was just under the George Washington Bridge and I would sit outside every night and look out over the waters of the Hudson. It was beautiful. I used to run back and forth across the bridge every day, maybe twice a day, just for the exercise. I loved it from the word go.

A guy called Mike Clarke, a friend of mine, told me about this job that was going at a place called Photo Engraving downtown, so I went down anyhow and got the job, and I stayed there for thirty-seven years. I was an expert engraver by the time I left; I was top class. The company was the third largest of its kind in the United States. It was in a huge building, which took over the whole block on 25th Street between Third Avenue and Lexington. There was this fellow there from Mayo, Tom Duffy, who took me under his wing straight away and we became great friends. He adored me. Even when he retired he'd always meet up with me on the 17th of March; he used come to the parade and he'd take me out to dinner. On my first day he said to me, "There's one thing I'm going to tell you, Jimmy. Don't be like other people. Never forget where you came from." That was the first thing he ever said to me. And like I said, I never did.

But I had a great time. I've a lot of great friends here. Oh, definitely we went dancing. The Jaeger House, of course. There was another place then on 59th Street, near City Center. I loved the set dances, especially the Caledonian, a great Clare set. They were the best dances. Then, after that, we'd go to Ireland's Thirty Two. Of course, I never drank. I never even tasted the stuff. After making my Confirmation, I was coming home from the Church and this old man met me on his bicycle. That time it was very hard to get a bicycle you know. He was cycling away anyhow and I was running alongside him. Next thing he asked me did I take the pledge. I said I did. He asked me was I ever going to drink and I said I wasn't. Then he said you're going to join the pioneers. He turned around the bike on the road and brought me down to Corofin and there and then I joined the pioneers and I have never broken the pledge to this day. I've never drank a drop of alcohol since.

I'm down there in JC Mac's bar on 238th Street every night playing cards and I don't drink. But everyone thinks I do. When my in-laws met me for the first time they thought I was half cut and if I went into a bar with another fellow this minute and ordered a soda and a beer, the bartender would automatically put the beer down in front of me. Every time, I tell you, every time. But, no I don't touch the stuff. If you asked me what a beer tasted like I couldn't tell you.

I was a member of the Clare Society here for a while and I played hurling for the Clare club in New York. I am a member of Rangers Football Club, a past member of the Clare Hurlers, Miltown Malbay Club and the Claremen's Association. I was also president of the Clare

Football club for a term. They had a good team. I've never missed a Sunday in Gaelic Park. I'm the only one that never missed a Sunday there to this day. Even when my daughter, Margaret, was baptized there in Visitation parish, I went up to the Park after the church to see the games. I didn't want anyone else to tell me about the games. I wanted to see them for myself, and then I went down home again for the party after.

Gaelic Park was great. The Park was the greatest thing ever for a bunch of Irish boys coming out here. When you think of it, over at home we'd have to change for a match at the side of a ditch and leave our clothes in the bush and when you'd come back they'd be drowned. If it rained you were finished and you'd have to change back into wet clothes again after. Over here we had real dressing rooms and a shower. Imagine a shower after the game and being able to get back into dry clothes? I thought it was great. And not only that, but you could go into the bar after and have a few drinks if you wanted and something to eat and even a dance or two. It was great. It was definitely great. Sure there was never anything like that in the whole of Ireland back then.

Yes, Gaelic Park was fantastic. Don't let anyone ever say anything against the Park, because it was just brilliant. The crowds were unbelievable. Everyone knew one another. I knew everyone that came into the Park. They'd come out new from Ireland and if they played in the Park or even just came down to watch a few games, you'd know them right away. Everyone was together. Everyone helped one another. I'm sure they do today too, but nothing like back then. People were closer altogether. Every county got on, because everyone was the same. Nobody had any more than the next fellow. We all worked hard and we all made the same money, everybody was the same.

I went home after four years; probably when I got married. Sure I go back all the time now. And of course I went back to bury my parents and my brothers and sisters. That's a very sad place to go. We also lost our daughter, Finola, some years ago and that's an even sadder place. We often thought of retiring in Ireland, but when you have kids born and raised here, it would be too hard to go off and leave them. We did go back one time to stay, you know. We lasted thirteen weeks. It was completely different. James was only four that time, he's thirty eight now. You couldn't get used to it. You'd go for a cup of coffee in the morning, and this was Ennis now, not West Clare, and at nine o'clock in the morning there'd be nothing open. You could starve or die of thirst in the place, but nobody was open. Then the job here called me and asked me was I coming back, that they'd have to give my job away if I wasn't, so we decided to return. I had a job got and all over there, in Centrex, got it straight away even though there were guys who were waiting years to be called. I couldn't settle, so we came back here, and I've not regretted it.

Our Wedding Day, July 7, 1962

Here's a picture of President Clinton and me taken at Eliot Engel's annual dinner for the Bronx Democratic Party. I love that man, President Clinton, and he loves us, you know. I had seven pictures taken with him that night and at one stage he looked at me and said, "Jimmy, I just love the Irish." It brought a tear to my eye. Here's a picture of me being presented with Doonbeg Man of the Year at their dinner in The Kerryman's Hall last November. A group of us started up The Doonbeg Society many years ago and we used to have our meetings in The Terminal Bar there on 242nd Street.

This is our wedding picture. How did I meet Ann? Oh! No, do you have to remind me? You'll give me a headache remembering.

Ann: Did he mention that Tommy Boland and the boys came on the honeymoon with us? And I would hate to tell you what was done. Yeah, Tommy and the wife and Mike Griffin and the girlfriend all came along with us. We didn't know a thing. Tommy says to us at the wedding, "I'm coming to Atlantic City with you." And he had a car. Oh! This big car. You pressed these buttons and everything. Nobody had a car like it in 1962. It was a grand car and we slept along the road and stopped for something to eat and finally landed in Atlantic City at four o'clock in the morning. They had no place to stay, but they took us to our hotel anyhow. We thought we mightn't get in if there wasn't anyone at the desk. Anyhow what happened was, the two boys stayed outside the door and told us to be sure and come out and tell them if we got the room or not, but we never went down near them. I don't know how long they waited, they must have got tired in the end anyhow, him and Mike Griffin, and they went off and got rooms in Erin's Café.

They came back a few hours later and wangled the phone number out of the desk clerk and rang us up first. Jimmy said to me don't lift it; it's them. But I thought maybe they had breakfast for us or something so I lifted the phone and of course, that's how they found out what room we were in. Found us out, they did, and insisted that we go up to their place and stay beside them. They were in rooms 32 and 33 and had number 34 fixed up for us. The person hadn't moved out so we had to wait a while for the room to be prepared. As soon as it was ready and we were booked in, all of a sudden they were very tired and insisted that we all take a nap before we went out. So I was there in the room anyhow brushing my hair in front of the dressing table and through the mirror I noticed this wire going from the wall under the bed. I got down on my hands and knees to investigate further and what did I find only a tape recorder on the floor. And even worse than that, next thing I heard breathing outside in the hall and when I opened the door the two lads nearly fell into the room on top of us. Look what I had to put up with.

Ann with brother Bill, Jan 1961

That wasn't the worse part of it. During the week anyhow they said they'd take us to a show. A cowboy show they said it was. I was delighted of course; I had never been to a show in my life. I thought I'd love to see a cowboy show. We went in anyhow and sat down in the front seats. Front row seats we had no less. Next thing the curtain came across and this fellow came out and started telling dirty jokes. After that then they rolled a bed out on to the stage and I thought what sort of a cowboy show is this. What was it only a burlesque; a strip show no less. I enjoyed it anyhow; sure I'd never seen anything like it. Griffin had his cap out at the end collecting the girls' telephone numbers. It was shocking. Well, Jimmy here was raging. "What kind of a Catholic are you?' He lit on poor Tommy. "You call yourself a Catholic?" We went for something to eat after in White Castle's and he wouldn't speak to any of us; he was so mad. We all walked up the street in single file and none of us speaking. And that wasn't the worst part. We left our entire luggage behind. We were doing so much messing in the parking lot, taking photos and what have you that we left the bags behind. We never missed them until we got back to the Bronx.

I don't know what made him come to America, but I know why I came. My brother, Bill, was here at the time and he was married and they were young. I think he was only eighteen when he got married out here and anyhow he was called into the army and he wanted someone to come out and stay with his wife, Jean. My sister, Mary, said she didn't want to go, and Bridget said she wasn't going, so I said I'll go to America and see what it's like, thinking I would go and come back again. I was supposed to go in December, but I said I'll not go before Christmas. Instead I flew out on January 17, 1959. Pat Duggan met me at the airport and when I walked up the steps to 567 West 191st Street, off Broadway there in Washington Heights, I thought Bill and Jean owned the whole building. I couldn't understand why the door was wide open and I thought sure anyone could come in here and murder us all. We walked up all these flights of stairs to their apartment on the fourth floor and all I could think of was how well they were doing, owning this big house.

I hated the place at first and wanted to go home after two weeks. New York was a very lonesome place when you didn't know anybody. Bill was away with the army and Jean was working all the time in Schrafft's restaurant so one morning I went off looking for a job in the telephone company. They had to write all the subway stops down for me, but I found my way up to 215th Street where I met a lovely woman, Mrs. Elliot, she's dead since, and I told her I was looking for a job. I filled out the application and didn't I get called the very next day and was told to report to 140 West Street for an interview and they offered me a job there and then in their branch on 50th Street.

It was as easy as that. I started off as an operator and eventually was moved into the billing department. The only thing I didn't like about it was the split shifts. I'd go in at eight in the morning, work until twelve, off till four, and then back again until ten or eleven at night. That's the only part I didn't like, but I loved working there and stayed until the day I got married. I met a few girls from home and they took me dancing with them. None of them lived near me though, some lived in Brooklyn, and some lived in Queens. Oh! But I missed Derry terrible. I was sorry I ever left it.

Anyhow, I was taking home fifty-one dollars a week, and my apartment was sixty something a month. But I got a great start. I got in touch with this man whose brother was married to my aunt, my father's sister, back home in Ireland. He and his wife owned this big apartment on 170th Street and I'd go down to dinner there every now and then. It ended up that they were going to Ireland on a holiday and they asked me to come down and stay in the place while they were gone. They had boarders who rented out rooms from them, and my friend, Eamon Gribbins, and I went down there and stayed for a while to take care of things. Later on when I was getting my own apartment in Jean's building, they took me to this warehouse to look at furniture. I had enough money saved up by this time and when I went to settle the bill, hadn't they paid it already. Oh! They were awfully good to me. They had no family of their own and they were so good to me. They gave me a great start.

Jimmy says it was because I was hungry looking at the time. That they took compassion on me, and that he did too. I was hungry looking. I was as thin as a rake. He was lucky to meet me. We met at the wedding of Maura Aherne from Clare. I didn't know her. I didn't know anyone. I'd never been to a wedding here either. But Jean worked with Maura in Schrafft's and she was invited to the wedding and she took me along with her. Jimmy happened to be at the wedding and he sent this guy, John O'Dea, over to ask me for my phone number. He said he was afraid I'd run away if he came over himself.

It was another six weeks before I made a move to go out with him. Every night he'd call me and he'd fall asleep on the phone and I'd hang up on him and leave him speaking to himself. I tell the truth, I tell you. Then there was this dance for this priest, a Father Morrissey, and I decided being a good-living person to go along and support him. Jimmy was there and he walked me home that night. We went out on a date to the Jaeger House and I didn't like it at all. It was too rough. We met these fellows on the stairs with blood down the front of their white shirts. I said never again. Well, that was a great start. I had always gone to City Center; there was a much more reserved type of person there. He came with me once, but he didn't like it. He said that you had to be a certain type of person to go to City Center; that they were a bit uppity.

It suited me because it was down beside where I worked. I'd get ready on a Friday when I went home during the split hours and I'd come back to work half ready for the dance that night. There'd be always someone to come back up on the subway with me, either Betty Mackle, or Anne Healy, a Mayo girl. There was always someone to accompany me home. If I had to travel by myself, everything would be all wrote down, all the stops, although I often got on the wrong one and ended up in Brooklyn a few times. We had great craic. We'd be coming up from 86th Street on the subway and one of the guys would be hanging out of the bars along the platform like a monkey and we'd be laughing at him and then the cops would come along and shift him.

Jimmy didn't come to Derry until after we were married. He had never been in the North before, but he liked it and they liked him, even though they all thought he was drunk half the time. If he acted civilized, they wouldn't have thought that. Wait till I tell you the best one though. When we were getting married, I sent home for my papers and when they saw the name Chambers they thought he was a Protestant. They weren't going to send the Baptism Certificate until they checked it out. But our parish priest said he knew that I wouldn't stray from my religion. I used to write to him all the time. Then he came out a few years ago and we lifted a collection for him at the Derry dance to build a new church in St. Mary's Parish in Bellaghy, where I come from. There's a picture of it up on the wall, beside Sugán

City, if you don't mind.

I joined the Derry Society fairly early on with Eamon Gribbins who was a lad from home. I don't go to all the meetings now, but I keep up my dues and go to the dance every year and the Communion breakfast and things. Rose McGurk was one of the founding members, but in her time they only met in each other's houses. By the time I joined they had started meeting in the Irish Institute down on 48th or 49th Street. These societies were a great help to the Irish at the time.

Derry was a beautiful place to grow up in. Everyone know'd the other. There weren't as many troubles back then either. Not that I can remember anyhow. Tommy Diamond is a cousin of mine. He'll be the Guest of Honor this year at the Derry Dance. Tommy was the first man to bring the Minor Cup to Northern Ireland in 1965. He played in Croke Park nine times and never lost a game there. And the boy that boxes, John Duddy, is coming over too. He'll be appearing in the Gardens on March 16 and will be an honored guest at the Dinner.

I didn't think Clare was that much different from the North. They had a party for us the first time I was there. I sang "The Sash" and this man threw his cap on the floor and said to Jimmy, "I can't believe you married an effin Protestant." He went crazy. Sure this fellow Jimmy here put me up to sing it. I wouldn't have had a clue. I didn't mind it that much when we went to live there. My friend, Mary Boohan and her husband, Pat, had moved back too. They were Supers over on Bainbridge and I liked being near her, other than that I wasn't bothered with Clare or Derry one way or the other. It's hard to go back when you've been here a while. My daughter, Margaret, now she'd move back to Clare in the morning, but my other daughter, Clare, she wouldn't. She'd be more for the North.

There were 350 guests at our wedding. The reception was in McGarry's, in White Plains somewhere I think. Six of us on the honeymoon, and I had no choice in it. Its funny how both Jimmy and I came to St. Elizabeth's Parish when we arrived first and that's where we got married. None of the families from home came for the wedding. There was no one coming out here that time for weddings. There's the wedding party. Maureen Halloran, I used to work with her in the telephone company; Peggy Masons; there's Anne Healy, a girl from Mayo; and Jean, my sister-in-law, Jean McPeake. There's my brother, Bill, whom I came over to. He's dead now. We bought the dresses some place downtown. Wasn't Jimmy a fine looking man? Wasn't I ever so lucky?

Interviewed at their home on Bailey Avenue, Bronx, New York; February 8, 2006

Jimmy & Ann with Mary & Pat Bohan

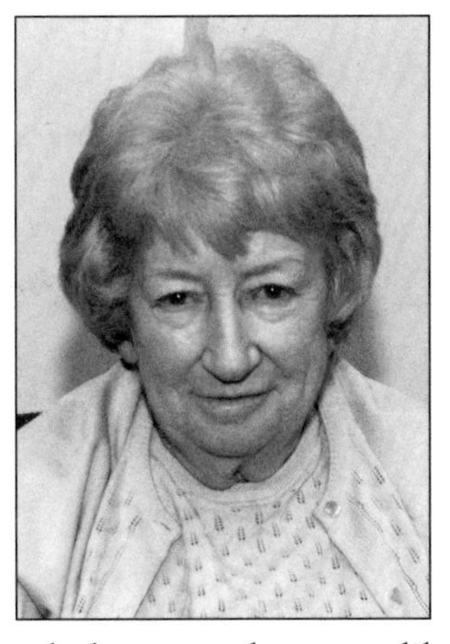

Peggy Murphy, 1956

You could say I do everything backwards because I was born in America and in 1948 I went back to Ireland with my family. Although I was only thirteen years of age, I can still remember that sunny day in April when we set sail. My aunts and cousins came to the house to say goodbye and there were more down on the pier to see us off. The whole atmosphere was like that of one big party. I had received a doll for Christmas—a Madame Alexandra with a pink dress and straw hat, and she lay in my arms the whole way to Ireland. At that time girls of that age still played with dolls; they were not going with boys so much. Now they're always with the boys.

We sailed on the S.S. Washington; it was just after the war, and I was so excited to be going to Ireland. We arrived in Cork city I don't know how many days later and headed straight for Ardgroom, a small village huddled at the foot of Hungry Hill, where we stayed with my grandfather for a while. His name was Cruger Murphy, a nickname they gave him because there were so many Murphy's in the area. We eventually bought a farm close by, on the Bantry coast about three miles outside the town, overlooking Bere Island, and settled into Irish life. I loved it. My father bought my brother and me two Raleigh bicycles and when mine broke down I'd have to walk along the old road to school.

I started at the local convent where young girls from Kerry came to be nuns, but there was too much Irish so I moved to the Technical School around the corner and had great fun there cooking and sewing, and one time we threw a water bag out the window on top of the caretaker and nearly died laughing at the look of shock on his face. I used to love going to Mass on the horse and trap. I would always sit up front on the mahogany bench and my eyes would be red from the hairs of the chestnut horse, called Pet. My brother also had a lovely collie dog like Lassie, whom he was called after and they would head off together over the hill to collect the turf and to visit his friend who lived in Seapoint. That's a real holiday resort now with chalets and all for the holidaymakers.

When my grandfather died it was the first time I'd seen anyone in a habit, even in a coffin, and they placed a square of brown material over his face. I missed him so much, as he was always kidding with us. He'd tell us to go pluck a nettle, just kidding like; sure I had never even seen a nettle before. Shortly after our arrival, my mother brought me up to her home place in County Carlow, and left me there for three months with her Aunt Kate. I remember the first time I visited Kate's cottage and I thought they were all so strange sitting around the fire poking at it with a stick. I thought they were stirring the flames or something. But they thought I looked funny too in my new navy coat that reached down to my ankles. I was dressed in the American fashion of the time called the long look.

My aunt would make tea every night for the stragglers coming home from the pub and I would have to dance for them. The Purcell brothers would be there and my cousins and Aunt Kate would play the melodeon. Then sometimes we'd go over to the wooden stage in Tinacarry to dance. I loved the taste of the tea out on the bog and there was a candy store down beside the church owned by a brother and a sister and in it there were lots of different biscuit tins with tons of different varieties. You could just go along from tin to tin and select whatever kind you wanted. My favorites were the chocolate-coated Irish cookies. The ice cream was different in Ireland too, with more ice than cream. We missed America though and used to wait for the parcels with the candy and the coloring books.

After I don't know how many years we sold the farm, the same people still own it, and we moved to England. I was old enough to go dancing then and had a great time going around all the ballrooms, especially to the Garryowen in Hammersmith, which was my favorite. But eventually, when I was twenty one years of age, we moved back to America again, back to the same parish, Ascension on 107th between Broadway and Amsterdam, where all of my aunts and cousins still lived and there are still some of them there to this day. In fact it is the same parish that Sister Christine Hennessey grew up in and she still meets my cousins when she goes back for reunions. I had always wanted to come back to America, so I was happy.

Despite my mother's promise never to venture over water again, eight years later, we set sail once more, this time in the other direction across the Atlantic from Liverpool on the Holland-American liner called the Ryndarn. We had a great time meeting all the new people. When we went to dinner we would have name cards to tell us where to sit and we sat at a different place every night so that we could meet different people each time. It was at the end of September 1956 and there were a lot of people leaving Ireland and England, and at that particular time of the year, there were a lot of teachers returning after the holidays.

I don't know where I started working first, but I eventually ended up in B. Altman department store where I worked for twenty-seven and a half years until I retired there about fifteen years ago. They were down on 19th Street, but then they moved up to 34th Street and Fifth Avenue. It was a very elegant store with an enormous central light court, large display windows, and all the latest inventions such as elevators and escalators. They were the first major employers to install rest rooms and a subsidized cafeteria for their employees, the first to introduce a shorter business day and Saturday closings in the summer; and the first to actively encourage schooling for younger employees by providing funding for their education.

The best though was the thrift shop for employees. It was in a big room and it would open at ten o'clock in the morning and we'd all line up outside in the hall and the minute they opened the doors we'd all run in and we wouldn't know which way to turn. They would sell coats and jackets and suits for five dollars, ten dollars. It would have everything they had upstairs only for much cheaper. Then they had a thing called the "nine fifteen." That was discount code and we could buy any of the merchandise for much less. We'd get it wholesale; we'd pay what they paid for it. I always came home with a shopping bag. Every night I'd come home with a shopping bag.

It was the most beautiful store at Christmas time. The carpet would roll along the whole block from 34th to 35th Streets, from Park Avenue to Madison. We had our own display department and we did our own windows and everything. We supplied our own electricity for the music and everything. The school kids loved working there too. They would get holiday work in the gift-wrapping department. And then there was a lunchroom for employees. We'd get lunch for a quarter, a whole lunch for twenty-five cents, coffee for five, a piece of pie for ten. They also served a lovely afternoon tea up in the Charlesford room. And what a medical department they had. There was a full-time doctor and three or four full-time nurses for the staff. It was the best store that ever was.

It closed in 1989. Australians took it over. The new owners had been real estate people. They started buying up real estate and they were spending the money they made from the store, but then they wouldn't be able to pay the vendors for the merchandise, and then they went down. It was a very, very nice store. It was run by the Burke's who were nice people too. They were very wealthy, but they weren't wealthy the way they carried on. They were very simple people who led a very simple life.

AICC creative writing workshop

When I wasn't working, I loved to dance. The Jaeger House was the best; it was more Irish. They were fussier in City Center, and the music was more American style. You'd stand there and they'd look you up and down. You'd think they were buying something. All we wanted was a dance. There were a lot of Paddys there, but we had our favorites. One night this guy asked this one beside me out to dance and she refused him and then he had the nerve to ask me. And when I said no he asked us if we had wooden legs. "The Stack of Barley" was my favorite dance. That's when you have two girls to one guy. My girlfriend and I would jump out onto the floor without waiting to be asked and wait for someone to join us. Then she would dance down one side of the hall with him and I would dance up the other. It was great fun altogether.

Today I lead a quiet life in Woodlawn and enjoy visiting with my brother and his family. I have not been to Ireland in many years and will hardly make it back there again, but I can still remember, as if it was yesterday, cycling along the coast road to Bantry, with Bere Island bobbing in the bay beside us and Hungry Hill hovering overhead.

From written notes and conversations at Aisling Irish Community Center creative writing workshops; November 2005 - May 2006

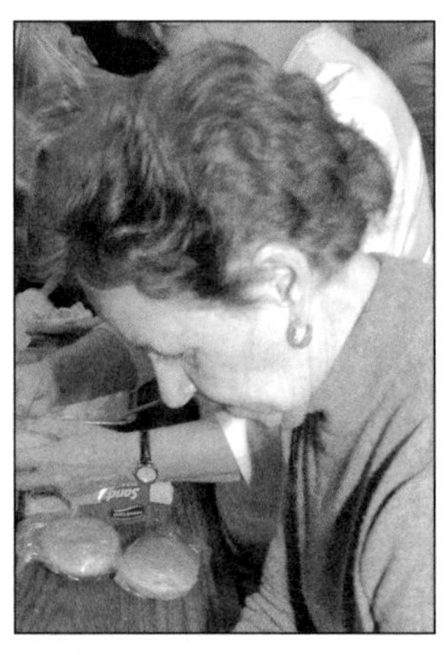

Bridget Glendon, 1956

I came to America in October 1956 flying from Eyreshire in Scotland to Idlewild in New York. The first thing I noticed was all the leaves on the ground and I thought the place was very dirty altogether. My Uncle Pat was waiting at the airport in his tartan tie and that was the only way I was going to recognize him, as I had never met him before. He had left Donegal about forty-five years previously along with his two brothers who were never to return, although he did once. Their mother had died at childbirth on her thirteenth baby when Pat was nine and my mother only three years of age. Times were hard for them and they had to leave eventually. Mammy would always talk about these brothers she hadn't seen in so long and after a few years working as a priest's housekeeper in Edinburgh, I took a notion to come and visit them. Pat paid half the fare and took me down to his home in Philadelphia. I've been here ever since.

I came on a Tuesday and was working by Thursday. Right away I was able to get a social security number, no problem whatsoever, not like the trouble they have now. I found a position as a cook with a wealthy banking family on Chestnut Hill. The first day I went along to meet the lady of the house – a lovely Southern lady, and she said the job wouldn't be available for another two weeks. So I said, "I'll get something else." I laugh now when I think of how brave I was. However, she agreed to pay me immediately, as she was afraid to lose me. So that was a good start – two weeks paid vacation. In the meantime I stayed with Uncle Pat in Bethlehem Pike and cooked him a steak dinner every day either before or after his shift in the local Ironworks. I also went dancing all over Philadelphia; that's all I loved to do was dance. We would all take the bus home and once, at about two o'clock in the morning, I was walking along the street by myself, as everyone else had been dropped off, when a police car stopped and asked what was I doing out so late. Next thing I knew they offered to drive me the rest of the way home and all I was worried about was that Uncle Pat would be watching out the window and see me getting out of the cop car.

Very soon, anyhow, it was time to start my new career. It was my responsibility to cook for the family and for the staff downstairs, which comprised of a Butler, Chauffeur and Kathleen, the maid. I had my own quarters in this fabulous mansion with every luxury you could imagine. My employers made sure that everything was to my liking in my accommodations and when I complained that there was a taste off my plates I was immediately supplied with a set of dishes complete with creamers and all the trimmings. Then she asked me was there anything in particular that I missed from Ireland. "The television," I told her. Sure I never had a TV in Ireland, but nonetheless a new set was put up in the dining-room and Kathleen and I enjoyed many hours in front of it. On my first St. Patrick's Day here she presented me with a kilt and a sash to match and made me wear it as I marched with Donegal in the Philadelphia parade. The following year I was excited to march with my county in the New York parade and was proud to wear the same uniform.

After a year or so the man of the house died and his widow decided to move to a smaller home. She offered to fix me up with work on Long Island or in New York City, but I settled instead with another couple further up Chestnut Hill. This time I was employed as a personal maid and it was my duty to take care of my lady's clothes. I also had to travel everywhere with her. They had an apartment on 67th Street and Park Avenue in New York and would spend two to three days a week up there. That was my introduction to this great city and its dancehalls. We would arrive up on a Tuesday morning and I would be dancing in City Center Tuesday night. Sometimes I would take the train back to Philadelphia after the dance in Manhattan, wait for Mass in Laverock and report straight for work. There would often be two car loads of us traveling back on the train. My lady's husband would know I hadn't slept at all, but warned me not to tell her. It wasn't because she would be mad at me; more that she would be concerned. They were so good to me. If it was raining the husband would escort me down to the bus stop under his umbrella. Or they would often send the limo to the station in North Philly for me if I was returning by train. I was living the high life, I'll tell you. It was a big change from the priest's house in Scotland.

The family had another house in Maine and usually spent the summers there, but when I didn't want to accompany them that first summer, they let me stay by myself in the house on Chestnut Hill. I worked in the local rectory filling in while people were on vacation. I could be upstairs, downstairs, in the dining-room; I was even a butler for a couple of weeks, and a cook in the kitchen, and all the while still living in the lovely house up on the Hill. Another time they went to Australia and New Zealand and wanted me to go with them, but I didn't, and I was often sorry after.

During my visits to their home in New York, however, I spotted this very nice Irish man who worked as a doorman and sometimes operated the elevator in the apartment building. One night I asked him where I would find some candy and he accompanied me to the candy store across the street. I discovered that his name was Jimmy and he was from County Kilkenny. Then he moved to another building and I searched every ballroom in New York looking for him. I could not understand how I could never get him in a dancehall. Of course, I discovered later that he wasn't a dancer. Out of the blue that Christmas, 1958, I received this big card at the house in Philadelphia and lo and behold it was from Jimmy. I got his address from the Super in the New York building and sent him one back, but between Christmas and New Year's Eve he came to our building one night to visit some of his pals and it happened to coincide with one of our visits to New York. Annie, the cook, and I were about to go down to her apartment on Grant Avenue and we bumped into him in the foyer. We each took one of his arms and before he had time to protest, we ushered him out of the building and down to Annie's, and he only there to say hello to the boys. That was the start of it anyhow. In a way you could say I kidnapped him.

We made a date that night to go to the movies on 86th Street, and were engaged on April 27, 1959. That summer, however, I accompanied my employers to their house in Maine and didn't see Jimmy for three months. It was unusual, but I guess I felt that if he was going to be there; he was going to be there. He was still there anyhow when I returned on September 12 and we were married the following November, the fourteenth to be precise, in the Seven Dolores Church. We had a big reception afterwards in Laverock and I wore the most beautiful dress that I had seen in a shop window in downtown Philadelphia one day and knew it was the one for me. After that I moved back to the Bronx with Jimmy where we settled in the Sacred Heart parish in Highbridge. By then he was Manager in a building downtown and I had several jobs in various houses around the city until I became pregnant with my first daughter, Theresa. When she was a year old I made my first trip back to Ireland after five years.

I grew up in Milford, outside Letterkenny, County Donegal in St. Bridget's parish in Golan. I was one of seven children and we had a wonderful family life back there on a small farm near the sea. It's funny though because none of us learned how to swim; in fact hardly anybody did back then, not even the fishermen who made their living on the water. As a result there were a lot of tragic drownings in our area. We had plenty of fresh fish to eat, however, especially herrings, which we bought from a man who came around with it in creels balanced on the back of a donkey. It was then cooked over an open fire in a wire mesh container held by a long handle. We'd wash it down with buttermilk. I remember my father's boss from the County Council coming to see him one day and he brought him in for the fish dinner. Daddy said he talked for days after about the grand feed he got and all the beautiful children sitting around the table.

Then on a Sunday my mother would kill a chicken, as we always had to have something special that day. She would drain the blood from his head, before removing the insides and plucking him. When you think about it, one chicken to feed nine people? Nowadays, one person would eat half a chicken by themselves. She made the most gorgeous stuffing with oatmeal and flour and she would bake it in a roll, like a pudding, which she would cut up in round pieces to serve with the chicken. The Christmas dinner then was something else again. She was a great cook. It was from her that I learnt it; I had no proper training at all.

We walked the mile and a half back and forth to the church on Sundays and my father would have the table set for breakfast when we came home with nine cups of water waiting for us to drink after receiving Communion. I don't really know why he did it, but it was a fashion he had. I suppose we would be fasting since eight o'clock the previous night and would be dying with the thirst. Then at Christmastime it was beautiful altogether when we'd carry little lanterns along the road to midnight Mass and you would see the procession of lights for miles and miles.

Even though my father had a job on the roads with the County Council, a ganger they called them, we had to work very hard on the farm. Many are the days I would have carried a load of turf down the mountain before I started school, and still be on time too. The school was a two-roomed structure with a Master and a female teacher, called Miss Campbell. When I was about eleven years of age, poor Miss Campbell fell sick on the road to school and died a few days later. We all had to go to her Wake. I can remember well seeing her lying in the coffin and for some reason I put my hand on her forehead, which I could have sworn was still warm. I've often wondered since if she was really dead at all.

Birdie and Irish Volunteers for the Homeless, AICC

My parents were both local and had a lovely, happy marriage, even though my father was a lot older than my mother. They went to the same school and the same church and knew each other all of their lives. I can remember Mammy coming home from the town with what they called a stardust shirt she'd bought for Daddy. It had these little dots of glitter sprinkled all over it and when he fit it on he swung her around the kitchen floor and they started to dance. That was the fashion at the time. He would always give us half a crown to go to the local dance in Milford and that would get us a soda too. Then there would be concerts in the town hall. We had great times.

Everyone emigrated though. All of my family went to England, but most of them returned home to Donegal to settle down in the end. Out of the seven of us I was the only one who came here and my brother who stayed in Canada. Originally I only went as far as Letterkenny to work in the all boys St. Eunan's College. Sometimes I would have to work downstairs setting tables and upstairs fixing the rooms, making the beds and that. Boys are very lazy you know. They even had a pot under their beds, which we would have to empty. Then the cook left and they gave me her job. One time an Aunt came home from Edinburgh and I decided to go back with her, as I needed a change. That's where I became a housekeeper to five priests and they were so good to me. I often had to go to the local prison with them when they would be saying Mass and I would carry the suitcase with the vestments and the Host and everything. When that prison door would bang shut behind us, I often thought we'd be in there for life. One time I saw a nice dress in a shop window and the priest gave me the money to buy it. When my brother, John, died at twenty-seven, two of the priests came home for the funeral with me. In fact my four brothers all died under the age of fifty, whereas my two sisters and I have lived long lives and are in great health. Mammy lived until she was ninety and her brother, that Uncle Pat whom I came to, was ninety-six. Wasn't that great and he brought up without a mother? So I was the only one to come here, but I never regretted it, and never wanted to go back for good. This is where my family is.

I have two daughters, Theresa and Carmel, who were both great musicians. They played the fiddle and the accordion and won hundreds of medals for Irish dancing under Martin Mulvihill, their teacher. We went to Ireland every year for the fleadh, which could be held anywhere in the country from Dublin to Donegal, to Cork and Kerry. One time in Dublin our troupe won so many competitions that the other contestants joked when we were leaving, "Go home and don't come back." There could be thirty in a group waiting to dance at any given time out of a troupe of three hundred. It was great for us though, as it gave us the opportunity to go back every year. I was always very close to my sisters and still am; all the miles across the Atlantic never changed that. They came to visit me many times too, as did my mother. I brought her all over. She loved her visit downtown Manhattan to Radio City Music Hall to see the yellow Rolls Royce about which a movie had been made at the time.

My daughters were also very good students. Theresa became a nurse and Carmel a teacher and between them I have five grandchildren whom I'm very proud of. We didn't go to Gaelic Park that much; someone was always getting hurt over there with the hurling. Nor did we frequent the

Catskills because we never had a car. Ireland was always our main port of call.

Then when Jimmy was only three months short of retirement he died. Everything changed after that. He was called down to work one Sunday to let people into the building to inspect the water tanks on the roof. It was a cold and frosty morning in December when he left and he must have run all the way down to the subway because he collapsed on the platform on the Mosholu Parkway station, while he was waiting for the train. The only way they could identify him was by the U.S. Army dog tags around his neck, which he'd worn ever since completing his Military Service. His colleagues kept calling me from the job wondering where he was and I would say, "He must be there; he left ages ago." Then the Transit cops came rapping at my door. They said they wanted to talk about Jimmy. I said he was at work. They asked could they come in and next thing they showed me a picture of him lying dead on the platform. Of course, I fell into a heap in the corner. When I came to they called my daughters for me and waited with me until the girls arrived. We'd had a lovely life together, Jimmy and I, and were married for forty-one years.

Now I live alone in Woodlawn, but thankfully at seventy-eight I'm still very active. God has been very good to me. I come to the Aisling Center every Friday to the 'Young at Heart' group and I also volunteer with the Irish Volunteers for the Homeless and have been coming down here now for four years to make the sandwiches. I have a great group of friends; in fact this morning eleven of us went for coffee and biallys in the Bagel Café up there on McLean Avenue after nine o'clock Mass in St. Barnabas. I still return to Ireland twice a year and have just been there celebrating my sister's 50th Wedding Anniversary. To think that a couple of months after that wedding all those years ago, I left for America. She re-enacted the whole marriage ceremony again, with me as bridesmaid again, and a limo came to their house to pick us up for the church. Afterwards there was a reception for eighty-seven guests in some castle up there in Donegal. They're all so well off over there now, it's great, not like when we were young. I hope they don't give the country away though. In twenty years time it could be a different story with all the new people they're letting in. I won't be around then anyhow, so it won't bother me.

Besides Ireland I also love to visit other countries too. I was recently on a cruise to the Caribbean with a group of sixteen from Yorktown Heights and very soon we'll be leaving on another one to Newfoundland. I've traveled all over England and Scotland and Ireland too. I even climbed Lough Derg for the third time a couple of years ago, and I loved that. When I think of all those years ago in Golan National School when the Master would invite his pupils to examine this big map of the world he had up on the wall. We would have to pick out the places we wanted him to talk about, and I would always reach for Russia or some out-of-the-way area that nobody had ever heard about. "Bridget," he would say, "you are going to be a traveler. You are going to travel the world." And he was right.

Interviewed at Aisling Irish Community Center,
Yonkers, NY; August 10, 2006

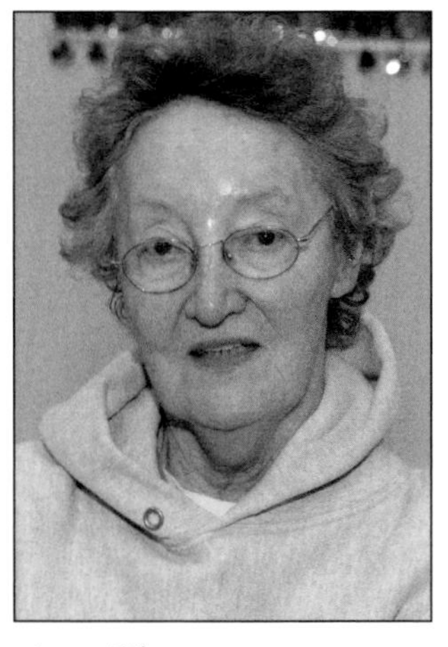

Pat Sheehy, 1956

I left Ireland in November 1956. I went from Dun Laoghaire to Holyhead and on to Liverpool to hook up with the Franconia, which then went on to Cobh to pick up the rest of the Irish passengers. It was a rough crossing and most people were sick. I traveled in steerage and it was the first time in my life that I became aware of class distinction. There were so many signs around the ship alerting steerage class that there was no access to this or that area, whatever was available only to First Class. They were the elite. It was the last voyage for the Franconia, as she got stuck in a sandbank outside Liverpool on her return to England and that was that.

I shared a cabin with three other ladies and I must have been very naive, as I was shocked when I saw my roommates taking off their wedding rings every night to go down to the ballroom. We were so innocent I don't know how we survived. They must have wanted to make believe they were single, but I don't know why they were traveling without their husbands. Overall I enjoyed it though. The boat was like a floating hotel, the first bit of luxury we had ever sampled. It cost quite a bit of money, but it was well worth it. There was dancing every night, movies, beautiful meals served by waiters in tuxedos and tea with freshly baked delicious pastries rolled out on trolleys every afternoon.

I remember arriving at Pier 92 in Manhattan and seeing the Statue of Liberty for the first time. It was an amazing sight, a lovely experience. We drove up the West Side Highway with my Aunt and when somebody tried to cut her off in traffic she exclaimed, "What a fresh kid." I had never heard that expression before. It was the first time I had heard that word "fresh" used in that context.

My first job in New York was at B. Altman's, a lovely store on Fifth Avenue. Ah! I still miss that store. I loved it. I went for interviews to Altman's and Lord & Taylor's. I got both jobs, by the way, but I took

B. Altman's for $40 a week compared to Lord & Taylor's for only $39 a week. It was on 34th & Fifth Avenue. I started in November and I was there when they rolled down that great big red carpet for Christmas and put up the beautiful Waterford crystal chandeliers. It was magnificent. I think it was the most beautiful store at Christmastime, and I think a family called Burke owned it at the time. They were dedicated to the store and the employees. I was working in the Christmas catalogue department and of course my accent was still very new and very Irish and most of the people calling up to order from the catalogue weren't expecting to hear a brogue on the other end of the phone. I remember someone called up looking for a vest. And, of course, in Ireland, a vest was an undergarment, and I got very confused because she wanted a waistcoat. There were loads of other incidents like that, I'm sure, but I enjoyed working there. So that was my introduction to working in New York. I stayed there for only three months and then I got a job with the New York Telephone Company.

Although I met my husband very shortly after arriving I still loved going to the dances. I loved the Jaeger House the best. The men stood on one side and the women on the other. There were seats on each side too, but I remember I always used to stand because I was so tall. I seem to recall that I never sat down because I was afraid somebody really short would ask me up to dance, so I used to stand all the time. Years later when I worked down in that Rose Hill building, I met a lady called Lucy Jones. She was a lovely, lovely Black lady, and we became close buddies and she told me she was the hat check lady in the Jaeger House for years, but I didn't remember her. She was a great lady and she only died last year.

Before I left Dublin I worked in the Civil Service in the Post Office department. It was a very monotonous, tedious job, sorting savings accounts numbers. My friends in the office were members of a youth group called An Óige, and they were forever going off on hitchhiking weekends. I don't know whether I was a snob or not but the idea of roughing it never appealed to me until one time they were only going as far as a hostel in Enniskerry, County Wicklow, and I agreed to accompany them, as they were taking the bus. As soon as we stepped off the bus, however, the heavens opened and we were forced to hitchhike. I couldn't get over how nice people were, driving out of their way to take us to our destination, and I was hooked.

A few weeks later we were on our way to the Puck Fair in Kilorglin and thumbing somewhere in County Limerick when a car pulled up driven by a man who was to become my future brother-in-law. When he heard I would be shortly leaving for New York he asked if he could give my number to his brother who was living over there? I consented, giving him my aunt's number and, on Christmas Day, shortly over a month after my arrival, I get this call from a man with an Irish accent who simply said, "Happy Christmas." I thought it was another Irish male friend of mine who had sent me a very nice Christmas gift. "Oh! Thanks for the present," I gushed, without thinking, and after the confusion was cleared up, I discovered he was Joe, my Joe, and we eventually decided on a date, but didn't get to actually meet until the following February.

What first attracted me to him was his pioneer pin, as I always swore I'd never marry a man who drank. We quickly fell in love, became engaged the following Christmas and were married that September; the 11th in fact. Joe also died on September 11th in 1990, so I will never forget that date for a number of reasons. My only child, Mark, was in the Twin Towers on that fateful day in 2001, but luckily he got out alive.

Recently whenever I hear Ireland mentioned in any conversation I have a yearning to go back. It's not that I don't like my life here in New York, but it's as if I have a foot in each country, like Atlas, and I have never been able to make roots in either. It's the nomad in me I suppose; there's a gypsy in me somewhere. Joe and I did pack up and moved back twice. His dream of owning a farm was quashed when he realized how much hard work it entailed. Both times we just couldn't settle there and came back to New York again. Some people were homesick from the start or in the early days, but for me it's only recently that I've begun to miss Ireland.

I grew up in Dublin, in St. Columba's Parish in Drumcondra, but I particularly recall the school holidays of my childhood, which were spent in the little village of Glynn in County Limerick, where my mother was from, and coincidentally my husband. It had always been my dream to go back and live there one day in this little cottage on the banks of the Shannon, but I never did make it. I remember the scent of the tea roses that grew in abundance around the cottage and the aromas of boiling bacon and cabbage wafting out from the kitchen. I remember the tang of the apples in the orchard and the whiff of the paraffin lamp as we lay in our beds at night. But most of all I remember the pong of the cowshed that floated through the Irish country air and for me that was the sweetest smell of all!

Written and recorded at Aisling Irish Community Center, Creative Writing Workshops, Yonkers, NY; November 2005 - May 2006

Postcard "Cunard R.M.S. Franconia 20,341 tons"

Mary Carrigan, 1957

I came to America on the Britannica. I left Cobh on April 6th, 1957, having traveled down to Dublin from Ballyfarnon in County Roscommon, in the parish of Kilronan. We lived on the other side of the mountain from the Arigna coal mines, where my mother was from. I cried the whole way to Dublin that day and a woman asked me was I going to England, and I sobbed, "No, I'm going to America." I was only nineteen at the time. My aunt met me in Dublin and put me on another train for Cork where I had to make the connection for Cobh.

Some people got sick on the boat and had to stay in bed for the whole six days, but I was more fortunate. I had a wonderful time dancing on deck. I made a lot of friends and I still keep in touch with one of them, Mary O'Riordan. I have the menu from the boat and many autographs of the other passengers who signed it for me. I was very lonely when I landed, saying goodbye to everyone. For the first few months, I lived with an uncle in Bayside, Long Island, before moving up to 87th Street in Manhattan to St. Gregory's parish.

I loved New York immediately, as I was able to find a job so fast and make a good living. I was the oldest of seven children at home only making two pounds and five shillings a week working in a store in Ireland. The village of Ballyfarnon consisted of about fifteen houses and each farmer had about thirty acres of land. I came to America for a better way of life, and an uncle, Jim Gilroy, paid my fare. I was homesick at first until I made my first trip home in 1959 for my twenty-first birthday. I was fine after that.

My first job was as a waitress at Schrafft's. I was in the branch down by Penn Station and I hated it so much. I didn't know the names of any of the food. One day a customer asked me for a screwdriver. I went into the kitchen looking for the actual tool and hadn't a clue where I would find a screwdriver. Imagine my embarrassment when they finally told me it was a drink. I was really happy to leave there and take up a position with the New York Telephone Company where I stayed until I had my first daughter.

I met my husband, Thomas, in Gaelic Park, the year after I came over. Not at the games, but in the bar after. There used to be a dance there on a Sunday night. There used to be a huge crowd at Gaelic Park and everyone would be dressed up. The men would be in their shirts and ties and the women in dresses. We weren't allowed wear slacks into the park back then. And we were forever getting our hose caught in the wooden benches. Every Sunday night you'd have a run in your nylons going into the dance. There were always collections at the gates too and the Irish were great for throwing in money. I also danced in the Jaeger House and in City Center.

Mary, aged 11, in her Irish dancing costume

Thomas and I got married and began our happy life down on 176th Street. We had three children: Ann lives in Florida; Kathleen and Thomas are both here in Yonkers. I have four grandchildren, all boys. My husband's death was a sad time in my life, but raising my children brought me immense joy as does being with my grandsons. I am happy now taking trips with family and friends, especially to Ireland, and I enjoy Fridays here in the Aisling Center.

Written and recorded at Aisling Irish Community Center creative writing workshops, Yonkers, NY; November 2005 - May 2006

Mary Judge, 1957

I came on a boat called the Saxonia in 1957, which took nine days to reach Worcester, Massachusetts. My two brothers accompanied me to Cobh and I was very lonely and homesick at first, but eventually I made a lot of friends on the boat and we had fun. We went dancing and enjoyed good food. My cousin met me at the pier and took me to see my Aunt Bessie who was in hospital. She wasn't that sick and was home in a few days. I lived with her and Uncle Ambrose for a while and got a job in a Woolworths five and ten store. My cousins would have to help me with the coins and get me to practice making change. I went to school at night for three years and fortunately got my high school diploma. That was a great experience, as I got to meet a lot of Americans. My second job was at St. Vincent's Hospital where I worked as a secretary to the building engineer. He was a Mr. Harney and my aunt knew him, of course. That's how you got anything; it was who you knew. It was a great job because I was in with all the men. I was in constant contact with all the construction workers who would be calling in about various jobs.

During this time I would regularly come down to New York to visit my cousins who had moved here from Ireland, so I regarded them as my real cousins so to speak. I will never forget the tall buildings when I first saw Manhattan. It was a bit scary, but the Empire State Building was some sight to see. I had so much fun with them especially at the dances like City Center that I decided to move down here altogether and started working in a bank. I stayed there for three years before eventually ending up in the New York Telephone Company as an operator. There were branches all over and they needed operators all the time. Everyone was using the operator for everything back then. You'd be so busy; there'd be one call after the other. We would be sitting in front of these big boards with wires hanging from everywhere and we had this really tough supervisor who gave us a really hard time. The day she stood behind me, placed her two hands on my shoulders and told me to stop talking, I knew I had to get out.

I went home to Ireland a lot on vacation and to England too, but I never dreamt of staying in either place. Back then the countryside in Ireland was very remote. The houses were all far apart and the only time we got anywhere was to cycle into the village to shop or something. I was born and raised in the parish of Geevagh, County Sligo. My father was from Conway's Cross and my mother from Coolmine. My mother passed away when I was very young, leaving me and my six brothers. She'd had an asthma-like attack and when we came home from school my father told us that he'd had the doctor for her. We all went to bed and when my father woke the next morning, she was gone. We could hear him crying all through the house; it was a terrible shock. My older brothers eventually left for England and I stayed at home to mind my father. When he passed away, it was time for me to go. My brother got the farm and there was no work for me so what was I to do?

Mary's U.S. Citizenship photograph

A lot of people that time went to England first, but everyone seemed to like it better here in America. I know I felt at home right from the start, as there was always so much to do and we always had company. Like I said, the Irish countryside was too isolated. People were friendlier here too and everyone banded together because we were all in the same boat. I never married. I did have a few offers and even wore a ring for a week, but I never wanted to disrupt the nice lifestyle I had. There was one boy back home, but he had to go to Dublin for work, so that was the end of us. He's married now with a family and I've often bumped into him over the years and we've remained friends.

At the end of my career I was working in advertising at Saatchi,

Saatchi, the advertising company. I finally had to retire because they flopped. I think the 1950's were the prime time for emigrating. It was an adventure. You learn so much when you travel.

Written and recorded at Aisling Irish Community Center creative writing workshops, Yonkers, NY; November 2005 - May 2006

Mary (2nd from left), brother, Eddie (left) and friends at the ESB Ball in Cork City, the night before she left for America

Jean McPeake (Walls), 1957

I remember when I came to New York. It was in July 1957 and the weather was so hot. We had never known heat like that back in Ireland, nor had we ever experienced the cold that we got the following winter. I don't remember the name of the boat only that I was sick the whole time and I vowed there and then that I would never get on a boat again, and I never have, not even when we were married first and all the young couples would be going on fishing trips, I never accompanied them. I came with my boyfriend, Bill, before we were married and I was only eighteen years old.

When we docked in New York the lights from the city were something else. We slept that first night on board, separate quarters mind you, and were not allowed off until the following morning. For years I kept in contact with the girl I shared a cabin with. She moved on to Preston Avenue with her aunt and uncle; I can't remember her name, but we've lost touch now. My Aunt Rose thinks I came to her because Bill stayed with her at first, but it was really to my sister, Ann, in St. Jude's Parish, Inwood, that I came. It would have been from Rose though that I heard about America, as she had been in Brooklyn for years and was always very good to my mother, sending parcels of clothes and bed linens from Montgomery Ward, where she worked. She would come back to Derry on visits too, always beautifully dressed, with Uncle Eddie who was tall and handsome with the most gorgeous American accent. I couldn't wait to get here.

My first impression of New York was the enormous highways with all the cars and how fast they were going. I can remember my first time on the subway, and I did not know what to do. I often got lost and ended up in Brooklyn and all sorts of places. My children laugh when I tell them that now. I hated the place at first and vowed I'd go home as soon as I'd saved the fare. But I made it and now I would not live anywhere else in the world.

My first job was waiting on tables in Schrafft's on 46th & Fifth Avenue. I did very well there and made lots of money. A quarter was a regular tip back then and if you made ten dollars in the whole day you'd be doing well. The older Irish waitresses would hide the silverware on us and weren't any help at all. But I didn't care I loved it there except for the fact that I had to work the holidays. I didn't like that at all. Bill worked in the Safeway supermarket before he moved on to A & P. Then he was drafted into the army and sent off to Germany. On one of his leaves home, two years after getting here, we were married in St. Elizabeth's Church on 181st Street. On another leave I paid his fare to Ireland and met up with him there. We stayed in the Heights for years where we reared our two daughters, Deirdre and Margaret. Deirdre went to Mount St. Ursula High School and Margaret to Cathedral High School from where she went on to Fordham University to graduate with a degree in business. She came top of her class and gave the commencement speech. She is now a Vice-President in a company and Deirdre works for lawyers. I have two granddaughters, Erica is an RN and Kristen is about to start College in September.

"To Bill, with all my love, Jean."
Taken in the Cloisters, a week
after Jean arrived in New York

I have gone back to Ireland many times, to my family homestead in St. Mary's Parish, Desertmartin, County Derry, but the last time I was there was three years ago when my sister, Rose, was sick. I would go to the hospital every day to see her and then she died two days after I came back. It would have broken my heart to go back for her funeral, and it breaks my heart to this day. That is the reason I probably haven't gone back even though I have a sister, Joan, still there. We lived in the country and my mother died from cancer when I was thirteen. She was sick for three years and it was just terrible to see her suffer. The doctor or the nurse came every night to give her morphine for the pain; it was pitiful. Then my father lived until he was eighty-four. There was never really any trouble in the North back then. Of course, Catholics were discriminated against, especially when you went for a job. They'd ask you what foot did you dig with; the right or the left. The Protestants always got the government jobs. But even after the Troubles began in the seventies, my sisters, Rose and Joan, didn't have any bother. My brother, alright, lived in a real IRA community, but he wasn't involved. His father-in-law had an IRA funeral and his daughters all wore berets, I heard, but other than that we didn't know much about it.

Bill was from Bellaghy and we were married for thirty years. It tore my heart out when we parted. We remained friends though and I always had him over for the holidays and took care of him before he died three years ago. His sister, Ann, came over to keep me company in the early days when he was in Germany and we are still friends to this day. My breaking up with Bill didn't affect that. She was a devil altogether and married Jimmy Chambers who was a handsome man back then, still is.

Another Bronx rooftop! With sister-in-law, Ann, June 1959

In the meantime, I met this nice Italian man, Ralph, and we were together for twenty years. He was the nicest man in this world with hands of gold. I met him when I was working for this other Italian, Sal, who had polio and I used help him with his laundry and house cleaning. Ralph was painting his apartment one time and he suggested we all go out to dinner. So all three of us went down to where the River's Edge is now on Bronx River Road, I can't remember what it was called then, but they had music and Ralph and I danced, and that's how it all started. Then, when he was fixing his daughter's apartment three years ago, he had a heart attack and dropped dead on her floor. I can still see him as clear as a bell. I tried CPR, which he had taught me himself, but I couldn't bring him back. I still miss him so much. His anniversary Mass now will be this Friday morning at eight o'clock. And my kids loved him. He would do anything for those kids. Even Bill liked him and would call him when he needed a ride to the doctor.

Everybody passed away the same year – my sister, brother, Bill, Ralph and Rose, all within six months of the other. If I didn't go crazy then, I'll never go crazy. Then I was diagnosed with lung cancer two years ago, went into remission, but now have it back again. I'm receiving chemotherapy and sometimes can be very sick from it. I'm in good form now today and not going to feel sorry for myself. I have to be strong. Whatever the Man above has laid out for me, so be it.

Written and recorded at Aisling Irish Community Center creative writing workshops, Yonkers, NY; November 2005 - May 2006

L to R: Unknown, Marion Reilly and cousins, Patricia and Kathleen Brady
RMS Brittanic (1958)

Jerry Cregan (third from left) and company on board the SS New York (1958)

Oliver O'Donnell and company on board the SS America (1960)

Dancers at City Center ballroom, New York, 1955

Martin O'Malley, 1957

I came on the Corinthia, one of the Cunard White Star liners. I had been working in England, and booked the passage from there, then came back to Ireland and picked up the boat at Cobh on the 27th of January 1957. I don't remember too much about Cobh except that it was very high up from where we stood on the tender. The town was climbing up the side of a hill. The sea was wild and the crossing a bit treacherous, but that didn't worry us. We were drinking and dancing for six days. We didn't spend too much time on deck, but I was introduced to Seven and Seven—Seagram's Rye and Seven-Up—by an old man who was returning after a vacation and he was bringing back a niece with him. She was very tiny, a very cute little girl. I often met her in the Jaeger House after, but I never met the old man again. So we'd be drinking Seven and Seven together every night. It was a nice drink then. I wouldn't drink it now.

Anyhow the trip was just beautiful. We were sorry to leave it in the end, as it was like a holiday, a beautiful long holiday, the first one we'd ever had in our lives. I was real lonesome getting off at the other side, as I had made so many friends, some of them I still know to this day. There was great dancing. It was like a cruise. It WAS a cruise. I was lonesome getting off. I'm not kiddin' you, I was lonesome. You paid for your passage and that was it, after that all you paid for was your drink. But things were cheap at the time.

Manhattan was not such a spectacular sight as it is now. There were not as many tall buildings, especially around Midtown. It's much more built up now. The Cross Bronx Expressway wasn't even there then. They must have ripped up about nine neighborhoods when they were building the Expressway. They picked up houses and took them away on the backs of trucks. It was amazing the way they were able to do it. It ploughed through Parkchester dividing Olmstead Avenue where my sister lived. It cut her off from the Safeway supermarket across the street.

She could not get across to it the way she used to, but had to take a footbridge, which was further down the street.

My first job was with the A&P supermarkets packing shelves. Then I started working the night shift in the telephone company mopping floors along with a fellow who changed the sand in the big ashtrays beside the elevators. It was humiliating work really. There was a fierce amount of women in the telephone company back then and we'd be hiding on them coming off the day shift. How could you ask a girl to dance at the Jaeger House if she knew you mopped floors for a living? But I took my chance early and got out quick.

Martin (center) and friends at Round Tower Ballroom, Holloway Road and Seven Sisters, London, 1955

In January 1958, only a year after arriving here, I was drafted into the army. It was after Korea. They had the draft for a long time, well into the sixties. And I still couldn't become a citizen after coming out of the army. I think that was one of the most unjust things. I had to wait five years like everybody else. I was over there in Germany and anything could have happened to me. Here I was an alien, ready to fight for the country and I still wasn't good enough to become a citizen. That's the truth, and I often thought that was very unjust. There were three Tipperary brothers—Mike, Jimmy and Denis who joined up together because they could get citizenship immediately after they came out, but because I was drafted, I couldn't. I could never see the sense of that. Anyhow I started off in boot camp in New Jersey, Fort Dix, for eight weeks and then they made me a cook. Sure I hadn't a clue how to cook, but I was a cook until I got out of the army. When the Tipperary brothers would start complaining about the slop I was dishing up, I'd say, "Well you chose to be here. I didn't!"

After Fort Dix I was in Germany for a year and a half. I'll tell you something I didn't mind that at all. I was always waiting to get out of it, mind you, but it was a pleasant enough duty. You were on a day and off two. We had an old car; three of us, Tom Kennedy, John Carty and I bought the car, an old Opal Kapitan, and we'd drive around on our day off. I traveled to London three times and Ireland twice during my eighteen-month duty. I also went to Paris and I honestly never thought I would see the Champs Elysées again. Last year, however, when I was visiting my brother, Tony, in England, he and his family took me and my wife on the fast train to Paris for lunch. I stood on the Arc de Triomphe and looked down on that very same spot where I had strolled nearly forty-five years before that, and the memories came flowing in.

When I got out first I had a part-time job in St. Nicholas of Tolentine High School. It was a grand job cleaning the classrooms. One day I was walking down 207th Street to grab a slice of pizza before my shift, when I bumped into a man called Paddy Lynn coming out of Clarke's bar there on the corner of Broadway. He was insisting on me coming in for a drink, but I couldn't, as I had to go to work in St. Nick's. "Don't mind that place," he persisted. "Come on the buses with me. I'll get you a note no problem."

He was such a nice man; I couldn't refuse him. He got me the note from this Roscommon man, you had to be recommended by someone, and I landed myself a job on the buses. Man alive, I cursed him more after. I couldn't stand it, man alive. I hated that job. First of all, I had no experience driving. I had a driver's license, but how I got that is another story. So I was a cook and I couldn't cook and a driver and I couldn't drive.

I got on a bus in Manhattan the first day and I didn't know where I was going. There were so many people hanging around my neck, and I was so slow making change, trying to sort out the dimes and the nickels and the quarters, and these ones screaming at me, "Where is such and such?" And I'd say, "I don't know, Mam." And they'd roar at me, "You're driving a bus and you don't know where it is?" And I'd say to them "That's right Mam." It wasn't easy, I'll tell you. But I survived twenty-three years of it. There was great money in it and great benefits and you could always drive the night bus every now and then to make a few extra dollars. I went on the buses in 1960 and I retired in 1983. At the age of fifty, I had my twenty years service put in and I said goodbye. Thank you

Paddy, I said. I had made it. It was a good job to get out of, I'll tell you; they had a great pension package and that, and I was able to put my six children through Catholic school and send them to college.

I did the usual round of the dancehalls, the Jaeger House, City Center, the whole lot. We had great fun at these dances, the waltz, the foxtrot, the jitterbug. There were these three brothers from Kerry and one of them was like a machine on the floor. He used to dance with this girl all the time and she was some dancer. That's all they ever did was dance. I don't think they ever went out with one another or anything. They were just mad for each other's dancing. It's a pity some of the women didn't learn how to dance. They'd be stepping on your toes and tripping over you and everything. Some of them were terrible snobs, you know. They wouldn't want to dance with you. There was this guy one time and he asked this one up to dance and she looked him up and down. "No," she said. "I'm very fussy about who I dance with, I'll have you know." He then looked her up and down and replied, "Well, I'm not. That's the reason I asked you."

Then we'd go down to Wright's cafeteria after, on 85th Street. You'd get your breakfast or a hamburger or whatever you wanted. Oh! A hamburger and fried onions at one o'clock in the morning! I thought that was the nicest thing I'd ever tasted when I came over first. Then we'd go down to Ireland's Thirty-Two on Third Avenue and 77th Street. It was sort of a bar and there was a place to dance. The Jaeger House would finish at one o'clock and then we'd go down to the other place. I never got robbed on the subway going home even though I'd often fall asleep and not wake up until Pelham Bay, and I living at Parkchester. I'd pass the stop and have to cross over at Soundview. Then I'd fall asleep again and pass Parkchester again on the way down and I'd have to get off and come up again and I never lost a watch, a wallet, nothing.

I met my wife, Annie, in this apartment building I lived in over on Post Avenue after I moved out of my sister's. It was in bad shape, man. You couldn't get an apartment unless you were getting engaged or getting married, whatever. I was none of the above. So another guy's girlfriend came with me sporting a big lump of an engagement ring. We went into the Super who was from Ballina, and I gave a month's rent and said I was getting married to this woman and that was it. He gave it to me. Oh, But, man alive, it was in bad shape.

My brother-in-law was working on Madison Avenue and he told me of a building they were tearing down there on 86th Street. I went down and found this lovely combination sink. You wouldn't look at it now, but it was grand that time. Then I looked up and spotted this lovely cabinet on the wall. As the building was coming down, you see, I figured I'd have the cabinet as well. I shook it and it started to come away, so I gave it a couple of more shakes and down it came. When I was cleaning it later I felt something right in by the corner of the door and I thought it was a spring. I got a screwdriver and pried it away and what do you think it was but a diamond ring. To find a lump of a diamond like that in 1960 was something else. I cleaned it up and got the paint off, it had been painted over in the cabinet, and I scraped it across a mirror. Lo and behold, it left a big streak.

A blustery day in every way – July 29, 1961

To make a long story short, I got $500 dollars for it, no questions asked. My aunt was a housekeeper for this woman whose husband was a jeweler and he bought it from me. It was probably worth more, but five hundred dollars in 1960 was a fortune. It set me up.

This friend of mine, Jim Conmy, May he Rest in Peace, became my roommate and Annie was living with Conmy's girlfriend in another part of the building. The girls had just moved in and they'd brought this linoleum with them, auld dry crap, and our job was to put it down. As we were finishing the job the door opened and this lovely girl walked in.

"When you have that done you can put another piece down in the closet while you're at it." I had never seen her before and I thought, "Cheeky!" She was Anne Coen, from Galway. We started going out shortly after that and were married in 1961. Conmy ended up marrying his woman too, so it turned out to be a great arrangement.

I was dreaming of home last night and I woke up dreaming of it, about buying a place in the next parish over from us, the most beautiful parish you ever saw, Lacken. The church was built at the edge of the strand and when the tide came in it covered the beach with water for about three miles, dividing Lacken from the neighboring parish of Kilcummin. People would arrive for Mass in ponies and traps, asses and carts, whatever, and if the tide was in they'd have to wade through the water to get to the church. They would be in their bare feet with their skirts and trousers rolled up around their knees. We also gathered sand eels on the strand there on a summer's evening. The men would strap buckets around their waists and gather in the eels. Man, there was nothing like the taste of those eels after they'd been fried. They didn't need to be filleted or anything because there was nothing inside them. Lacken was just beautiful though. The first time I brought Anne home she thought it was the most beautiful place in the world. But I wouldn't go back there now. I wouldn't go back if you gave me the whole county of Mayo. We were just too poor.

I grew up in the village of Kilbride in the parish of Ballycastle, on the Killala peninsula, County Mayo. At that time, there were about fourteen houses in the village and the farms were very small. Talk about poor; we were all poor. My mother was from the same parish and she met my father locally and they seemed very happy together. I had two brothers and two sisters, and actually my twin sister died at birth and I didn't discover that until many years later. I feel though that I missed out on not having her with me all this time.

When I was just twelve years of age my father developed tuberculosis. He was sent to Peamount Hospital in Dublin and we were never to see him again, as he died a year later. I remember the day a neighbor came to tell me to go get my uncle. I knew was something was wrong and my feet didn't hit the ground as I ran all the way to his house. It was this uncle who brought the body back home. After that my mother never seemed to stop crying and that was a terrible thing to watch. We were now worse off than ever before and the eldest of my two brothers had to work outside the house to earn a few shillings. I helped around the farm, but it was very miserable work and didn't bring in much. I had a great godfather though. He was a neighbor of ours and a little bit better off, his wife was a schoolteacher and my father used to do odd jobs for them on the farm. He used to cut their hair too, don't ask me why, but he must have been good at it.

Anyhow this couple had no children and they were so good to me. Every Christmas, Easter and birthday I got the grandest present from them and my two brothers and two sisters used to hate me, hate me they did, because they would get nothing. And the funniest thing, this man always insisted on sewing his oats of the 1st of May, whereas my father wouldn't harness a horse or anything on that day; he said it was bad luck. It's funny the things you'd remember.

I remember November's Eve pelting heads of cabbage at people's doors and running away. But some people wanted the cabbage, so we never threw it at them. Instead we threw turnips, which would burst the doors open, and we'd have to run all the more. Then at Christmas my mother, God rest her, would go into town and say she was going to buy the Christmas. The Christmas box was what the grocer would give you as a present. But, we wouldn't get much mind you; there'd be no turkey or anything, maybe a goose. Turkey my foot. God, but we were poor. We were so poor, man; we used to have what we called potatoes and point for dinner. In the past my father would have killed a pig and hung him in the kitchen to cure and you'd get the grandest smoked bacon. Later on all we had was the potato and we'd just point at where the pig used to be!

Anyhow, when I was seventeen I got work reclaiming land around the area. It was a wet, dirty job so in 1954 I set off for London where I worked on the British Railway. A lot of our generation left Ireland that time. They came to America and they went to England too. I'll tell you, we had two villages together, Kilbride and Carrowmore, and we used have country dances. Sure there was a dance nearly every night, and there were about thirty girls, and it went down that there was only my sister left. Imagine that, between the two villages, between about thirty houses, only my sister left.

At first we couldn't afford to go home so we'd go to the Catskill

Mountains instead. Ah! The Catskills. The Catskills were beautiful altogether. We'd go there at weekends and for vacation in the summer. Two week at a time, and we'd all pick the same two weeks – the last in July and first in August. We'd be dancing every night, dancing all night, out all night. We'd sleep until twelve o'clock and then lie at the pool all day. There were guys and girls out having a good time. You'd meet everyone there that you'd meet every other day of the year in the Bronx. Even after we were married and had a family it was a lovely place to go, and the kids loved it. I had a Volkswagen bus one time and us men would fill the cooler with beer and soda, pack the kids into the bus; the women would stay at home chatting, and we'd go to the drive-in, lay a blanket on the ground and watch the movie. They were great times. I'd be so happy driving up the thruway to be getting away from the buses; well I'd be on a high. And the kids would be waving at the other kids in other cars. Ah! It was great. We loved it. Sure the whole lot of us went up there, every single one of us. There were probably five or six establishments at that time and every one of them had a crowd. That'll tell you how many Irish went up there. That was where we went, the Catskills. There was no place else to go. We just couldn't afford to go home.

I have a sister, Rita, there yet and a brother, Tony, in England, so I like to go back occasionally to see them. It all turned out great though. The kids have a great bond with Ireland. Sure if you asked them what nationality they were, they'd say "Irish!"

My daughter, Ann Marie, is a teacher and is married with four children in New Jersey. Una was a teacher in Special Education and she was doing her thesis when she got pregnant. She was going to Columbia University for her doctorate and had to give up then when she had the second child. She now has three children and lives in Croton-on-Hudson. Teaching is a nice job for a girl. It depends on where you are though. Imagine trying to teach in DeWitt High School? There's a teacher I used bring up the Grand Concourse in the bus in the morning. She used always sit up in the front with me, as she was probably afraid to go to the back. "How do you teach them?" I asked her one day. "We don't," she said. "We just try and keep them from killing one another."

As for the rest of my children, Eileen is married is New Jersey with four children and Theresa is in Connecticut; with three. Patrick, an MD, is a Lieutenant Colonel in the U.S. Army and is teaching medicine in the

Medical School in Bethesda, where he lives with his wife and two daughters. Martin is a Jesuit priest and is moving to Germany soon to complete his Doctorate. We have sixteen grandchildren whom we spend a lot of time with and enjoy immensely. I credit my wife with how well our children turned out, she was always there for them and would stay up late at night to make sure they were all home safely. She was also the disciplinarian, but I was the ultimate boss!

We lead a quiet life now in Woodlawn, and I enjoy coming down here to the Aisling Center as a member of the Irish Volunteers for the Homeless group. It's nice to be able to give back to the community that gave so much to me.

Interviewed at Aisling Irish Community Center, Yonkers, New York; January 16, 2006

My beloved Mayo – Dún Briste, Downpatrick Head

Carmen Purcell, 1957

When I was a child my father worked for a while on a ship that took him from Belfast to Rio de Janeiro and back. When he came home he'd bring us Tee shirts bearing the American flag and coins like quarters, nickels and dimes. That was the first I ever knew America existed. Later on I became familiar with it through the movies and always associated it with the good life. For many people in Ireland, America was the one out we all had. That is why when the Franciscan Sisters of the Atonement visited the schools in the 1950's to recruit novices; I decided to join. And that is why I came to Graymoor in Garrison, New York, when I was only fifteen years old, to become a nun.

We sailed on the Britannica in September 1957. There were three other novices with me and two nuns. I was sick the whole way over and only on the Thursday of that week was I able to eat. The nuns even allowed me a glass of brandy, although I was a pioneer, anything to ease the nausea. We had also been inoculated against smallpox before departure, and our superiors were hoping that the shot would quiet us down for the journey. They thought the four of us wild and in need of calm. We traveled with a family called O'Connor who was returning to the States after a holiday in Ireland and we all stood on deck as the ship pulled into New York harbor. I will always remember my first sight of the Statue of Liberty welcoming us ashore and how it was bronze in color; not green like it is today. I stayed in Garrison for ten months and enjoyed it immensely, especially mixing with all of the other nationalities. There were seventeen potential nuns in our group that year. But the homesickness was too much for me at such a young age, and I was advised to return home. I realized that I did not have a calling for the religious life. My true vocation was for nursing.

Having trained in Yeovil, Somerset, I returned to the States in July 1964, as a fully fledged nurse. I had completed my midwifery in the Jubilee Hospital, Belfast, where I was born. I would often look at the beds and wonder which one my poor mother gave birth in. She would probably have known. I applied to an agency that was recruiting nurses for America and was assigned to a position in Washington D.C., not New York where I really wanted to be. After seven weeks my brother-in-law here hooked me up with four girls on Bainbridge Avenue, and I got a job at Jacobi Hospital. Of course I had to take all the state exams at the time in order to practice in the U.S., which annoyed me at first. I was only twenty-two and indignant that I was already a qualified nurse. But it worked out great because later when I wanted to go to Lehman College for my Degree in Nursing, I was glad to have my state boards.

I loved New York the minute I set foot in it. Of course, I was homesick, and I missed the Northern accent so much, as you'd hardly ever hear it here. I would follow people in the street just to hear them speak. There was hardly anyone coming over from the North back then. It wasn't until after the sixties that they started leaving, after the Civil Rights Movement took force. But that first St. Patrick's Day I was in heaven. When I saw a contingent from County Down marching up Fifth Avenue my heart soared. I was elated. To think that we were Irish and Catholic and we were allowed to march in a parade. And everybody loved us! That was even more surprising. The last Catholic parade I had seen was when I was only five years of age back on the Falls Road in Belfast.

Four of us lived on Hone Avenue, in St. Francis of Assisi Parish, off Bainbridge Avenue. There was Roisin McGraigue and her brother, Patrick, who were in the Tyrone Society. In fact he was secretary with Marilyn O'Neill from Riverdale, and they were all into that at the time. Theresa Kelly from Sligo was the fourth roommate and when Roisin and Patrick went home, Theresa and I were left with the big rent so we sublet an apartment on University Avenue from an Irish family who were going home for six months. We then got another apartment on Valentine Avenue and 201st Street and there we stayed until I got married. We went to the Red Mill a lot, the Tower View, City Center, The Trocadero, all those little Irish enclaves. Dancing was the big thing; and Irish weddings, but social life was just for the single people. Once you got married the social life ended.

I met my husband, Andy, at the Red Mill on Halloween night in 1965. I wasn't dressed up in costume; I suppose I should have been. He's from the village of Gortnahoe in the townsland of Urard on the

Tipperary/Kilkenny border. The nearest town is Urlingford. The name of the place means garden of grapes. I wasn't that good at the Irish, but what the nuns taught me, I remembered. I could say my prayers in Gaelic, and sing St. Patrick's hymn. I taught my children any of the language that I did know, that was my part for standing up for my Irish roots, and when they came first at the feis one year, I was so proud. Raising my four daughters has brought me great joy and they are also proud of their Irish heritage.

I was only here a year when I went home. Oh! Dear I felt that the place would disappear if I didn't see it soon. I was so homesick. After that I went home every year for five years. My daughter, Nuala, named after my sister, was born in County Down in August 1968, as Andy and I both wanted our first child to be born in Ireland. We gave her the Mountains of Mourne for her birthday. Everyone came to her Christening, Protestants and all. That was unheard of over there, as it was a Sunday and traditionally they didn't dance or attend parties on the Sabbath. That was before Bernadette Devlin and the Civil Rights Movement began. After I got married and we bought the house in Woodlawn, it was sixteen years before I saw Ireland again. I had a young family, four little girls, and I didn't want to annoy my sister, Nuala, with young children, as she also had a family of her own. We were very close always. We could even finish each other's sentences and I could nearly tell what she's thinking right now. We would write one another letters and they would cross in the mail and I would have answered her questions before I even got her letter. I missed her terribly, especially when I was raising my children. I would love to have been near her then.

On that first visit to her home in Kilkeel in 1984, I saw the British soldiers for the first time. It was like a mad ballet. They were running all over the place and three of them came over to our car and stuck a gun in the window. Nuala kept pleading with me not to say anything and I didn't. All I could think was that these are real guns. She said she didn't take any notice; that was the usual there. I was shocked. Here we were in a little town on a sunny Sunday morning and soldiers in camouflage were pointing guns at the citizens, including the children. It was a real shock.

My rebellious nature was nurtured on the Whiterock Road in the parish of St. Therese, in the predominately Catholic area of Andersonstown, Belfast. The Protestant children in the neighborhood wore uniforms to school and were always better dressed than we were. They also lived in nicer houses. We were told not to go near the Shankill or Donegal Roads, but we were never told why. When I was eleven I started to skip school to hang out in the Falls Park. As a result I was sent to St. Louis Convent in Armagh for three years. Upon my return I started to become more aware of our fearful environment. I knew there was a gun in the drawer at home, but I dare not ask about it. All I know is that it ended up in the river Lagan. My mother took me to a sweet shop one day and she told me not to say anything; that she would do all the talking. It suddenly dawned on me that she was afraid of these people. That was my first inkling that as a Catholic I had no chance. Then one Sunday morning my father was listening to Radio Eireann and something came on about the IRA. I asked what was the IRA and my mother became very agitated. "She'll get us all murdered," she cried. That was the fear at the time; that if you even mentioned anything like that, you could get killed. That was my second awakening.

Studying for nursing exams on the grounds of Taunton General Hospital Somerset, 1962

I had initially applied to a hospital in Lisburn for nursing, but it was well known that more Protestants than Catholics would be accepted. After I had trained as a midwife in the Jubilee, I had a six week wait before leaving for America. I browsed through the Belfast Telegraph and The Irish News for a little job to tide me over. Anything that appealed to me I circled, to discover that only Protestants could apply. That wasn't even a shock to me then; now it annoys me.

Three days before I came here in 1964, in one final act of rebellion, I went into the local record store in Belfast. It was July, just before the Twelfth and I asked for "Kevin Barry" and the "Soldier's Song" to be played. The guy had never heard of either of them before. It wasn't right what I did, but I was glad, and I wasn't afraid. Nor was I afraid of the doctor who gave me the medical examination for my visa. He asked me why I was going to America when the Queen had educated me in England. I replied that my better question was why you are here, and why is she here, when I'm leaving Ireland and I was born here. He wasn't going to pass me; he left the room for a while and came back smiling sarcastically and reluctantly gave me a clean bill of health.

My father was in the old IRA back in the twenties and we were sometimes well off, but more often poor. He worked one time as a cab driver for Ulster Hire, which was a Protestant outfit. He traveled all over the country and knew all the roads, even in the South. He taxied around movie stars like Judy Garland and Bing Crosby until Ian Paisley's father got wind that he was a Catholic and threatened to boycott the cab company if they kept him on. He was let go. He worked then for a while on a boat that sailed between Belfast and Lancaster until eventually my parents moved to Lancaster altogether where he continued to work on the boats until 1971. By then it was getting too dangerous, as there were regular bomb threats and one of my brothers persuaded them to join him in New Zealand.

I traveled over there to see my mother before she died, as I figured she'd brought twelve children into the world; the least I could do is be there for her parting. On that trip I also spent time with my oldest brother who had left Belfast in the fifties to join the Merchant Marines and eventually moved to Sydney, Australia. He is now retired in Tasmania. Another brother settled in Brisbane. Of the two that became ship's stewards and ended up in New Zealand, one was killed in a car accident at the age of twenty-two. My father returned to Belfast after my mother's death and passed way in 1999. Another sister who lived in Dublin died in 2004. Four of my mother's babies died at infancy. Our large Irish family has known a lot of loss.

From America it was very good to see that Irish Americans were willing to help the situation in the Six Counties. All I can say is that we hope that all the money that we raised went to the right places. I think hopefully that it really did. I always kept in touch with what was happening in the North. In the seventies people became more fearful, I think. They weren't as friendly with one another anymore. Nuala wrote and told me that some of the Protestant stores would not serve the Catholics. The

Catholic businesses could not do the same, as they were too dependent on customers from both sides. I followed closely the success of the Civil Rights Movement and how the IRA became slowly involved when simple rights were being denied. I admire Gerry Adams for the work that he does, I think he has great courage. And I really admire President Bill and Senator Hilary Clinton for all the work they did for Northern Ireland. They really stood up to the plate. Of course President Kennedy had been our great hope. We really thought that he could have helped us without resorting to violence. I remember the night he died. I was doing my midwifery on the Lisburn Road, which was a dangerous spot, and I think it was one of the saddest and most sickening nights of our lives. All hope for Ireland was shot with him. When I lived in Washington D.C., I went to the White House every day to look through the gates hoping to see his brother, Bobby, but all I saw were President Johnson's dogs!

I finally did see Robert Kennedy one day here in New York on Fordham Road with Hubert Humphrey when he was campaigning. I was just getting on a bus going up towards Jerome Avenue and I spotted their truck turning around the corner from the Concourse in the direction of Alexander's. I jumped off the bus again and nearly fainted at the sight of him. He was standing up on the truck waving at everyone, and of course I thought he was looking just at me. I nearly died. I saw him again on the St. Patrick's Day parade when he was running for Senator of New York. I saw Gerry Adams too, when he was in Rory Dolan's that time and he showed us the film of the Maze Prison, where he himself had been. Governor Pataki was with him that night. That was my first taste of the political side of things.

I worked at Jacobi Hospital for twenty-three years and then got a job as resident nurse at Macy's where I stayed for eight years. We mainly carried out drug tests on prospective employees where we would be especially busy around Christmas with all the extra workers for the vacation. We also had to take care of customers who became ill or were injured on the premises. I even had to make depositions in court sometimes when there were law suits against us; and, of course, we took care of the store employees when they were ill. Our Director, Grace Sells, always insisted that we be called Executive Nurses, thus giving us the same status as the store's executive staff. She was marvelous. I stayed there until Macy's was taken over by the Federated Department Stores who did away with the medical center. Grace took me with her to Meridian Healthcare where I would be sent out as a per diem nurse to various major companies. I was working in Morgan Stanley at Number 5, the World Trade Center, on September 11, 2001.

Shortly after reporting for duty at 8:45 a.m., I heard what sounded like the rolling of furniture on the floor above. Then I heard people running out on the corridor and I stuck my head out the door to tell them be quiet, that the Supervisor was due any minute. They were all running in place; there was no pushing or anything; and they seemed to be crying. I heard the word "bomb" being mentioned and someone cried, "Nurse, come quick." I checked the bathrooms and locked everything away, the filing cabinets, desks, office, everything. Here are the keys. I keep them in my pocket to this day and take them with me everywhere I go, as a reminder. We filed down the stairs; we were lucky to be only on the sixth floor and I held hands with a little girl behind me. Moira Smith, a Transit Authority secretary, was on one of the landings and she told us to keep going, not to look back. She didn't want us to see the people falling from the windows and the Plaza full of dead bodies. She then proceeded back up the stairs and was never seen again. I'll always remember her smile and her beautiful red hair.

As a nursing student at Yeovil General Hospital, Somerset, 1960

By the time we got out on the street the second plane had just arrived and I thought it was the fire department coming to help. After all America was magic and I was sure everything would be fine in the end. Then I saw the top of the second building flare up like fire crackers. The cops were screaming, "This is not a circus," as they urged us to move along. We were steered into Dey Street, too many of us for that tiny alleyway and when another boom sounded and more flames leapt out of the second tower, we all fell to our knees. I thought I was going to be crushed up against the walls of the Century 21 department store.

There were cell phones everywhere. I grabbed one and my fingers were sore trying to dial the number at home, but to no avail. I later mailed the phone to its owner who worked at Goldman Sachs and he sent me a twenty-five dollar gift card for Macy's. I still had my white coat on, as I walked in the direction of Brooklyn Bridge, not knowing where I was going when I met this lady, called Colette, whom I used to treat for her asthma. We walked the whole way across the bridge together, to her home in Flatbush, Brooklyn, where I drank Jamaican wine, my first drink in twenty-five years. I hadn't touched a drop since my youngest daughter's christening. I stayed there until the subways started running again and eventually made it home from Atlantic Avenue to Woodlawn that night. All I could see for weeks was the white smoke and the people dropping from the sky. I prayed to God that I wouldn't go mad.

Imagine coming all the way from Northern Ireland to experience terrorism in my beloved New York. The experience brought home to me the insanity of people fighting in the name of Religion for there is no sign of any country on the communion host. I saw priests and ministers and people of all persuasion and race run to help one another that day and it gives me great hope. New York is still magic and it will never lose that. Apart from the sacrifice of leaving my family, I will always be glad that I came here. I wish it was as easy for the young Irish here to become legal as it was for us. It's very hard to watch them at Christmas on Katonah Avenue when you know they would love to be back home. The Irish built the railroads here; they should not be railroaded by the U.S. government now.

I am delighted with the changes back in Ireland, with the beautiful houses and the beautiful roads, especially in rural Ireland. The Irish people deserve it. I'm sorry I'm not there to enjoy it, but I'm glad they are.

Interviewed at Aisling Irish Community Center,
Yonkers, New York; March 02, 2006

Jerry and Marion Cregan, 1958

Jerry: I came in September 1958 and I think it was the sorriest day of my life. A semi-final was being played that day between Kerry and Derry and naturally, being a Kerry man, I'd love to have been there. And Kerry lost, which made it even worse. Anyhow we got into the hackney cab—my father, my mother, and my Auntie Sarah. Lanigan's hackney cab it was that took us to Cobh. We had to stay the night and I remember going up the hill to the big cathedral and then back down for the bite to eat and I thought that my mother didn't know I smoked, you see. So every now and then I'd sneak out for a cigarette and one time Auntie Sarah followed me. "We know you smoke." She whispered, handing me a few fags. "Haven't you been stealing our butts for years?"

She was a big smoker and so was my mother, you see, Lord have mercy on all of them now. Anyway, I got on the boat the next morning and that was it. I always figured that I'd only come for a few years and that I'd go back.

Marion: He thought he'd make his fortune.

Jerry: No, not really. I never really wanted to come in the first place. I never, never wanted to come here. But that time there was nothing. The best pay I ever got in Ireland was the red ten shilling note and you'd have to foot a day's turf for that. There were no jobs back then in farming communities or in a country place.

Marion: Didn't your teacher want you to continue school?

Jerry: Yes, she did. She came out to the Cross one day to see Dada and said to him, "That boy should go on to college," or secondary school or whatever it was. But I never did.

My father had been here for years before me. In fact, on one of his trips back his boat was one of the first to come upon the Titanic after it sank. He was in the American Army for thirty-three years and had served under General Douglas McArthur's father in the Philippines during World War I. His younger brother, Steve, was killed on November 9, 1919, two days before the Armistice was signed. My grandmother had asked my father to look after him, so he was always upset about that.

Dada returned to Ireland in his early fifties, married my mother, a local girl much younger than he was, and they had eight children. Six of us emigrated here. So, I didn't want to come, but I had an American passport through my father and I was all set. Somehow or another I wound up anyhow on that boat.

Now I come from the mouth of the Shannon, in Tarbert, County Kerry, and my uncle, Eugene Holohan, was a fisherman all his life with a licensed boat and net, and he fished for salmon. I was quite used to water, to boats, to fishing, pulling in the nets, and all that. I was fine on the ferry, but the next thing this ship started to move and I started to heave with it. I was sick as a dog.

There were four of us in the cabin; two were here before and going back after a holiday and two of us were going over for the first time. I was in the top bunk and not feeling too good. I slept through the night, however, but the minute my feet hit the ground the next morning, I was sick again. I had to stay in the bunk for a day and a half until one of the guys dragged me out of the bed and took me up to the bar. Now, up to this I had never drunk except for stealing an odd glass of sherry from Mama at Christmas. Anyhow yer man ordered me a brandy and I knocked it back. Then he took me back to the cabin and introduced me to the shower. A shower? What was that? And this is no lie; I walked in socks and all. I got drenched. I had no idea what a shower was.

But from that day on I got to know every inch of that ship, including the swimming pool, the Captain's deck, every tier of it, the pursers quarters, the movie house, everything. There wasn't an inch of the ship that I didn't know. Outside the cabin door there was a diagram showing how much we progressed west every day. One morning I noticed that the ship was going south. I ran up along and asked one of the crew, "How come we're going south?" He explained that there was a hurricane coming up the east coast of America; it was September, remember, and we had to go south for a while to avoid it. I suppose I drank on the ship and went dancing.

Marion: You played cards didn't you?

Jerry: Oh! That's another story. Dada had given me enough money to take me to Syracuse to my Auntie May's where my brother and sister were already staying, but I got into a card game and lost the fare. Ah! Anyhow, I got off the boat and I went up and stayed with Mrs. Moriarity, where my brothers Steve and Josh were. She was a Kerry woman who had a rooming house on 161st Street and Nelson Avenue, in Highbridge.

Marion: That was a real Irish neighborhood that time.

Jerry: So Mrs. Mor said to me, "You can stay one week; you can even stay two weeks; but after that, if you're not working, you're out." She gave everyone the benefit of two weeks without paying until they got a job.

Now I had only ever seen one Black person before that and he was selling medicines at the Listowel races. Whatever few shillings I had that day I bought a bottle of something for Auntie Ellie's rheumatism. The next Black person I ever saw was on Nelson Avenue.

Anyhow I was not quite eighteen years of age so I had to get working papers before I could even apply for a job. My brother told me how to manage the subway, which was an awful ordeal altogether. When I got on at 161st Street, the train was elevated, you see, above the street.

Marion: That same thing happened to me.

Jerry: I went downtown, got the papers on 18th Street, and walked all the way back up to 34th Street to B. Altman, which was one of the finest department stores in this country that time, if not in the whole world. There was a man by the name of Burke who was President and he always gave consideration to the Irish for jobs. I got hired there and then, and made my way to the station for the train home, but I couldn't find the subway anywhere. I went out into the middle of Herald Square to this cop who was directing traffic because I couldn't figure out where this subway had disappeared to.

He said, "It's over there in front of you." I thought he was mad, because I couldn't see it anywhere. "But sure," I said, "When I got on the blooming thing up in the Bronx it was up there." I pointed to the sky. "It's gotta be up there," I insisted. "It was up there when I got on it." He asked me was it my first time and I said it was. He left the traffic in the middle of Herald Square, this is no lie now, he left the middle of the blooming traffic in the middle of Herald Square and escorted me over to the station where I could take the D train, which was now underground, you see. I hadn't noticed that on the way down.

Marion: The very same thing happened to me. I got on the train in Queens and it was over ground. We had to climb up these steps from the street to get on the Number 7 there in Sunnyside. I didn't notice that it had gone underground by the time we got into Manhattan. Just like Jerry, when it was time to go home again, I couldn't find the train anywhere. I was looking for the steps and the elevated tracks, but there was no sign of them on 34th Street. I asked a nearby cop for directions to the station, and he told me it was only a block away. I walked down the block, looked up at the sky, and could see no subway. I went back up to the cop again and told him there was no subway there. He said that there was, of course. Well, surely I would see if from here if there was? I can't see it. I was persistent. I could see it in Queens before I got on it, why can't I see it now? He looked at me, "Is this your first time?" "Yes it is," I answered.

An American Wake in the Cregan kitchen the night before Jerry left

He was just about to come off duty and offered to escort me back to the station. He walked through the gate without paying and I followed suit until the token booth operator snarled at me, "You need a token, use the turnstile." When I got out on the platform, I couldn't figure out how the train was now underground. We just hadn't taken any notice when we'd arrived in Manhattan earlier, I guess.

Jerry: We were only sixteen, seventeen years of age, you see, we'd never been anywhere else before in our lives. I hardly had been in Dublin, except as a child. It was a shock.

Marion: It was a shock. It was a shock to the system. They used to call us greenhorns, well, believe you me, we were greenhorns. Well, I was anyhow. I had never even seen electricity before. I went to work for a woman up in Scarsdale and she handed me a vacuum cleaner and I didn't know what it was. I was scared stiff of it; the noise alone. Oh! My God, what am I going to do with this thing? It was scary. It wasn't until I went home three years later that the electricity was just coming in. It was then that my family surprised me with a bathroom.

Jerry: We had no indoor plumbing, you see, no toilet, no, nothing like that, back in Ireland. There were very few cars too. I use that as the excuse as to why I've never learnt how to drive to this day.

Marion: I remember going to Dublin with my cousin, Cissy Brady, to get our visas for America, and to do our medical examinations. We had to go to this neighbor's house in Cavan to have a bath before we left.

I came in January of 1958, nine months before Jerry, when I was only sixteen years old. I can't think of the name of the boat, but I know it was the Cunard Line. The others were older than me. Cissy was nineteen and Kathleen was the eldest of eleven and her mother had died young and she'd reared the rest of them. Then she went to England with this boyfriend, but he decided to go off to Australia and I don't know what happened, but she came to America anyhow with us. She was older by that time. And another woman from home also came along with us. We traveled from Ballyconnell in County Cavan to Cobh in a taxi. My father came with us, but not my mother.

It probably cost a lot; I don't know who paid for it, but I always sent money home, so I think I well paid for my passage. I never realized we were poor because everyone else was in the same boat. We weren't that poor; we had a farm of land and we always had plenty to eat. When my sister came out I was going to pay for her, but my uncle paid instead. That's the way it was, one paid for the other.

Anyhow, Daddy had told the others to take care of me. We shared a cabin and I was in the top bunk. It was so hot the first night that we left the door open and just pulled across a curtain. In the middle of the night I heard a rustling on the floor and I was terrified. I lay fixed to the bed and didn't know what to do about all this noise. I didn't know how to turn on the light, but, finally, got the courage to do so and there was Kathleen kneeling on the floor, rooting through the trunk, flinging things all over the place, looking for the blessed candles she'd packed.

"Oh! Daughter, daughter, the ship is going to go down. Oh! Daughter, daughter, if we ever get there, we'll never get back." She was in such a state sprinkling Holy Water around the cabin and searching for the blessed candles. "Oh! Daughter, daughter," she kept crying out to me, wringing her hands with worry. And she supposed to be looking after me?

As well as that I was the only one of them who never got sick. I was tired carrying bedpans up to the cabin. In the dining room I was put at a table for nine and oftentimes I was the only one who showed up for breakfast every morning. And they supposed to be looking after me?

I had a great time though. I loved the boat. I loved the food too. It was so different from what we were used to, which was only meat and potatoes up to that. Well only potatoes most times, and meat only some of the time. And the dancing, of course, was great altogether. There were a lot of cute guys on board too.

Jerry: Now Mar.

Marion: I suppose I was in awe of it, but I enjoyed the boat thoroughly. I was free!

I was very disappointed with New York at first. We headed straight for Elmsford in Queens to an aunt and uncle and I thought it was a desperate place altogether, very shabby and run-down. After all, I had thought the streets were going to be paved in gold. They didn't even have a house, only an apartment. I was surprised because my cousin, their daughter, had come to Ireland before that, and she spent a year with us. It was a gift for her graduation and she was the real yank with beautiful clothes and everything, so I was very surprised when I saw where they lived. I had thought they were very wealthy. They probably had money, because they had a grocery shop and a bar at one stage, but I couldn't figure out why they were living in an apartment, in what was not a very fancy neighborhood.

Anyhow, they had jobs already got for us in three different houses in Scarsdale. I lasted a month! The family I was working for had three kids who were nearly as old as I was and I supposed to be minding them! But I had never been on my own before and I was too scared to stay in that big house alone, so half the time they had to get a babysitter for me! Anyhow it didn't work out.

I then went to the telephone company and I loved it. I stayed there for five years and they sent me to school to train for this big job, but in the middle of it all I decided to go to Ireland for three months and that put a dent in my service there. I could've gone back to it, I suppose, but I never did and I always regretted it. That was a big mistake, Jerry always said, as I would have had great benefits and a good retirement package. But I didn't like the way we were treated like children sometimes. We had fun though and I made a lot of friends, some of whom I'm still friendly with today. I became a receptionist/telephonist next and then the company went bankrupt and after that I went working as a waitress. I spent thirteen years in the Greentree restaurants on Bainbridge and Riverdale Avenues until I finally retired from formal employment. I now take care of two adorable little girls, Rebecca and Aisling Kenny, and they keep me going, let me tell you.

Jerry: I became a stock boy anyhow with Altman's in the pillows and cushions department. Needlepoint became my specialty. Well, I learned more about sewing in that job, and ended up as an Assistant Buyer. The customers were very high class. One of them was Gene Tunney's wife. He was a well-known boxer who fought Jack Dempsey a couple of times. Then, of course, all of us had to register for the draft by law and I wound up in the U.S. Marine Corps and did my time in the reserves in Parris Island in South Carolina.

I was doing my basic training when President Kennedy was shot. They never told us for a day and a half, which, I think to this day, was a mistake. They said it was part of the training. It was during my time in the south, from Parris Island to Camp Lejeune in North Carolina, that I saw how badly the Blacks were treated in this country. I remember one Sunday going to the USO for a few beers, and afterwards Dinny Burke— an Irish American lad— and I went for a walk. When we got to the railway station he wouldn't come any father so I continued on alone and believe me you, there wasn't a place in Kerry or in Galway or anywhere else in Ireland at the time that was as poor as this neighborhood I walked in to. I was shocked by how those people were treated, which was very, very poorly. Even in New York back then the only time you'd see an African-American in a bank was either mopping the floor or taking out the garbage. You'd never see them in behind the counter. Today is Martin Luther King Day—now he was a great man for his own people.

After I came out of the army, I went to another company,

Whitman's. More cushions.

Marion: No wonder he's always giving out about the cushions I buy. Well I went to the dances. City Center was my favorite. A whole group of us hung out there. I always thought the Jaeger House was kind of rough; there were supposed to be a lot of fights there. Brendan Ward played at City Center, Joe Nellany from Sligo, Brendan Bowyer, now he was great. A lot of bands came out from Ireland and they were always the best. There was always a crowd no matter what. The guys would be on one side of the hall, the girls on the other, just like Ireland, and when the dance was called there'd be a big hustle; and then they'd charge like bulls.

Jerry: Now Mar, we did not! How about us? You'd eye up this one in the corner and make a beeline for her and ask her does she want to dance, and she'd bark at you, "No!" And you'd have to walk all the way back across the floor again.

Marion: Sure you should have just asked the one beside her.

Jerry: Maybe. Then there was the Tuxedo Ballroom on a Sunday afternoon in the winter. There was a guy with a lame leg who used to play there. Of course, it was Gaelic Park in the summer. You'd watch a game; get your dinner there too if you wanted, and then dance all night. They were great years. They were absolutely great.

Marion: Sure anytime was good when you were young.

Jerry: I suppose you're right. Anyhow, I met Marion on a blind date.

Marion: That's right. His roommate used to go out with a friend of mine, she later became my roommate and she was going out with Jerry's friend, Pat, and he used to say to me you must meet this guy. Jerry used to be a recluse. He didn't go dancing much.

Jerry: Now Mar.

Marion: Well, not that much. The pubs had come on the scene at this stage. The Uese was on 207th Street; they used to have good bands. It was down the road from the Old Shilling. There was a strip of bars there on 207th Street just like today's McLean Avenue. So anyhow this fellow, Pat, said I should meet this guy; he thought we'd get along;

Jerry: We used go to Bainbridge, didn't we, Mar? And the Red Mill, we used to dance there too.

Marion: I never danced with you in the Red Mill.

Jerry: Oh?

Marion: My sister met her husband in The Red Mill, but I never danced there with you. And Bainbridge was after we got married. So Jerry called up to the apartment one night anyhow; we were supposed to go to a movie. I don't know whether we did or not.

Jerry: Oh! Well now she probably started me off on a paint job or something like that.

Marion: Jerry! You never painted for me. I thought he was kind of cute. But my first impression was that he had a lovely personality. We knew each other twelve years before we got married. We certainly took our time. It wasn't steady always; it was off and on, but he was always in the background, and I guess I was always in the background for him too.

Wedding Day, March 17, 1979

Jerry: One time Marion needed this paint job done, you see, and this fellow, Cahill, he was a carpenter and he wasn't working very much at the time agreed to do the painting. So Cahill went and he got the paint brushes and rollers and he painted Marion's apartment. She gave him her phone number at work and he called her. Now, he was a quiet kind of a fellow, and Marion asked how much did she owe him? Ah! He says, just get a piece of paper, and jot down everything as I shout them out. He called out all the supplies he'd bought and told her to tot them up and add thirty dollars for himself. So Marion got back to him anyhow when she'd done the calculation and said she thought she owed him two hundred and odd dollars. "Girl," he said. "I think you forgot to carry the one!"

Marion: He knew exactly how much it was. He wasn't that quiet!

Jerry: But we had great times. Rockaway Beach used to be great too. Dancing again. I loved Rockaway.

Marion: The places we stayed in were dives, but the atmosphere was great at night.

Some places would ask us for identification so often I wouldn't be served, as I was too young, and they wouldn't let you sit at the table unless you had a drink. They were very strict about that. They wouldn't throw you out or anything, but they'd make you feel uncomfortable. I didn't drink until I was twenty-one.

I was here three years before I went home. I had a lot of baby fat when I left, but I was so skinny by the time I got back. My mother said if she'd met me at the airport she wouldn't have known me. She thought I was too thin, but I guess it was because I had no Mom's cooking. She soon fixed that. I guess they called me the Yank; they thought I had lovely clothes and all, but I had no desire to stay. Jerry always says that he thought he'd only be here a couple of years before he went home. My mother also thought that we'd be back. I was the first one over, then my sister followed eighteen months later and my brother after that. But she always thought that Ann and I would be back within five years. She thought maybe we'd set up a business at home or something. She couldn't believe we stayed here.

At sixteen I didn't know what I wanted to do. I had always wanted to be a nurse and when I was fifteen I had my appendix out and what I saw there put me right off. Then my aunt and uncle were home that year on a visit and they suggested to my parents that I come over and stay with them for a while. And that's kind of how it happened. Mam said to me did I want to go and I said I'd try it for about a year anyhow. But there really wasn't anything in Ireland for me. My parents couldn't afford to send me to school and I didn't really want to work in a shop. I didn't want to be an apprentice to a shopkeeper, which was all the choice I would have had. So even though I didn't necessarily want to come, from very early on I regarded New York as home.

Ireland today is definitely not the Ireland we left. It's very European, but it's great. I feel that Ireland could be any other country in the world today; there's nothing to distinguish it as Ireland really, except family. We travel a lot. We were in Greece last year and China, and we're off to Italy in the next couple of months.

Jerry: I was on the Great Wall of China last September when I heard that Tyrone beat Kerry in the All-Ireland. And it was a Dublin man that told me. I'll never forget that. I wish I had been home for it. I do think though that New York was the best choice, out of all the places we could have come to in America. Even though I didn't want to come at all, I am glad that it's here I came to. I was here for about two years before I went home.

Marion: We didn't have the money to be going home. We weren't earning that much money when we came over first. What were you earning, Jerry, in a week?

Jerry: Oh! I was earning about forty dollars in B. Altman's and out of that they took taxes and social security and I came out with thirty something dollars. In fact I think I still have a pay slip from back then somewhere. It wasn't that much money at the time.

Marion: Well, it was more money than we'd ever seen, but we had to pay a lot out of it.

Jerry: Guys in the telephone company would have been making much more. I tried everything to get in. I'd have mopped the floors, anything.

Marion: I wasn't making that much with them. Of course, women weren't paid as much as men that time. Then I had to go to Continuation School one day a week.

Jerry: I tried college for a while, NYU believe it or not. I never had a high school diploma or anything like that. I took the test for the cops too when I got out of the Marine Corps and I went to a school here where they'd prime you up on how to pass these tests, and you had to pay for the damned thing. It turned out to be simple math and I decided I didn't need to pay to figure out that. I wound up very high on the test, regardless, and I was called for an interview, but I had to have a license to drive. I went down to the Department of Motor Vehicles and told yer man that I only needed the license to get into the cops and that I knew how to turn the key and how to drive around the block; but, I wouldn't be able to park the damned thing. So he gave me the license anyhow.

Marion: Not only that he gave him a lorry license.

Jerry: Yes. Anyhow to this day I have a license and I still don't know how to drive.

So I went down to Thomas Street for the interview for the cops anyhow, and I'll always remember the man who interviewed me. He was Jewish and he told me off the bat that my education in Ireland was not equivalent to a high school education here. And I said, I beg to differ, that my education in Ireland is better than anything I could get here. I said, look at the test, and look at the score. Oh, no, he said you have to have a leaving certificate or whatever. I said sure how come nobody told me that when I applied for the Marine Corps? I pointed out that they were letting in all these minorities with lower scores than I had. He said to me, I think you're prejudiced. And I said I don't know how you figure that out.

He wanted me to take the GED, which is equivalent to the leaving certificate; it's funny I never did that in the army, I don't know why. He wanted me to go out to Stephen's Institute in Hoboken to study for the damned thing, but I disagreed and appealed to the Irish Consulate, but they wouldn't approve it for me. So I was thumbs down then, and I after doing all these pull-ups and sit-ups and everything. It went according to your ability to run, jump, everything, which was no bother to me. But anyhow, I didn't get on the cops, and maybe it's "Thank God."

Marion: Thank God is right. I don't think you would have suited the cops anyhow, and I thanked God every day that you didn't get it.

Jerry: But I would have been long, long retired. Anyhow, I made a different career. I eventually went into the lumber business—a big change from the cushions, let me tell you—and that's what I retired out of. I ended up in Dyke's lumberyard for thirty-seven years and I thank God every day for it, as I did very, very well there. But, nonetheless, I'd go home to Kerry in the morning and walk my two greyhounds, and I'd be happy out. I never wanted to come. Now don't get me wrong, I love this country, but the changes that have happened in the last ten years or so I'm not at all happy about.

Marion: He's not in favor of President Bush.

Jerry: No, in fact I even threatened to go home when he was elected again. This country was loved all over the world; then they made stupid mistakes invading Afghanistan and Iraq, and now they're going for Iran.

Marion: They don't have the personnel to invade Iran. There'll be conscription into the army again if they do that.

Jerry: Perhaps. Well, I'll tell you, when I look back. Now I am not computer literate or anything, but I would not give up my childhood in Ireland, out walking with an auld dog, snaring an auld rabbit, or hunting, compared to sitting inside and watching an auld video the way they do today or clicking on an auld computer. Even though we had no luxuries growing up, I would not exchange one hour of my childhood for anything they have today. No way. I have two dogs at home now and they'll be coursing next year; following a live hare and I'd give anything to be out walking with them every day.

Marion: And he blames me. He said he'd have gone back if it wasn't for me. But it was destiny. I guess it was in our destiny to travel across the Atlantic Ocean just to meet one another and settle in the Bronx, and I don't regret any of that.

Jerry: Me neither, Mar.

Interviewed at their home on Post Road, Riverdale, New York; January 23, 2006

Honeymooning in Miami

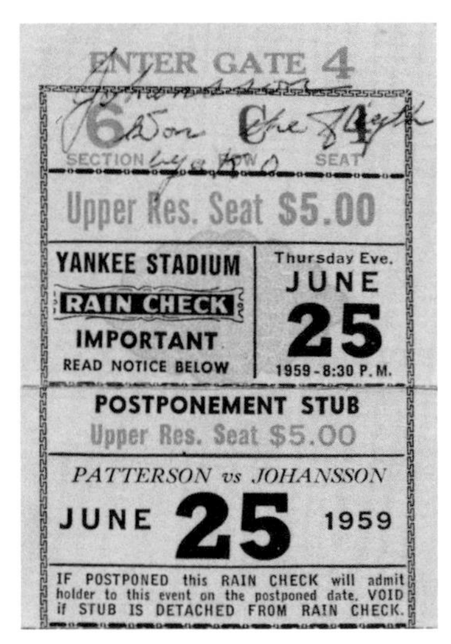

Ticket to Yankee Stadium to see Johansson beat Patterson, 1959

Ticket to Madison Sq. Gardens to see Ronnie Delaney win the world record for the mile, 1959

Pat and Phil Murray, 1958

Pat: My wife and I flew from Shannon to New York on October 15, 1958, about a month after we were married. We stopped to refuel in Gandor where the temperature was zero degrees. I had never experienced such cold before and could hardly breathe walking across the tarmac, dressed only in a light, tweed jacket. We then flew a thousand miles south to a sizzling eighty degrees in New York where they were having an Indian summer, and I had never experienced such heat before either. It was incredible. The whole trip took twenty hours and when the plane landed everybody applauded. They were so relieved to hit ground, as for most people it would have been their first flight and everyone was nervous and white knuckled. It would have been such an unusual thing back then to fly across the Atlantic.

I was happy, however, because I had always wanted to come to America. It may have had something to do with the fact that my father, Lord rest him, had intended coming when he was a young man and newly married to my mother, but she became pregnant with my sister, Peggy, and he couldn't leave her. He had two brothers who fought for the British Army during World War I and the person for whom I'm called, the original Pat Murray, was killed in France when he was only nineteen years old. The other brother, Jem, came to the Bronx and disappeared. He did keep in touch with my father for a while, however, and had encouraged him to come too. That would have been back in 1927 and he had his down payment for the ship, but he couldn't leave my mother who was to follow him out. So I think from listening to him all my life, I always had the desire to see America.

I loved Ireland, but I always had a tremendous admiration for this country. From the time I could read, when I was six or seven years old and the United States had just entered the Second World War, I always felt that it was the great bulwark against worldwide oppression by fanatics, and I still believe that today. We're still engaged in a worldwide struggle against an evil power. I know most of Europe doesn't agree with that and unfortunately many Irish don't either, but people forget very easily. They're protesting in Ireland about the soldiers stopping in Shannon, but Ireland or Europe wouldn't have the freedom it has now if America had not stepped in to help them in 1939. It was then and still is the most powerful nation in the world. I am unwavering in my support for President Bush and history will prove us right again.

I was so happy when I landed in New York that day in October 1958. It was thrilling. And even today after forty-eight years I love to visit Manhattan. It is the most exciting city in the world. I love to walk down Broadway and see Times Square and yesterday, for the first time since we came here, my wife and I marched up Fifth Avenue in the St. Patrick's Day Parade, under the Limerick banner, which is her native city. However, that first day my brother-in-law, Harold, a Marine, met us at the airport and we stayed that night in a hotel near 34th Street. We got up early the next morning and climbed up The Empire State Building, which was another thrill, to stand on top of what was then the highest building in the world, and now again, thanks to the Arabs, it is the tallest building in New York. Back in Dublin, where I grew up, the highest building was a five-story Georgian tenement.

Of course, back then the Irish and Europeans had a preference over other nationalities when it came to immigration, but President Kennedy changed all that in the sixties. Now it's uncanny that his younger brother, Ted, is fighting to reverse immigration laws in order to legalize the Irish today, not that many of them need to come here anymore because the economy is so much better over there. However, in those days, you had to have a sponsor and Harold had to show even his bank account to the U.S. authorities before they would let me in, and my wife's aunt, Nora, who had come here in 1923, claimed her in. She also had to prove that she was a woman of substance, and we had to sign a document that we would not become a ward of the State during the first five years until we became eligible for citizenship. We could not claim a penny for compensation of any sort until we became citizens, which we did five years down the road.

Harold drove us down to Philadelphia the following day to Auntie

Nora's where we settled in a small apartment on Walnut Street close to the heart of the city. Apart from me playing Gaelic football for a short while, we never really immersed in a native Irish community there. Although I worked for many years in the local bar, Walsh's, owned by Harry Walsh from the Falls Road in Belfast; it was mainly an American neighborhood. Harry was a bootlegger during Prohibition and when it ended, he was the second publican to get a license to operate a tavern in the city of Philadelphia. By the time of his death he was the oldest licensee in the city. They had that bar for twenty-five years by the time we arrived, and they were very good to us. I had no bartending experience, but it proved to be a great supplement to my income from working in a warehouse and selling shoes part-time.

My wife, Phil was very, very lonely for home. She spent a lot of time on her own, because I was always out at work, and after we had the three children, I think she felt even more isolated. I had decided at a very early stage that I wouldn't even think of going back. I steeled myself not to think too much about my parents and home, which I know sounds cruel now, but I had to look to the future. Of course, I had thought that we were going to do very well very quickly, and that we would be able to go back every year on vacation, but that was only a pipe dream. Reality soon set in. Those were the years of the Eisenhower depression when work wasn't that plentiful here and the money not that great. You couldn't even buy a job. I was determined to succeed, however.

It was very tough trying to juggle three jobs and take care of this small property we eventually invested in. It was a small rooming house, but I wasn't a great handyman so it was very hard to maintain. What killed it was the rising cost of crude oil, and when the crunch came in the early seventies; our profit margin was wiped out trying to heat the place for our tenants. We did dabble in real estate again and eventually bought our own home a few blocks away on Chestnut Street and although my wife doesn't agree with me, I think these small investments helped us in the end. Many of the people I worked with were Jewish and to this day, I think they are the nicest people you could meet. Coming from Ireland I had the impression that all Jews were rich, but many of the shoe salesmen whom I worked with had less money than I had, and I the immigrant. Their advice was always to save for our children's education. They told me to make sure that my children got a better education than I did, that that was how the Jewish people succeeded in America. And I never forgot that. That was one of the things we strove for and Thank God they are all well educated and all doing much better than we ever did. We're very happy about that. But they do know about their Irish heritage, as do our grandchildren, and our Italian-American grandchildren are very aware of their Italian heritage too.

After six years Phil went back with our first two children. I didn't go back until 1968. Ten years without seeing my mother and father. It was such a strange experience going back after that length of time. I took a bus from Limerick to Dublin and I couldn't get used to the place. I thought the people sounded funny, the buildings were very small and the sky was so low and dark. There's always a hint of the storm clouds in Ireland. I called my mother from Bus Aras, a bus station there near the city center, and took a taxi out to Rathfarnham, where she had the big breakfast ready for us. The house looked so much smaller than how I had remembered it, the rooms seemed so tiny when I wandered through them that day.

I spent the whole month catching up and when it was time to go back again, I had started to become re-acclimated to the place. Of course, the pubs hadn't changed that much, which was a relief, not like they have now. They're like something out of Las Vegas now; Ireland has become so Americanized. It was such a joy to see my parents again though, but so strange, because by then America was my whole experience. Maybe it was because I was so deprived that first ten years that now I want to go back all the time. I'd go back today at the drop of a hat, and of course I always love to see my brother, Pierce, who is also my best friend.

I grew up in the historical hamlet of Rathfarnham nestled at the foot of the Dublin Mountains. Rathfarnham Castle, which dates back to Elizabethan times, is one of the few remaining examples of Tudor architecture in Ireland, and the village was originally formed around it. My father was born and raised in this ancient parish and could trace back his family there for seven generations. We lived on St. Mary's Terrace, a row of houses flanked by the very famous South County Dublin pub, The Yellow House. As a matter of fact, the Walkers who originally owned the pub, built the Terrace in 1912, and my father, who was about eighteen at the time, saw these little red-bricked homes being erected, with a fireplace in every room, and he thought they were so beautiful. Little did he know that he would one day raise his family there or that my brother, Pierce, would be still living there almost a hundred years later? My father was a baker with Landy's, a small bakery in Dublin, so we had a moderately decent living. We weren't poor; at least we didn't know we were poor. I guess we were poor, but having a trade was a good thing then. One of the young bakers who apprenticed under him was called Joe Brennan who later went on open his own business and become one of the wealthiest men in Ireland with Brennans Bakery whose motto still is "Today's Bread Today."

Another famous resident of Rathfarnham was William Butler Yeats who lived there in his declining years, where he was a source of derision for the local children. He had long white hair and always carried a blackthorn stick, even though he was confined to a wheelchair at only seventy years of age. Now we would all have learnt the poem, "The Lake Isle of Innisfree," in school, and we would run down the street to taunt him with, "You will NOT 'arise and go now,' Willie."

My father trained with Padraig Pearse in the grounds of Scoil Eanna. He would always say that Padraig Pearse was the first man to show him how to cite a Lee Enfield rifle. Pearse was called after the great American revolutionary, Patrick Henry, and did not change his name to Padraig until he became involved in the cause for Irish freedom. My father didn't fight in the Easter Rising though, preferring to take the side of the Redmondites, forerunners of the Fine Gael party, who were not in favor of the rebellion. John Redmond preferred to preserve peace and hold out for the Home Rule that was promised by Lloyd George, who, of course, reneged on that. My father was a member of the regular Irish Army as a Military Policeman, stationed in the Curragh. They kept prisoners there in the camp and he was guarding them. One night, during the Civil War, he was doing sentry duty at the wall when bullets started whizzing by him, probably from a sniper. He always told us, "I did what any sensible man would do; I lay down on my stomach and waited until it was all over."

All his life he remained faithful to Fine Gael and my mother was strictly Fianna Fail. She was from Wexford, the daughter of a stonecutter, where she worked as a seamstress. Her sister married Joyce Conlon, a very famous Gaelic football player for Kildare. In fact he won two All-

Ireland medals for them back in the twenties, probably the last time the Lilywhites were victorious. The Conlons had a little teashop at the back of a candy store in Newbridge where my mother eventually came to work. My father would go in there with the other soldiers for a cup of tea and that's how they met. They married in Newbridge and then moved back to Rathfarnham.

In later years my aunt and uncle's oldest son, Peter, joined the Irish Army during the Second World War. He drove a truck on the bomb squad and a German mine washed up on the beach in County Wexford, which coincidently was his ancestral home. Peter had a crew of three bomb disposal guys in the back of the truck and he drove them up to the beach. His orders were that he was not to leave that truck because he was the driver; that the other three would diffuse the bomb. After a while, however, for some reason he strolled down to the beach just as the bomb exploded. The other three soldiers were killed instantly, and he was badly injured. A couple of days later I made my Confirmation and my mother took me into Dublin city to see the movie "The Casbah", with Charles Boyer. When we came out of the theater on O'Connell Street the evening newspapers were just going on sale and the headline board stated in bold letters, FOURTH SOLDIER DIES. She knew it was Peter and she started to cry.

Cruise's Hotel, Limerick City, 1955

My father, very strange for a Dublin man, was strictly GAA. He never watched rugby or soccer, which to him were foreign games. As a result, Pierce and I played Gaelic football for Pearse Brothers, called after Padraig and Willie, who resided at one time in the area, and started the well known Irish speaking school, Scoil Éanna. In 1950, when we were about nineteen or twenty and our team in the lowest division in Dublin, Junior C, we won the championship. There was such excitement. We all went back to McGrath's pub afterwards and stood on the wooden bench, filling the cup with lemonade and whiskey, and my father was so proud, as he was one of the selectors. You would think we had won the All-Ireland. Pierce can still name every one of that team. Eight out of the fifteen are now dead.

Another hobby Pierce and I enjoyed in those days was lifting weights in a local gym. People don't believe me that we had a gym in Dublin back fifty years ago, but there were two in the city at that time, for wrestling and bodybuilding. Of course you were considered a weirdo in Dublin then if you lifted weights. They were free weights; there were no machines or anything, and we would go there three times a week. We were also big Dublin followers in those years. Interestingly, after many years of struggle, they finally won the All-Ireland the year we left, when they beat Down.

That was my last visit to Croke Park for a long time. I didn't go to many dances then. I had met Phil on a holiday in Galway and I considered her my girlfriend for many years, even though I only saw her every couple of months when she was playing the field down in Limerick. Then she dumped me, sending me the "Dear John" letter and I almost died. I couldn't believe she was giving me up. I was devastated, absolutely devastated. About a year later we reconciled and shortly after we married and came to America. She didn't want to come at first, but I talked her into it and I think she's happier here now. I know now she's happy being surrounded by her grandchildren. The only thing I regret about coming here is that my parents didn't get to spend much time with their grandchildren. I realize now how lonely that must have been for them. But there was no way of knowing how prosperous Ireland was going to become. Back then it was a very depressed, primitive country. I felt that we would have much more opportunities here.

I had attended the local technical school after national school, from where I matriculated, and I took a lot of night courses in bookkeeping and accounting in the High School of Commerce in Rathmines. My first job in Dublin was with the Mooney chain of pubs as a payroll clerk. Then they opened a bottling plant where I became a manager, which was very interesting as I learnt a lot about bottling beer and operating hydrometers to reduce whiskey. That knowledge, however, wasn't much use to me in America, where I could only sell the stuff, and of course, I spent a lot of time drinking it too. But my basic education in Ireland and the strong work ethic gained there contributed to my ultimate success in this country.

In 1972, Mickey Walsh, Harry's son, who was a Ward Leader at the time, a non-paying political position, said he would get me a job with the City of Philadelphia. The first job he wanted me to take was that of Deputy Sheriff, and although I had been a member of the FCA at home and could operate a rifle, I had not that much experience with guns, and it was required that one have some knowledge of firearms. But I was fortunate because then he got me a job with the Revenue Department as a Revenue Investigator, which was well paid. I took several Civil Service tests over the years and management courses and eventually became very educated in taxes, and after many promotions, I ended up as the second highest ranking civil servant in the City of Philadelphia. I was the Chief Enforcement Officer in the Revenue Department and placed second in the test for that position, the only candidate that did not have a university degree. I credit my Irish education for that.

My life here also took another path when I became involved with one of the people I had met in the gym in Dublin, a Kerry man, Dan Kelly, who was an Irish wrestling champion. He came to America to wrestle. At one time he wrestled against Primo Carnera, the Italian, six foot seven, whom they called the Ambling Alp. A lot of professional wrestling is faked for the show and according to Dan, Carnera who was then almost fifty, was arthritic. Dan said if you threw him down, it was called a fall, unknown to the audience you would have to lift him up again. Anyhow, Dan had his own carpentry business, but he also started promoting wrestling matches and Irish shows over here and for about ten years we were partners in show business.

We were the first to bring The Chieftains to Philadelphia to The Academy of Music and of course, before that, we had the Clancy Brothers and Tommy Makem there many times. I will always remember that Sunday night in 1963 when they first appeared on The Ed Sullivan Show in their Aran sweaters. They got very lucky, as some other act had to cancel and they ended up playing for sixteen minutes, which was very unusual. They were a fantastic act. They were, and I think they still are the greatest folk group to come out of Ireland and they also revived interest in Irish folk music. We also had The Wolfe Tones, Hal Roach, and Carmel Quinn. We also had Siobhan McKenna, the well-known Abbey actress; perform poetry readings during the interval when The Chieftains were playing. We had Geraldine Fitzgerald who was born in Leeson Street, Dublin, and became a very famous movie actress in the forties; she even had a small part in Doctor Zhivago. When the Clancy's split up, Liam and Tommy went out on their own; they were always a sell-out whenever we had them.

I used to introduce the shows and we would become very friendly with the various acts, going out for dinner and that afterwards. The Clancy's never liked singing after their show was over. If we went into a bar, they would never sing impromptu, they never even brought their instruments with them. One night Paul McCartney was in the same hotel, and he was actually quite friendly with Liam, but by the time we got down to the bar where he had seemingly been playing the piano for a couple of hours, he had already left. The Manager said we had missed him by about five minutes. Imagine we had only just missed him. Isn't that interesting? But they were interesting times.

The first night The Chieftains played we all went back to the Holiday Inn after the show, where we were all drinking, of course. They had just come back from Russia where they had been playing with the Russian Symphony Orchestra and they had met Krushev, whom Derek Bell, a little guy from Belfast, said wasn't much bigger than himself. Anyhow he was playing the piano for us in the bar that night and next thing the waitress, who was anxious to leave, started harassing us to get out. Derek stood up and said, "I think I'll play a little Chopin." Next thing the waitress went over and slammed the piano down on top of his fingers nearly crushing them to bits. She didn't have a clue who he was, and didn't care, but she could have ended his career right then and there. We had some great times back then. Phil doesn't agree with me, but I know we made some money too.

Then on July 3, 1979, tragedy hit when our house was blown up and we lost everything. Two kids next door had been making fireworks, we were originally told, for the Fourth of July festivities, and it appeared that one of them had lit a cigarette and blown up three houses on the block, killing themselves and their grandmother. I remember the day so well, I remember exactly where I had lunch, in a restaurant called The Boardroom on 12th and Sanson streets, and I remember walking back to the office where I noticed everyone standing around looking at me. I didn't know what was going on. The Commissioner told me to sit down, that there had been an accident and that my family had all escaped, but my home was gone. As well as that, my daughter, Ann, was in danger of losing her sight, as glass from the TV had pierced her eyes. He then called Mayor Rizzo who got in touch with a Dr. She, the most prominent eye surgeon in the country at the time. As a member of the American armed forces, he had operated on Lord Mountbatten in the Burmese jungle during World War II when a sliver of bamboo had entered his eye. He had saved Mountbatten's eyesight and was now about to do the same for Ann. He operated on her that night and drove in on the Fourth of July to remove the bandages himself. He knew then that she was going to be all right. I'll always remember what he said about nurses, "You can always tell a nurse, but you can't tell them everything!" Isn't it amazing then that years later Ann ended up a nurse herself and married to an eye doctor? And Randy, our son-in-law, heard the bang that day, as he was just about to start medical school, and was moving into his new quarters.

A few weeks later, when I returned to work, Mayor Rizzo called me to see if everything was all right. He told me to keep my spirits up and that he was praying for all of us. That was the end of the conversation. Years later he was accused of taking bribes while still in office and there was a Grand Jury investigation into the case. I was called to testify and when asked if I had ever received a telephone call from the Mayor to give someone a tax break, I said I had received a call from the Mayor only once and that was on the day I had returned to work after two weeks compassionate leave when my home blew up in West Philadelphia. There was dead silence in the courtroom when I'd finished relaying the story and then I was excused by the Judge, a man called Bradley, who was part Irish.

The people next door all died in the explosion. It turned out that the two young boys weren't making firecrackers at all, but were actually arson bombers who had been chased out of Delaware County for doing the same thing, before coming to live with their grandmother, our neighbor. It was estimated later that they had six hundred pounds of gunpowder in the basement, and that one of the boys must have lit a cigarette, which caused the explosion. The poor grandmother's body was retrieved from the wreckage in various parts and taken away in a black refuse sack.

That was a terrible scene altogether.

But what I remember most about that day was that the Mayor sent a car to take me to the She Institute, and that's when I first saw Ann lying on the hospital bed, her face covered in bandages, and Phil sitting beside her with no shoes on, covered in dust.

Phil: I had been putting on my skirt; it was a wrap-over. All My Children was just ending on the TV and I could hear my son, Neil, teasing his little sister, Mary Beth, down in the kitchen. We were getting ready to go into town shopping for the Fourth, as that was the childrens' favorite holiday. I was standing sideways in front of the mirror when it started to split. I saw the glass crack once, twice, and then the windows started to snap. It was all in slow motion, and then I heard a boom. I thought it was an earthquake. I ran out of the room, down the stairs, which were now starting to wobble and the ceiling above me was starting to shake. A fireman was standing in front of the house, where our porch used to be, beckoning me to come forward. Neil and Mary Beth were already outside, but there was no sign of Ann. Neil went back into the burning house, he was only fifteen, and finding her temporarily blinded wandering through the flames, he carried her out onto the sidewalk. As we drove away in the ambulance, I saw the house cave in with the curtains still flowing through the windows, and I suddenly remembered I'd forgotten my charm bracelet. You know how there's one thing you always say you'd take with you if your house ever burnt down?

We were taken to the hospital, with Ann on a stretcher. Immediately after a brief check-up, she was detained but we were brought to the police station and questioned about the young boys next door. People said afterwards that shouldn't have happened. We were covered in black soot and shoeless, except for the paper slippers they'd given us in the hospital. There was a short interrogation as to whether we had noticed anything unusual or if we had seen anything suspicious being delivered or any strange trucks pulling up, which we hadn't, we never noticed a thing. We were brought back to the hospital only to walk into the room where Ann was being anointed. I spent two nights with her, which was just as well, as I had nowhere else to go. Here I was one night sitting there beside her bed, holding her hand, her eyes covered in bandages, and next thing I see Neil being interviewed on national television. I thought to myself, this must be a dream.

The worst part about it was that we were all on our own. Except for our young niece, Barbara, who was staying with us for the summer, we had no family here and I missed that terribly. I had always missed Ireland since the day I got here. I missed the tea and Kirby's, the little grocery store on the corner of O'Dwyer's Villas in Thomondgate. When I came over first I was afraid to go into the Penn Fruit supermarket in case I wouldn't find my way out again. I missed the way people were so quietly spoken at home compared to all the screaming they do over here. I had never wanted to come and had never needed to leave Ireland. I had a good job in Ranks Flour Mills in Limerick and a great social life going dancing all over the city in Cruise's hotel and the Stella ballroom with my friend, Eileen, whom I had known since we both attended St. Mary's National School on Convent Street.

I hated leaving my little sister, Maura, all alone with Dad, and was worried that she would be all right. My brother, Connie, was the only other member of the family left in Ireland, but he was living in Donegal with his wife and young children. Our oldest brother, Paddy, was a Christian Brother in England. My eldest sister, Betty, had been in England too, but then she left for Canada shortly after our mother died. A couple of years later a younger brother, Eamon, joined her there and Maura and I cried for weeks. We missed Eamon so much as there was always something going on when he was around. He was so involved in the Shannon Rugby Club, which our grandfather co founded, and I'd say he could have played for Munster, even Ireland, if he'd stayed., Mike had left for America about eight years before us and, was by then back from Korea and studying somewhere in the Midwest. Even though three of my siblings were living this side of the Atlantic, my only real connection to America up to then had been through the movies. I thought I would be like Doris Day sitting beside a swimming pool all day long, singing. Pat even made me give away my good winter coat, as he said we'd have lots of money to buy a new one. I didn't realize he'd have to work so hard for it.

I only worked for a few months and that was in the medical records department of the nearby Hahnemann Hospital, where I earned $84 every fortnight and where my first two children were to be born. But I got pregnant almost immediately and had to give it up. I was so lonely at first with only an aunt for company and I would have to keep the babies so quiet, as the apartment building was full of old ladies who would complain. In a way it probably would have been better if we'd come to somewhere like the Bronx where there were more people our age, but my father, who didn't want us to come in the first place, felt that we should stay with his sister, Nora, as their other sister, Mary, had been killed in Philadelphia the previous April while out walking her dog. Nora was still heartbroken.

I missed not having my sister around when my children were born and, of course, my mother, who had died about ten years previously. I used to think about that too, about how I went dancing every night when she was sick, as I didn't realize how bad she was. People didn't mention cancer back then. I felt guilty afterwards and would talk to the priest about it, as I had nobody else. There was no such thing as therapy then. Dad was devastated and spent every night praying in front of a big picture of the Sacred Heart. We weren't allowed listen to the radio and the following Christmas there were no presents or decorations. Maura and I had to wear black stockings and sew black diamond shaped pieces of fabric on the sleeves of our coats. It was so dark and dreary without Mam.

She was a quiet woman, but loved music and the movies. She played the fiddle and the mouth organ and every night when we were children we would have a concert in the kitchen where we would have to come out from behind the curtain and do our party piece. She also loved the movies and she and her mother, our Granny Lynch, would go to the cinema every week and if they really liked the film they'd stay for the second show. To heck with our tea! Their big favorite though was the Savoy cinema on Bedford Row where Connie, a boy soprano, would sometimes sing during the interval. To heck with our tea altogether on those nights! They also loved the Gilbert & Sullivan operettas in which the boys would take part. So even though they were great at cooking and sewing, they weren't your conventional mother and grandmother for their time. And to think that Granny Lynch lived into her nineties and Mam died in her fifties. She was a big loss to our household. Dad ordered a wreath of laurel leaves for her grave, as he said laurels were for a champion. I missed her terribly when I came here first. I missed everything.

I would yearn for the postman to bring me a letter from Maura and Dad. Even though he wasn't a very affectionate man, he was a great man for the news. As a family here we missed not having grandparents, aunts and uncles, cousins to share the Holidays with. There was no one there for Communions and Confirmations, my kids missed out on all that. Luckily, by the time the weddings came around, people were able to come over.

When I went back in 1968 for Maura's wedding I didn't want to come back again. I stayed for five months and it was really hard leaving again. My little boy had his first birthday there and my daughter missed her Daddy, but I still found it very hard to come back. It's become easier as the years have gone by, especially as my children got older and became involved in their careers. Ann is now a nurse, Neil a lawyer and Mary Beth is a Guidance Counselor in South Jersey. When Pat retired we also moved to that area, as our neighborhood in Philadelphia was deteriorating. When Pat was held at gunpoint outside our home, we knew it was time to go. We now enjoy the local gym, summers at the Jersey shore and rooting for the Eagles. Sometimes I think I could go back to Limerick in the morning and settle in as if I never had left. Then, of course, there are the grandchildren here whom I adore and would miss too much.

Losing my home, though, was the lowest point. We lost everything, every single thing, and our only possessions were the clothes we stood up in. We had no photographs, no children's mementos, no souvenirs from Ireland, no wedding presents, nothing—only memories. It was written up on all the papers where they called us the Irish immigrants and that is the worst part about immigrating, being so far away from home when something happens. Maura didn't even have a phone; we had to ring the local hairdressing salon to break the news to her and Dad. But, I must say the few friends we had here were very good to us, and we moved around from one to the other. We even stayed in a few hotels, until eventually we found a small apartment back on Walnut Street; back where it all began; back where we had to start all over again.

Interviewed on Fieldston Terrace,
Riverdale, New York; March 18, 2006

Oliver O'Donnell, 1960

I always say I came to town with the Mets. They were the new team in town when I arrived, as they had formed around 1960. I went to see them for the first time in the old Polo grounds, across the river from Yankee Stadium and I've been following them ever since. I love the Mets.

But my story starts six years before that the day I left my native village of Rosegreen, County Tipperary, to see an All-Ireland final in Dublin. Cork beat Wexford by the skin of their teeth that day and it was the best game of hurling I've ever seen; in fact it's the best All-Ireland I've ever been to and I've been to many. Those were the days of Christy Ring and the Rackett brothers, Bobby, Nicky, and Willie. They were the first set of three brothers who ever won an All-Ireland when Wexford went on to win in 1955 and 1956. Nicky Rackett was a massive big man; he could drive a ball through a brick wall.

Anyhow the next day I went down to the Curragh and won a few bob on the horses. I decided there and then I'd go back up to Dublin and head for England. It was hard back in my time; someone had to leave. There were ten in the family and no room for us all. So I hopped on the boat in Dun Laoghaire, landed in London, and never went home again, except for a visit. I wrote when I got there, but the family wasn't a bit concerned about me. They knew I was a survivor; I always was and I am to this day. It's an instinct in me.

London was booming at the time. It was just after the war and the city was still under construction. There was an awful amount of work. And the money was rolling in. You'd be working in one place and maybe take a break for lunch and another fellow would come along and offer you two shillings an hour more up the street and you'd down tools straight away and follow him. It was repetitious. You could do the same thing the following day and the day after that; every day in fact, and everybody did it. And they didn't care what you did. "Can you work?" is all they'd ask you and if you could that was it. I wasn't out of work for an hour the whole time I was there. One foreman looked at me and said, "What do you do?" I said I was a carpenter. "You're too young to be a carpenter," he says. "You're only a baby face."

One time I was working for this major construction group, McAlpines, I was one of McAlpine's Fusiliers, and a whole bunch of us were sent down to Southampton to finish up a project for this American chemical crowd out on the water. Every day we watched the major ocean liners leave for America and that is where I first got the notion of going myself. We saw the ships; there was one that went out nearly every day—at least four times a week anyhow—and we said it would nice go on one of those. Before we knew it we were applying. Along with two other fellows, Mike Griffin and Sean Reynolds, I went back to Ireland and booked on the S.S. America, which we boarded at Cobh. We forced a vacation upon ourselves by taking six or seven days to relax on the boat rather than flying, which would have got us here in much shorter time.

The boat was massive. It was as big as a football field. For the first few days the water was a bit rough and everyone was sick. Oh! My God it was unbelievable; you couldn't walk anywhere without seeing someone getting sick. Then it started to settle down a little bit, as soon as we hit quieter waters. But I'd say it was the food too. Not saying there was anything wrong with it; it just didn't suit us. We couldn't take it at all. It looked elegant enough—there'd be trunks of the most gorgeous looking fruit. There were apples like we'd never seen, and then you'd bite into them and half the time they didn't taste as good as they looked. But the service was something else; there'd be a waiter to every ten people. Every night we were treated to a banquet, even better than a banquet. All the wait staff was Puerto Rican; in fact it was the first time we'd ever seen Puerto Rican people.

On the last night there was the Captain's Dinner and every table had their picture taken as a souvenir. The cabins were a bit tight though, we were downstairs in a hole in bunk beds with railings on the side in case you rolled out of it, like a child's cot. I made sure I got the top bunk, as there was no way I was going to be cramped down on the bottom. I don't like tight corners. But I'll tell you, it was better than the boat to Holyhead where you had to sit on your suitcase; they didn't even have a seat for you.

Then there was the dancing. Every night there were two or three orchestras in a couple of different ballrooms; you'd have your choice.

There was more than one type of music. There were bars too that were just like the real pub scene you'd get anywhere. I met a woman from Shinrone, in County Offaly, whom I tried to court, and I often met her after; but, she eventually married an Offaly man. We docked in New York on the 5th of April, 1960, and I liked it the minute I saw it. I had a crack in my neck looking up at the tall buildings, but I was never a bit afraid of it.

Anyhow Sean Reynolds was a tremendous asset to us, as he'd been here before and he hooked us up with a place to stay. He had an uncle who'd been here for twenty-five years and we made straight for his place. Otherwise we'd have walked off the boat with nothing. They solicited you to come to America back then. We did all of the paperwork in England and Griffin's sister, Mary, claimed us out. She lived up in Rhode Island and I never as much as saw the place for about thirty years until I was driving out to Cape Cod one time and did a detour.

There was no need for us to go further than New York as Sean's uncle, Mick Reynolds from Mohill in County Leitrim, turned out to be a great mentor, and he hooked us up with everything. He had a big apartment on 197th Street and Briggs Avenue, at the very top of the Concourse. There were four bedrooms; it was a massive place, so we all had a room each. His daughter represented the U.S. in the Olympics for gymnastics and he had pictures of her all over the place. She obviously was very good at her sport. You don't get on the Olympic team on your good looks.

Mick took us down to the local 257 carpenter's union on the East Side of Manhattan on a Monday night and we were working by the middle of the same week. But he told us very quickly, "ye left yer mothers in Ireland, boys." We were then to fend for ourselves. Two of us stayed there until they day we got married, not to one another mind you, about four years later, but Sean returned home not long after he was conscripted into the army. He didn't go AWOL or anything; he just didn't choose to go. Griffin and I got lucky, as we were never drafted; in fact we never even registered. We all had to sign up as soon as we got here, that was part of the deal, but we were advised not to. I knew of fellows who were shipped out to Vietnam, and some who came back, but I didn't know them personally. There was only one chap who went out that I really knew, and he wasn't gone six months when he was killed. He was born in Liverpool of Irish parents and we knew him on the sites in London and met him again over here. The poor unfortunate was buried here in New York, over in Calvary, a year after he got here.

The work that we got was of a different type than we were in the habit of. But we took the first thing; we weren't going to be choosy. We had always worked indoors up to that, but now we were on the outside of the Borden Cheese building, which we took from the ground all the way up to the 46th floor, performing an operation called "goulash." The ironworker went up ahead of us erecting the girders and we were behind wrapping the beams with wood and filling them with concrete to make them fireproof. If you fell over you were history in a heartbeat. There was no skill to the goulash; any fool could do it. They outlawed the concrete and changed to asbestos later, as it was a quicker way of construction and cheaper, but if they'd kept to the concrete when building the Twin Towers they wouldn't have collapsed the way they did. They blew up like a bomb. The concrete would have withstood that heat. I don't believe you'd ever melt concrete no matter how hot it got. But that asbestos couldn't withstand the heat at all. They're going to change back now, as they learnt the hard way.

The three room mates: L to R, O'Donnell (Tipperary); Reynolds (Leitrim); Griffin (Clare)

But that's what we worked at anyhow, it was small money, about $2.79 an hour for a thirty-five hour week; not as good as we'd been getting in London. In fact, I had a side job and I made more from that. However, the money back then went further than the big money does now. You'd get a fine apartment for $100 a month. I stayed with the union for eight or nine years and then went out on my own. I stayed with the trade, just gave up the union. It was probably a mistake because they have great benefits, but that's it, I made the decision and have no regrets.

The social life was great back then. I wasn't that mad about the Jaeger House, but I loved the Blarney Stone, up in the 50's there somewhere, on Eighth Avenue. Maybe it's the first place you go to that you like the best. There was dancing seven nights a week there and again on a Sunday afternoon. There'd always be a bit of a crowd, especially in the wintertime. I danced to the great Mick Delahunty in The Blarney Stone, a man from my own hometown of Cashel. He'd come to the U.S. on a tour every lent, because there were no dances at home then, and he always spent a weekend in New York.

Then in the summer there was Gaelic Park. That is where my heart was; Gaelic Park was where the craic was. GAA was an instinct for me, you see, all my life, and it was no different here. We'd walk down from the Concourse on a Sunday, which only took about half an hour. We weren't long around though when we had our own wheels. Three of us bought a car between us within a year; not everyone had a car then, you know. We never looked back after that; we were on the pig's backside. Anyhow, I started off playing hurling for Tipperary—you naturally had to play for your own—and I played football for Leitrim. You were always better off starting off with your own county, even if you didn't play a second game with them, because blood is thicker than water after all. I did my best, I wasn't that good. It was just to fill a jersey really to keep the team on the field; to keep the team legal. You could start off with a handful, but you had to field a full team by half time or you couldn't continue. It was fifteen a side at that time, and you'd be thrown out of the championship if you hadn't made up that number to go on for the second half. You'd even be suspended for two years. You'd be gone. It was the same in Ireland, I'm almost sure; we took all of our rules from Ireland.

Gaelic Park was mighty though back then. There wasn't a Sunday there that you wouldn't meet fifty or sixty fresh faces. And you'd look forward to it. It was a fantastic place for meeting people. There'd be about ten to fifteen bartenders behind the bar and you'd have to be very familiar with them to get a drink because the patrons would be about eight deep at the counter. The dancehall was active back then too with Mickey Carton as the resident band. Sure Carton played for us for half of our lifetimes. I think he also played at the Jaeger House too; he was very good. Rock'n roll was jumping at the time; it was the Elvis Presley era, and there were women everywhere. I wouldn't say I was a Romeo; I prefer to say I was easily led! I loved to dance and that was a big plus with the women. And I considered myself well able to dance; the girls would always get to know a decent dancer and they'd never refuse you. I cannot understand today now, not at all, no dancing anymore. It's a joke. And the music is only noise. The television is the same; I've no interest in it at all. You couldn't keep me awake at eight o'clock in the evening now to watch anything on television.

The GAA over here though was much better organized and more competitive than in London. It was very dirty over there. I remember playing hurling there and nearly getting killed. It was crazy back then, but it has improved a ton. Then after a lot of hard knocks and fallings out, I became President of the New York GAA from 1983–1987. I've seen an awful lot of All-Irelands. I had the pleasure of sitting beside Jack Lynch the year Cork beat Galway. I was Vice-President to Mick Morrissey then and he always got the fine seats. Then, in 1990, I sat in the Dublin hurlers' dugout. I got lucky. Enda Gormley, the great Dublin hurler, worked with me one time and stayed with me too. He was best man at a wedding one day and couldn't go to a game. "You're the luckiest man in Ireland," he said, handing me over his ticket.

I've always loved the Dubs, and knew a few of the lads in the past, Johnny Twomey and them, and have always shouted for them. They'll win it this year. Kerry is gone and the Northern teams have nearly spun themselves out. They can't keep winning. Tyrone is still good, but they're missing a few of their key players. It's tough to come out of the North though, and tough to win it two years running. As I said the GAA is an instinct in me and in it you meet people from every county in Ireland. I can't believe they're letting soccer and rugby into our sacred ground. Let them go and buy their own stadium. I'd vote against it once, twice and three times if I could. Croke Park will be overworked from it all. We'll be dancing around these guys in a couple of years yet and the Dublin bars will back them up too, as there's big money in those games. I was at the first hurling All-Ireland to be broadcast in Loewe's cinema on Fordham and we had as big a crowd as Croke Park. You wouldn't get anything like that now.

Marriage got me quick; it did everyone back then; it was a normal thing. I met my first wife in the doctor's office. I had an awful cold and couldn't shake it off and decided to go to the first doctor I came across.

Dr. Willie Horwitz the plaque read and in I went. "I have a lovely Catholic girl for you," he told me, as he scribbled down a prescription, "A patient of mine. Irish-American. Will I give her your number the next time she's in?" And I being cheeky replied that I'd take her number instead. So I called her up, never saw her before, and arranged to meet her in The Killarney Rose on Fordham Road. It was a blind date and sure she fell madly in love with me straight away. I was married to that lovely girl for seventeen years until we fell out; seventeen years and two sons; now that's not bad.

Then there were a few more partnerships until I met my present wife, Eileen, one night in The Punch Bowl there on 238th Street and Broadway. She was after coming in from Woodside to watch an All-Ireland and was there with a few girlfriends when Frank Molloy called me over to make the introduction. I think the chief was trying to pick up one of her friends and probably thought he'd use me as an alibi. He knew I had a car and probably thought I'd be good for a lift somewhere. Anyhow I met Eileen that day and we're together ever since.

I was never a Romeo really! London 1954

America was good to me. I never cried a day for Ireland. I love it mind you and it's lovely to go home, but I never yearned to go back for good. It's Eileen who wants to go now. The only damper on my first year here was that my father, who accompanied me to Cobh, was dead within two weeks, and I didn't hear of it for a whole month until I received a letter from my brother. But I got over it. He was seventy years of age; at that time it was considered a good age; it's a good age at any time. Other than that I loved it here and always preferred it much better to

England despite the fact that the work was better over there. I think the weather was the main thing about here though. I was always a fan of the heat and after weeks of rain to arrive here and enjoy six months of glorious sunshine was something else. The summer of 1960 was unbelievable altogether.

Ireland today is a different Ireland and I won't fall into the category of knocking it. I think the prosperity is fabulous and I'm delighted for them. I hope it keeps going. Of course, having an eye for construction, the main thing I notice is the houses. One house is bigger than the other. You could travel from Donegal to lower Cork, as I have on numerous occasions, and there are houses everywhere. And everywhere you look there's a crane. There's not a piece of ground in Dublin but that you wouldn't see a crane. When I left Rosegreen there were three houses in it, one was our own; there was the church and a shop—Mother O'Neill's we always called it. Now there are sixty houses. Of course we got a big boost when Vincent O'Brien opened a stable down there, his land comes right up to the village, and he bought us a hurling pitch.

My brother is still in the home place and my sister, who was here for years, is now living in Cashel, so I go home all the time. Of course they call me the Yank, no question about it, but I was paid a lovely compliment the last time I was there when this fellow told me that I might as well never have left Ireland, my brogue was still that strong. I'm going to retire back there in another couple of months and I'm having awful second thoughts about it. I've been on sixty-four trips to Ireland since I got here forty-six years ago and I've looked forward to every single one of them. I even went for funerals and looked forward to going, but this time I'm not looking forward to it at all.

The prosperity is great though. The last time we were home Eileen's nine-year old nephew looked at me exasperated one day, and exclaimed, "Oliver I don't believe you don't have a mobile. You and Nanny are the only ones I know in the whole world who don't have a mobile." And his Nanny is eighty-six! We never even had access to a phone at all growing up in Ireland and his family have one each—seven of them!

The other thing that gets my dander up is the anti-American sentiment in Ireland. That puts me up on the high stool for sure. I've been told I'll get into trouble for it, and I don't care. I'm delighted that President Bush was in office when we went to war. That war wasn't popular, but what war is? War is never great, but it had to be done, and I'm sure the President doesn't gloat over it either. I'm happy he was there; that's what he was elected for; and I'm glad it wasn't that other wimp who ran against him, Kerry. And I believe he's going to run again, but I'll vote for Hilary Clinton in a heartbeat if she's nominated. I'd vote for almost anybody they'd put up against Kerry. I'm not a party man as you can see; I don't have to wear anyone's colors. I'll shout for whatever jersey I like.

So I came to town with the Mets. The polo grounds were where Cavan played Kerry in 1947. It was pulled down in the late sixties or early seventies, and then Shea stadium replaced the old World's Fair site and the Mets moved over to Queens. I had the pleasure of seeing one of their greatest fluky wins ever over the Red Sox in 1986. I got two fabulous tickets from this Jewish man I did a bit of work for. He always wanted to give me tickets for Broadway and the Opera and things like that. I wouldn't mind an auld show if I could pick it myself, but you couldn't pay me to go to the opera. Instead I asked him for a few baseball tickets and there was no problem whatsoever.

We were on the third base line, so close to the field that we could hear the players grunting. The Red Sox were up by three when Bill Buckner, the first base, let the ball hop in between his legs. The Mets supporters went mad and Buckner was nearly run out of Boston. They nearly assassinated him. It would've been the first time they'd won it in a hundred years—and they didn't get to win it again until last year. They thought they'd been cursed for selling Babe Ruth to the Yankees that time. He held the record for the most home runs for the longest time, until the steroid boys caught up with him. There were no drugs in Ruth, only whiskey, he was full of the stuff. So when they won last year, they broke the curse.

We were probably the last big wave to wash over from Ireland. They were coming in droves when I came; now they're hardly coming at all. I remember when we would pack three thousand into Gaelic Park on a regular Sunday, now if you ran an All-Ireland in it you'd hardly get ten thousand. We're at the other end of the economy too than Ireland. We feel we're not getting as much for our money as we used to. I remember getting gas for less than thirty cents a gallon; today you'd pay three dollars. We're taking a bit of a beating, but again we'll get over that too; we did before and we'll do it again. And the Irish will come back. It happened before in the sixties when Kennedy, it was Bobby really, as he was Attorney General at the time, reduced the quota, halved it in fact. There were about 15,000 a year coming in my time, from every county in Ireland. He got it down to seven or eight thousand. And we all thought that was the end of the Irish in America. But they came back, and they will again.

Interviewed at Dr. Gilberts Café,
Broadway, New York; January 2006

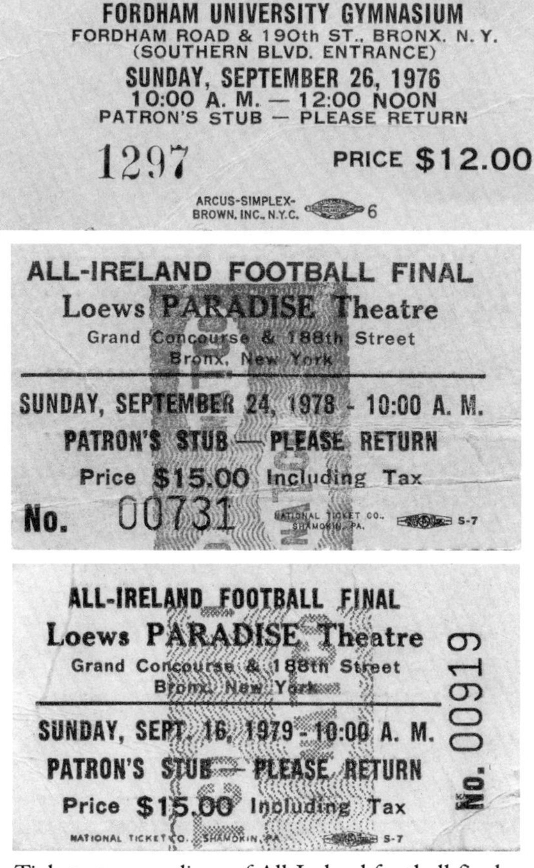

Tickets to recordings of All-Ireland football finals, 1976, 1978, 1979 in Loew's Paradise Theatre, Grand Concourse, Bronx, New York

Bill Burke, 1960

I flew into New York City in November 1960 after my sister had sent me the papers. The night before I left my hometown of Tubbercurry, County Sligo, my brother insisted that we should go up to Rooskey in County Roscommon to the annual Quinnsworth dance. Shortly after entering the marquee my brother and I were separated. Afterwards I walked to where we had parked the car and, lo and behold, it was gone. I hung around until all of the cars had cleared out and there was nobody left, only the band. They offered to take me to Athlone, which was about one hundred miles out of my way, and then decided instead to drop me off at a local boarding house. The ruffled landlady opened the door at 2:00 a.m. and demanded a pound before she would let me in. Luckily I had one!

At ten o'clock the next morning I found a hackney car that agreed to take me home. Time was of the essence, as my flight was at 2.00 p.m. from Shannon. After a short distance, I spotted my brother's car coming towards us and hailed him down. He was furious with me for not being at the car the night before and gave me hell for it. He had thought I got a lift from friends and had been up and down to Rooskey all night looking for me. Meanwhile, my father was pacing the floor wondering when I was going to get up and they had a job keeping him out of my room where he thought I was still asleep. My sister had even talked about issuing an SOS on the radio. Such commotion. Anyhow I arrived home, ran upstairs, shaved, ran downstairs again and left. My last memory of my father is him standing beside the kitchen table, looking sad. He was not an affectionate man, but he hugged me that day, as he said goodbye. I never saw him again.

My two brothers and two friends accompanied me to the airport. My brother, the driver, would not speak to me because of the Rooskey scenario, so, for safety reasons, I sat between my two friends in the back seat. They smoked the whole way to Shannon and when we eventually reached the airport I jumped out of the car only to discover a hole in the pocket of my good jacket where obviously one of them had dropped a cigarette butt. I had to carry it over my arm for the rest of the journey.

The flight to New York was uneventful until the pilot announced that, due to a snowstorm, we would have to stay the night in Gander. Upon landing we learnt that a bus was awaiting the passengers to take them to a hotel, but I declined the offer thinking I wouldn't have enough money to pay for the accommodation. I stayed at the airport all night by myself. At five o'clock the next morning the lights came on and the cleaners began their daily shift. They asked what the hell was I doing there and then kindly shared their breakfast with me. When the bus returned from the hotel the first one off was Maureen Armstrong, another Tubbercurry native, who told me that everything had been excellent, and free. So I had missed out. Later that day I arrived in New York, exhausted, and still carrying my jacket.

The next morning was a Saturday and my brother-in-law took me to his local laundry in Brooklyn Heights to drop off his shirts. He introduced me to the Chinese man behind the counter who asked me what type of work I would be interested in doing. "Anything," I shrugged. He then offered me a job working for him, pulled a business card out of his pocket, and told me to report for duty the following Monday morning. I assumed he meant in the laundry, but upon examining the card I discovered that he was a vice-president in the Bank of America. I showed up at his office on the Monday at nine o'clock, as requested, and an hour later I became a clerk in the International Department. That was forty-six years ago, and I have been in the banking business ever since.

Several things made me come to America. First of all, back in Ireland in 1960, you couldn't get a job. And even though my father was quite well off, he owned a farm and a garage in the town of Tubbercurry, there probably wouldn't have been enough for all of us there. Also my father was born in Manhattan. My grandfather came here from Galway in 1882 and my grandmother came from Tubbercurry around the same time. My father was born on 77th Street and Third Avenue; his parents were the Supers of the building. They returned when my father was about twelve or thirteen so he always thought of himself as American. One of his brothers was here and two sisters and he always intended coming back himself. I think it was a regret he had, that he never did. He was always going on about this country as the land of opportunity, and as soon as I graduated from school, he said to me, "Go to America." Then he died six months after I got here. I couldn't get back for the funeral because I had no money.

For the first six months we were enjoying life here. We got paid on a Friday and by Sunday night we were broke. It was hard to lose my father when I was so far away from home, but you become very tough very quickly when you lose your mother at twelve years of age. I had four sisters, the eldest one ran the house, but a young boy of twelve doesn't even realize how hard it is going to be without a mother. The only thing I remember about her funeral was my father insisting that we carry the coffin. That was pretty painful, but those memories have to run through you very quickly.

It's amazing how naïve we were when we came over first and how smart we thought we were. I was flung straight onto Wall Street and, believe you me, I was there for two years and I still didn't know what I was supposed to be doing. I had a fancy name, and my job was to check some documents, and I swear to God, I don't think I ever checked them, because nobody ever showed me how to check them. Even though I had my Leaving Certificate coming over, which would have been regarded as a fairly high standard of education at the time, I still had to do a few courses at the American Institute of Banking and Pace University. You needed that to compete.

It would have been unusual for a young boy back in Ireland at that time to have a Leaving Certificate. But, I'll tell you, in Tubbercurry there was no secondary school; only a technical school where you'd learn woodwork and welding and that, and the only other alternative was to go to the priests in Ballaghaderreen in County Roscommon, which was about twenty-six miles away. It was too long a commute for us so we had to board in. You'd go in there at about twelve or thirteen years of age, spend the next five years in it and then get out as fast as you could.

The priests at St. Nathy's gave us a good education, but nobody would put up with that lifestyle today. The food was exceptionally bad, and the conditions were exceptionally bad. There wasn't even any heat in the place. You couldn't get out until the term was over. You couldn't read a newspaper, you couldn't listen to a radio, and, of course, there was no television, so you were completely cut off from the outside world.

The only news you got was in a letter from home, or if someone came to visit, which my father did every week.

Out of six boys, I was the first to go to secondary school, and then my younger brother came after me. The only thing good about the whole experience was that the discipline was so severe; it was a great preparation for the business world. We had to get up at a certain time, be at class at a certain time, go to Church at a certain time, and when you came over here you could beat anyone with that sort of discipline. It also prepared you for the loneliness of exile. You would be very lonely for your parents in there. You were dealing with guys from twelve to eighteen years old and you learned how to survive very quickly. You learned how to get along with people or you'd get killed. Another thing was, no matter how bad things might have got here, they would have been twenty times worse in that school. Immigration was only child's play compared to it.

When I first started working in the bank, the people there had never heard an Irish accent before; they'd never even seen anyone from Ireland before. In the International Department there were mostly foreigners. There were Cubans from the Cuban Revolution and Hungarians from the Hungarian Revolution of 1956 and there were a lot of Orientals, who were vaguely familiar with the stage-Irish scene. First thing in the morning they'd greet you with "Top o' the Mornin'" and "Erin go Bragh," which got a bit annoying after a while, even though they didn't mean anything bad by it. I just found it highly insulting. As well as that, there were no other Irish people employed in the bank, but rather than me being a novelty, I was isolated because of it. I ate lunch by myself every day and because I didn't know how to order anything else, I basically ate the same thing every day, a ham sandwich and a coke.

I came from a different culture, so I didn't mix with anyone during the day except the cute Irish girls who came over from Schrafft's with the coffee; if I did I was just putting on an act. It was only when I came home at night that I got the chance to talk to people, as I roomed with my brother who was a bus driver and another lad. These were the people I could really relate to. And of course, we only socialized with Irish people.

There were two main dancehalls in New York that time. One was City Center. That place was huge altogether, holding up to a thousand people on any given night. If you saw a girl you liked you might never get a chance to dance with her. There was a famous band down there called

Brendan Ward who played modern music and then we had the Jaeger House, which was more traditional. Now when I came here first all we knew at home was Elvis Presley. All of a sudden I walked into Gaelic Park on a Sunday evening and everyone was step dancing. Now it was absolutely fantastic; but I hadn't a clue how to do it. The boys and girls from Connemara were absolutely dynamic at The Siege of Ennis and the old-time waltz and you felt like a real idiot beside them struggling with it. Nor had I ever heard of Coleman or any of those other Sligo fiddlers that everyone was talking about, but I became interested after I got here. It was the same with Irish history, of which we had learned very little in school. Then you meet these Irish-Americans and they know all about the Easter Rebellion and all of a sudden you want to know about it too.

I played the odd bit of football for Sligo, for only about a year, but I was at a disadvantage really because I originally came to the East Side of Manhattan, so it was hard to get up for training and that in Van Cortlandt Park, where all of the teams practiced. As a result, I only got up there on a Sunday. Then I got involved in the bank sports teams, we used to play softball, and I got more immersed in that world.

My first big career break came when I moved to the Franklin National Bank and was sent on an Executive Training Program. Most people coming out of that program would be upgraded to Clerk or Executive Clerk, which was really a glorified clerk, and they would never go any further than that, which was fine. But one day one of the chiefs in the Bank called me into his office and asked me to go up to Boston and deliver a package the following morning. He gave me a ticket for the shuttle and five hundred dollars expenses. At eight o'clock the next morning I arrived at the address he had given me and presented myself to the person I was to convey the parcel to. He asked me to hang on for a while, that there was someone else who wished to speak to me. I had no idea why, as really I was just a lowly employee of the Franklin at the time, so you can imagine my surprise when an Assistant District Attorney for the state of Massachusetts approached me. I was even further shocked when he announced that I was to be a witness for the state in a tax evasion case, and that if I left he would hold me in contempt of court. I was stunned. He assured me that they would prepare me for the interrogation and not to worry.

So I took my seat on the stand and swore to tell the truth, the whole truth and nothing but the truth, and I answered the nice man's questions about the package, that it was just a wire transfer for a safety deposit and everyone was very courteous and things were running nice and smoothly until the defense's attorney got up and tore into me. How old are you? How long are you in this country? What do you know about banking? Are you an expert witness? Of course I was getting all exasperated and you know when Irish people get excited they start using profane language. Seemingly, the South Boston jury was highly amused by my brogue—so much so that the judge had to reprimand them for laughing. I was sweating by the time I got off the chair and couldn't wait to get out of that court my nerves were that shattered. The DA met me outside with open arms. "You won the case for us," he smiled. "The Defense Attorney messed up because it was an all-Irish jury and they regarded you as one of their own."

I was astounded by this and even more amazed when I returned to New York and my boss congratulated me on the fine job I had done. He told me that he had purposely picked me because I had no clue what was going on. He explained that because I was a fast talker, he knew I'd talk my way out of it, and because I was ignorant of the situation; he almost used the word moron, that I was the perfect witness. He also told me that when I graduated from the Program he would make me a vice-president of Franklin National. I was probably the youngest of that rank at the time and with the least service, only six or seven years, and the least educated, as most of the other guys would have had university degrees or equivalent qualifications. But I got that lucky break and my career took off from then.

Before I took up the position with Country Bank, where I am now, I had been senior vice-president with the Bank of Ireland in their branch on Fifth Avenue. I think mentally I wanted to say I worked for an Irish bank because obviously when I was growing up in Ireland there was no way I would have got in. It was all who you knew back then; it didn't depend on talent. You had to come highly recommended by a bank manager or someone, so I think deep down I just wanted to prove a point when I moved to the Bank of Ireland.

I worked with them for several years and during that time I had breakfast with Joe Murphy, the Chairman of the bank here, just after he'd started Country Bank, and out of the blue he asked me if I'd like to go work for him in the Carmel office. I thought he meant Carmel, California, not realizing there was a town of that name Upstate. Anyhow I took the job and took one look around Carmel and decided to move the whole lot down to White Plains, where the headquarters still are, and eventually I opened branches in Woodlawn, Riverdale, Scarsdale, and finally, New York City. I credit our success to our huge Irish following and to the relationships I've built up with people over the years. I've been lending money for forty-six years and when you loan money to an Irish man, he'll never forget you.

The Irish are intensely loyal. I've set fellows up in their first home, first business, they're all big shots now, but I knew them when they were small guys. I have customers here who would probably get better rates elsewhere, but they still stay with me. And remember when I started there was no other Irish person in banking, not to my knowledge anyhow, so I might have been the first contact they had. Some of them ask me why they should do business with me and I say, "Did you ever meet the president of your bank before?" I am the highest ranking working person here. Basically the Chairman of the Board, of which I am also a member, owns the bank, but I run it. Country Bank is owned by an Irish-American family called Murphy so it was a break for me the day I met Joe, because prior to this I was just on the payroll, now I own a piece of it.

So that's how it was back then. In the beginning you took a job, and you went where it took you. All of the guys in the Irish community were making much more money than me in construction and the buses and the telephone company and that, but as I moved up, the gap narrowed, until all of a sudden I was making more than them. I sacrificed at the beginning, but then made up for it in the end. There weren't too many of us in the business world. Bernadette McManus, a Mayo woman, had her own personnel agency and she would place a lot of the guys in that type of work. During lunch time some of us would go up and chat with her, maybe we wanted to date her, I don't know.

Anyhow, there were very few of us. Then things changed. In the 80s, the new Irish came in and took the city by storm. They were well educated. They were smarter and more worldly, and they hit Wall Street like there was no tomorrow. They were well respected, there was no more "Erin go Bragh", or any of that crap, because they were better than anyone else down there. We have more survival instincts than somebody brought up here. I mean when you think about it, who would send their child at a young age to a strange country where they had hardly any connections? That's why we're killing the youth coming up now because we're not throwing them out there anymore. Sometimes they nearly look down on us because we had to emigrate and they hadn't.

The Irish Americans in executive positions have more respect for the young Irish born now too, as in my time they had learned from their parents and grandparents that we were all poor and primitive with no bathrooms and they had this notion that we were backward too. But we showed them that we weren't stupid. I know there was a lot of poverty in Ireland back in the forties and fifties, and immigration was chronic. My father had a hackney business and every time a boat went out he'd have three of four loads of passengers to take down to Cobh. Some of these people were only fifteen and sixteen years of age and he said it was heart wrenching watching these youngsters saying goodbye to their parents whom they might never see again.

I think it will be a crisis for America if the Irish stop coming, as they are the smartest race in the whole world. They are obviously number one in the restaurant business here; they're almost number one in construction and Irish Americans basically run Wall Street now. Look at how well all those guys who came over in the fifties got on? They were geniuses, and they're all millionaires now. Imagine if they'd had an education? They'd be running the country. Like me, they probably went to a two-roomed national school with a bathroom out in the wilds. There would be a few classes in each and the teacher would announce, "Now we'll have 4th class history." The boys would line up along the wall for their lesson, while the rest did their sums, spelling, reading, whatever. The dentist would visit once a year and examine us on a hard chair out in the hall. The story was that he got paid according to how many teeth he pulled, so there weren't many left with a mouth full. Then we had to supply the turf for the fire. I loved that job, as it meant a day off and we'd go around with a donkey and cart and fill it up with the soggiest stuff we could find. I apologized to the Master for that when he retired.

I think my parents would have been more proud of me being Grand Marshall of the St. Patrick's Day Parade than being President of a bank. When we were growing up my Aunt and Uncle here used to march for Sligo in the parade every year, and they'd be all dressed up in white uniforms with green capes, and all these pictures would arrive home and they'd be given pride of place in our house. Really when you think about it, Sligo probably didn't set off until four o'clock in the afternoon when everybody else was gone home. St. Patrick's Day in Ireland wasn't such a big deal; it was just a religious holiday, and as a result it didn't mean that much to me when I came over and to be honest with you, I always used to work that day, even though I'd probably celebrate later in the evening.

Anyhow I was picked to be 226th Grand Marshall in 1988; there were only two hundred and twenty-five before me and that morning when I went to Mass in St. Patrick's Cathedral, I swear to God, I couldn't get my parents out of my mind, just couldn't get them out. The memories kept flooding back. All day long, I thought of them. As I walked up Fifth Avenue later, that's all I could think about, is how delighted they would have been to see me lead the parade.

Ireland is a great place now, and obviously the economy is better than here almost. It has become a very modern society and the banking systems are probably better than here and basically the education system is much better, but I just couldn't bear the weather. No matter what time of the year you go home, it'll rain and I just don't know how much of that I could put up with. Obviously when I was growing up there it didn't bother me, but I just couldn't live in that climate again. You know here that once the 1st of May comes that's it, you basically will have summer until the following November; the winter may be severe sometimes, but it's short and you're guaranteed good weather after it, but not over there, you might never see a summer. My wife is from West Cork and we have a house there, so it is nice to get back every now and then.

America still has a great economy. New York is the financial capital of the world and there are still great opportunities here. Personally, I don't think we should be at war right now; there are too many young people being killed. It's all very well to say free Iraq, but are we willing to sacrifice our own sons and daughters for that cause? I read the paper there every evening going up home on the Metro North and every day a few more are killed and they're all only eighteen and nineteen years of age, dying in a foreign land they know nothing about. Look at all that were lost in Vietnam, for God's sake and afterwards the two warring factions became friends, and all these people died trying to separate them.

I had to register for the draft and went down to Whitehall Street;

they even sent me the subway token, where I got the roughest physical known to mankind. There was a written examination too and I would have been eligible for conscription except for my wife was pregnant, so I got out of having to join the army and I got out of going to Vietnam. I didn't know anyone personally who went, but a lot of Irish born boys were sent over and I believe they were exceptionally good soldiers. They were tough guys, strong and used to hard work at home; believe me I would have been able for Vietnam after being at St. Nathy's. When I went home one time the priests there had a dinner in my honor, so I suppose they were proud of me too in their own way.

I have been married twice. The first time was when I was twenty. I met Kathleen up in Gaelic Park very shortly after I arrived. At that time we'd play the games in the afternoon and then there'd be a dance in the evening. I was going to school at the time and didn't hang around very much in the park, but this one night anyhow I did and I met this lovely girl from Cavan. I eventually called her a couple of weeks later and she told me she worked for Chase Manhattan Bank, which was only about five blocks from where I worked. We were married about two years later and moved up to Riverdale to 251st Street and Broadway looking out on to Van Cortlandt Park, where we lived for six or seven years. We had a Jewish Super and he did me the greatest favor of all times. He would only give us a one-year lease so every year he would renew it and try and get more money out of us. This really got on my nerves after a while; being at the mercy of this fellow, so eventually we bought our first house up in New Rochelle. We had four children, two boys and two girls, and Kathleen then died from cancer at the age of forty-eight. That was in 1991, just when everything was starting to go great.

So that was another shock to the system, I had already had two major losses and this was the third. But, two years later I got married again to a girl from West Cork, Aileen, who worked with me at the time and we have two boys, Ross and Riley, one ten and one eight, so I am active again with little league, basketball, and baseball and all those things. It's better really raising a family the second time around because you have more time and more money.

It was hard, however, to watch my first four children lose their mother, just as I had. They were older than I had been and, of course, in Ireland everything was hidden so I didn't even realize that my mother was dying.

Here if you have cancer everyone knows it and they know the consequences. Everything is out in the open here, which is better really, but it doesn't matter how you lose your Mom, it's going to be hard. My son, Bill, is now in banking too, Robert is in business, Michelle and Liz are married, and we have six grandchildren. So life is hectic, but wonderful.

The first time I went back to Ireland was after five years, which was a long time. You have to remember at this stage I had no mother or father, I had been orphaned at eighteen, so there was no home really. My brother was in the home place, but he was married with children, so it wasn't the same. I had grown up with three guys in Tubbercurry; we went to national school and secondary school and all together and we were very close. But when I went home after the five years I found that I couldn't relate to them at all. We were completely removed from one another. I was very saddened by that, but other than that, I didn't' really miss Ireland at all, because really, home is where your parents are, or where you make your own family.

All of my siblings are still alive. One of my brothers goes into a Home every now and then when his arthritis gets very bad and if I go and visit him there he makes a big fuss, taking me around and introducing me to all the other patients, telling them all about me, how I'm president of a bank in New York, how I was Grand Marshall of the Parade, the whole lot. One day anyhow, after doing the rounds, we come to this old gentleman half asleep in his wheelchair and my brother nudges him awake, demanding, "Look who we have here. Do you know who this is?" Yer man opens one eye, squints up at me, and flops his head back on his chest again. "No idea," he mumbles, "but take him up to the front desk, they'll tell you who he is."

The Irish will always keep it in perspective for you. Sure after all these years, every time I go back to Tubbercurry, someone will surely come up to me and say, "Are you the lad who got lost up in Rooskey?"

Interviewed at the Country Bank, Head Office, New York City; April 03, 2006

Therese Crowe, 1962

I came to America in 1962 on the S.S. America. I traveled cabin class and it was brilliant even though we were only a day out in the ocean and I became violently ill. The Captain was doing his rounds and I asked him could he stop the boat and let me off. He laughed, but got me some medication all the same to settle my stomach. After that I had the best five days of my life. It was an experience everyone should have, as coming in a plane is nothing at all. We sailed from Cobh and when we arrived in New York we discovered that there was a strike in the place where we docked. There was pandemonium in the port and I thought people were going to kill each other. I had never seen anything like it in my life. It was diabolical and I wanted to go home straight away.

I made my way up to Connecticut all the same to my sister's husband's sisters and their aunt who was nearly one hundred. They were working in a big house belonging to the man who supplied oranges to Tropicana. I stayed there for a while and then I contacted this guy, Jim O'Rourke, whom I had met in England. He brought me down to Manhattan where he lived with his mother and two brothers. The three of them were in their forties and had never married, but they were very nice. He fixed me up with a place to stay with this woman on Amsterdam Avenue.

However, I knew these people living on Tremont Avenue in the Bronx, so I went up there and found these girls from home. One of them was in St. Francis Hospital on 138th Street and St. Ann's Avenue having a baby, so I decided to go down straight away and visit her. There for the first time I held my godson, Darren Hogan. A nun, Sister Marinatta, swept into the room and declared, "You're holding the baby like you know what you're doing." I told her that I was a qualified Children's Nurse and she offered me a job there and then. However, as they didn't recognize my qualification over here, they hired me as an Infant Care Technician, as I didn't yet have my full license.

I moved in with the nuns in the convent above the church and I got fifty three dollars a week, working six o'clock till two; off from two till six; then on at six again until ten o'clock at night, seven days a week. And when they were short of anyone they'd knock on my door and I'd have to go down again. Another nun, Sister Theresa constantly encouraged me to go back to school and become more fully qualified. I had only attended a school to learn children's nursing in Dublin and I wasn't state registered, but I said I'd think about it. However, after three months I wanted to go home because I was too lonely.

After spending a short time at home I continued on to England where I worked for a while at a hospital in Margate, Kent. I disliked England though. As a matter of fact, I disliked it intensely, and as soon as my eighteen months was up, I came back out here again. I returned to St. Francis Hospital from where I commenced my nursing career.

I'll never forget the time Mayor Lindsay wanted to close down the hospital. Mike Quill used to call him "Lintsley"; they fought like two tinkers. But Cardinal Spellman gave his coin collection to keep it open. I think Quill and Lindsey were friends too; sure Quill was a friend of everybody. He was a great man and went home to Kerry every year to keep up his accent. Anyhow, I was interviewed by this well-known TV reporter who still has his own show today on a Sunday morning. I won't mention any names. I was the only white person at St. Francis at the time and he asked me, "What's a nice girl like you doing in a place like this?" Then he proceeded to ask me out to dinner. Now I'd say he must be have been over ten years older than me at the time, but I went out to dinner with him anyhow

At that time I knew nobody and I wanted to meet everybody. Eventually someone said, "Go to Gaelic Park." Now my sister, Mary, Lord Have Mercy on her, knew every single thing about hurling. She could have written a book about it, but I knew nothing. I only went to a match if I knew some of the players. I had played in two camogie games as a child and this girl hit me twice in the ankle and I nearly broke her neck and that was the end of my camogie career. It was also the extent of my knowledge of the GAA up to that.

By this time Sister Theresa had got her way and I had returned to school once again, to the Hospital for Special Surgery. One Sunday after I graduated, I made my way to the Park. Clare was playing Cork, I think, and one of their players took a shot at the ball and whatever way he turned, he fell to the ground out there on the field. I knew the way he was lying with his leg underneath him and the way his neck was positioned that they shouldn't move him. "Don't pick him up," I roared from the stand and proceeded to run out on the pitch. "I'm a nurse."

The fellow's name was Chambers. He'd be a cousin of Jimmy Chambers who's there in the Park every Sunday without fail. They let me in beside the player anyhow and I splintered him with broken hurleys out there on the field. So next thing anyhow, I went into the bathroom and on my way out I met John Kerry O'Donnell, Lord have mercy on him. He complemented me on the good job I had done and asked me if I'd like to come up on a Sunday every now and then to help out. I said I would, anytime I was off. As I walked away, he yelled at me, "By the way, you won't get paid."

That was my first time in Gaelic Park and it hasn't been my last, let me tell you, I've been up there ever since. It must be thirty years now and, along with Jimmy Chambers with the cigarette stuck in his mouth, I haven't missed a Sunday. I could wring his neck for smoking. He and his wife, Ann, are great people though and his sister, Rita, lives in Thurles. She works in the County Home there. Although I don't think it's politically correct to call it that anymore.

It was through nursing that I became involved with Gaelic Park; not because of the GAA. I would go down every Sunday and help any player who got injured and it didn't matter what jersey he wore. I remember one year when Tipperary met Westmeath in the final and we were two points up. A young man by the name of Shane Dalton from Dublin was playing for Westmeath, and he hurt his hand. After I sprayed the hand Shane got the ball and scored a goal, and Westmeath beat us by a point. Our lads nearly killed me, but I made it very clear that day and I always have, that I'm a Tipperary woman outside the gate and I'm a nurse inside. I have to differentiate, as there no way on God's earth I'd have survived down there at all.

A Tipperary woman I am through and through; although I had the slight mishap of being born in Kerry. My father was a temporary stationmaster in Killarney at the time, and my mother gave birth in the station house. It's a car park now and I really think that there should be a plaque there for me somewhere. I was a premature baby. I was born at only seven months and, as there were no incubators back in 1934, I had be kept beside an open fire for four and a half months and bathed constantly with cotton wool soaked in oil to extend my lungs. My mother went down to Manning's in Fairhill one day to buy me a dress to lay me out and she went into the Friary and prayed that I'd be dead by the time she got home. She didn't want to watch me die slowly. I often used to taunt her with it after when she'd be scolding me for being bold. "Mammy," I'd say, "If I'd died that time, you'd be praying to me in Heaven now." My parents would look at each other across the fire. "Where did we get her from, Bridgie?" My father would shake his head.

Therese with her mother, Bridget, upon graduating from Nursing School

Everybody belonging to me was on the railway—The Great Southern railway. My Uncle Mick was a stationmaster, Uncle Tom was a driver, and my brother was a driver. A train went from Cork to Dublin one time with Daddy as the goods guard and Tom the driver. Two of my sisters served in the dining-cart and the ticket collector was my uncle as well. My parents were from Tipperary and it was to there that we returned shortly after I was born. Mammy came from Upperchurch and Daddy from Clonolty in the parish of Goolds Cross. There was nobody like our parents back then. They worked so hard and they never expected anything really.

I was raised on Croke Street, Thurles. The street is called after the great man himself, Archbishop Croke of Cashel who was the first patron of the GAA after it was started there in Hayes Hotel in Thurles back in 1884. I wouldn't give up my upbringing there for fifty million dollars. We had nothing, but we weren't poor either, at least I couldn't say we were. Nobody was poor. I don't think they were anyway, because we were all in the same boat. I remember a girl going to England and she came back with nylons and I thought that if I had a pair of nylons, I would walk up and down the street and nobody could stop me, and I believed that. I really did. We had everything and we had nothing. We used go out to

Grandma's in Upperchurch, and we'd come home with chickens and pig's meat, and all that type of a thing. My uncle Tommy would bring us in loads of turf.

Mammy would take the top off Dad's egg in the morning. She'd butter his bread or his toast. She'd put sugar and milk in his tea and she'd stir it and put it in front of him. This was the normal thing to do. And if he had to go out on the railway in the middle of the night, Mammy would get up and cook a full meal for him to take in his basket. When my younger brother came home from England one time, he said to her. "Why don't you let Dad do that?" Her answer was, "You live your life. I'll live mine." I kind of agree with that. I'm old-fashioned, I suppose, and I know people think I'm crazy, but I think a man should be taken care of. Now I wouldn't let him walk over me either.

I went to school in the Presentation Convent, Thurles. Sister Benedict from Kerry used to beat us with a big stick. She beat everybody; well they all beat everybody that time. And if you went home and told your mother, you'd be killed again. But not my sister, Mary, she never got the stick. She was a saint, Lord have mercy on her. Not like me. Sure if you dared me to walk across the River Suir, I would do it. The water was up to my chest one time, as I waded across, and a teacher going back to school after lunch took my boots, where I'd left them on the wall. I had to walk home in my bare feet.

Another time someone told me that if you put a frog in your mouth you'd never have a toothache. So of course I had to try that. And I sat up on a pig one time, and the pig nearly died. They had to bring a vet down from Dublin and put him up in Hayes Hotel. My younger sister, Philomena sat on the floor between my father's legs while he was reading the paper. "Guess what Tess did today, Daddy?" She chanted. "She killed Mrs. Cleary's pig." I was nearly being killed myself. I didn't realize that I was clotting the pig's blood the way they do for black pudding. Sure how did I know he could die? We had to pay for the pig anyhow.

After I left school I worked in O'Meara's Lemonade factory washing bottles. Master Denis and Master Basil owned it; they were the elite of the county; and I hated every minute of it. It was very humiliating to have to address someone as "Master" and even more humiliating to have to answer to the supervisor who was worse than they were. My dream had always been to be a nurse. One day Mammy told me that if I wanted to go to Dublin to do nursing, they would send me to Dr. Donnelly's in Bray. He was a man who used prepare girls for nursing, but you had to work for him as well. Talk about work. You were a maid really and then you were sent into St. Brigid's in Dublin for the nursing and then you had to go back to Bray again and do more work.

After finishing that course I went to England where I met this American fellow and I thought I was in love. Mammy did several Novenas that he wouldn't marry me. And her prayers were answered, because he didn't. I followed him to America anyhow. He drove a Jaguar, and this is how stupid I was, well, innocent really. I thought if I went to the Pentagon, where he worked, I would be able to find him by picking out his car. Now wasn't that brilliant? But I tracked him down all the same. He thought I was an apparition. We had a long distance romance for a couple of years between New York and DC, but we never married.

Actually I didn't get married until I was thirty-four. I met my husband at the hospital where he was an X-ray technician. He was supposedly of Irish descent. His grandfather was a valet to the Rockefellers, but I'd say he was more English than he was Irish, and a bit of German. I didn't want to get married at all, but sure I thought I was in love, again. We were together for ten years, all through his time in medical school and then he took off. I didn't know where he was for six months. I thought he was dead even though he left me a note along with his W2 to do his taxes. He took the car I gave him and said he'd keep up the repayments. And I still didn't get the message? I thought he might have had a heart attack because all of his family had heart conditions. I used to shovel the snow and mow the lawn so as he wouldn't have to exert himself or that he wouldn't drop dead in the chair like his brother and two uncles. I wouldn't do it for him now.

It was a terrible time though after he left and I was devastated. I'd seen him at work with this other woman all right, but didn't suspect anything because nothing had changed at home. Our house was still the same. I still got the flowers every Friday. I think the florist was more upset than I was. I couldn't go home, as my mother was sick and I couldn't lie to her, and I couldn't tell her the truth. I could never tell a lie to my mother. "You're lying, Tess," she'd say to me. "I'm not, Mam." I'd answer back.

Then I got a wire from her to say that Uncle Tom was dead, not to come home; that he'd been buried that day. That even further upset me, as I was supposed to take after him and he always stood up for me when I was in trouble. My husband eventually showed up like the second Resurrection, but he was with the other woman and our life together had come to an end. I must say though that I had a great ten years, and I have always wished him well.

My single life began again. I didn't go to the dancehalls that much first time around, because I was always at school. I've never even been to the Catskills. When everybody was out enjoying themselves, I was going to night school. During that time I got my high school equivalency here; I studied at the Hospital for Special Surgery; I became a licensed practical nurse, and I went on to become an RN. I got my associates degree in Nursing from the Hospital for Joint Diseases and Cornell's medical school. I was living at 2850 Webb Avenue in the Bronx where you had Kaplan Avenue and Kingsbridge Road. That's where all the craic was. Durty Nelly's was a great place. Then Joe Cornyn had a restaurant on Fordham Road and every Irish person used go to eat there. Joe Cornyn was great; he worked on the buses one time. Then there was The Recovery Room and The Archway, and they were brilliant. Everybody was one. There was no such thing as where you came from. Everyone went into the bar to see the bartender, not just to drink. They were fabulous meeting places. And everybody helped everybody else. It's still like that somewhat today. We're more united here than they are at home, in every size, shape or form. But any of them who came out in the seventies and eighties, I'll tell you something, have all done absolutely brilliant too.

Healing a young man in Gaelic Park

There are the Conroy brothers, Ian and Niall; they have a couple of bars downtown, Mustang Sally's, Mustang Harry's. You have Joe Graves, you have Tony O'Brien, Rocky Ryan, these are all young people and they all have their own businesses. They worked hard and they got what they wanted. It's a great country for that. You can be what you want and go for what you want. But you can't be bending your elbow every evening either.

I took care of Joan Crawford in my day and Frank Sinatra's uncle, and what's that one that was married to the Prince? Wallis Simpson. She came in to the Hospital of Special Surgery for a Keller procedure, which was to straighten out her toes. A lot of the patients were often taken underneath to the New York Hospital to have a face lift. I took care of Mr. and Mrs. Goodman of the Bergdorf Goodman store. I spent three years with Mrs. Goodman and two years with Mr. Goodman up in their estate. They were absolutely out of this world. She was magnificent. He was Jewish and she was Catholic. She was born in Spain and raised in Cuba, had been married, divorced and had a child. Walter Winchell, a famous New York writer, wrote that the Spanish beauty would not last six months. But they were married for fifty-two years. When they died, Father Michael Walsh, a priest that I went to school with, who was an Irish Chaplain in New York, presided at their funerals.

Coming to America was a great experience for me. Ireland has changed a lot and it is great to a certain extent. It's great for education and I approve of that. A lot of them don't know the value of money and they're spending it. They all have credit cards and they're maxing them out to the hilt and if anything ever happens to this tiger, I'll tell you something, it'll be a disaster. That would be a pity really, as we've come a long way. But there's no place like it all the same. I used to go back all the time when my parents were alive; any time I had a week off. I used to be crying so hard coming back on the plane, people would ask me did somebody die? So, at last, I'm returning. I'm going to retire at home. This should be my last year here. I'm looking forward to it really, because you can always be done without. They tell me they'll miss me in Gaelic Park, but I doubt that. A lot of the young nurses today though don't want to do it for nothing. But it has been a great experience for me.

I was the first Irish woman to be honored by the GAA here, and the first Irish-born woman from New York to get the President's honor in Ireland, from Sean Kelly, last year. That was a great honor for New York. This award is for the people who work behind the scenes. That famous Limerick man, J.P. McManus, and I were honored together, and he was brilliant. You would never think he was one of Ireland's wealthiest businessmen and racehorse owners. You wouldn't think he had two pennies to rub together. We were down in Cork up to our necks in muck at that awful Páirc Uí Chaoimh and I said I'd never set foot in this place again. J.P. said if Limerick meets Tipperary in an All-Ireland final and it's played in Cork, would you not come? I said I wouldn't. "Well, if they do," he laughed, "I'll send the helicopter for you." Sean Kelly said he probably would. J.P. is an awful nice man.

That's the thing. You meet such nice people all the way through. I used to work down in the South Bronx doing shut-ins. That's when the patients couldn't come out and I'd go to their homes and take their blood pressure or whatever. A lot of their young neighbors were helping them and nobody knew anything about it. They would take them to worship – to the Synagogue on a Saturday or to the Church on a Sunday. Nobody hears about those people at all, but I have met their like all though my career

I've been involved with the immigration issue since day one. In the eighties it was the IRM with Sean Minihan and now we're rooting for the ILIR. Please God President Bush will do something for them, if we're not all killed first. The GAA is suffering here terribly because of it. They're stopping them at the airport and everything. How can a Jewish immigration official at Shannon airport know if someone is a Kilkenny hurler? Somebody must be telling them. These lads are not even getting paid for coming over to play ball. We just give them a good weekend. We're only trying to keep our culture and heritage alive here. With the help of God things will work out. I am a member of the County Tipperary National & Benevolent Association of New York, which is a great organization altogether and has raised money for several people in need. If someone has any links to Tipperary at all, and knows a member of this Association, they can apply for help, especially with medical expenses. I wish every association had such a service. I am a delegate for the Tipperary Hurling Club and the vice-chairperson for the New York team. And I still do the volunteer nursing at Gaelic Park every Sunday.

Who would have thought a hundred years ago that a woman would be elected as delegate in the GAA? As for today's Tipperary team, we're living in hope and dying in despair. The big GAA Banquet will be held next week at Astoria Manor. Danny Doohan, a Donegal man, who owns

Ned Devine's up the street there, is our guest of honor. I have the letter from the Archbishop of Cashel and Emily, a patron of the GAA at home. Every year he sends a letter to the honoree to be put into the journal. I will get it framed and present it to Danny and Sheila.

I met the love of my life seventeen years ago when I was at home at a GAA function. This fellow was winking at me and when I discovered who he was, hadn't I courted him one night years before, when I was only sixteen. We got together and have been so ever since. He's good people. I've been very lucky in that respect. I may not have been born rich or beautiful, but I was born lucky.

I have a house bought on the road to Holy Cross and I'd love to get a piece of land and set up a hospice there. I have a dream. I'm like Martin Luther King. In fact, I'd love to do it in every county in Ireland, because the people in the country can't always get to Dublin. I'll come back out to America to get the money. That's my dream now. As Archbishop Clifford says, anything is possible.

Interviewed at Aisling Irish Community Center,
Yonkers, New York; February 14, 2006

Gaelic Park, September 2006

Denis Mulcahy 1962

I came to America on the 14th of March, 1962, when I was seventeen years of age. With me was my good friend, Denis Coughlin, who just passed away recently. I had two brothers here already over in the east Bronx, near the Bronx Zoo, in St. Thomas Aquinas parish. There was a big bus depot there that a lot of the Irish guys worked out of, over near Southern Boulevard, which was already a bad neighborhood back then. But we had been working in England prior to that and when we saw my brothers' apartment on Vyse Avenue; we thought it was the lap of luxury. Ten people would have been crammed into a place like that in London. It was very expensive to rent a little flat there and you had to pay for heat and other utilities on top of that. For the people with families it was very hard altogether. Coming over here and seeing what the guys could afford, it was completely different. Really people couldn't do enough for us as far as jobs and that was concerned and that's what impressed me most about New York.

Den and I started working up in St. Raymond's Cemetery just taking care of the graves; gravediggers I suppose you'd call us. There were a lot of Irish guys working up there too, for some of them it was a side job, but we had to get five years in at something until we were eligible for citizenship. Then we could apply for the Police Department or something like that, which was my main ambition at the time. My brother, Pat, who is back in Ireland now, was a police officer, as were a lot of the Irish guys. It was a good, secure job, with good benefits and a pension, and that's what people aimed for back then. I'll tell you in those city jobs you'll never become rich, but you'll always have security and a good living. That's why some of my children have followed in my footsteps, even my two daughters. Maureen, who lived in Ireland for five or six years—in fact my granddaughter was born in Newry—is a Sergeant in the 34 Precinct in Inwood, and Tara is a court officer at Manhattan Criminal Court. I like to see girls independent because if marriage doesn't work out then they have their careers to fall back on. My son, Sean is a detective with the Emergency Services Unit. Denis Jr. chose another field, that of accountancy, and is now a partner at Deloitte Touche, one of the largest accounting firms in the world. He's done very well.

In order to become a police officer I had to have a high school diploma so I studied under the scrutiny of Frank O'Connor for the equivalency. Frank, a Kerry man, was down there on 23rd Street and 8th Avenue on the 2nd floor. He was very reassuring and gave us a lot of encouragement, unlike a lot of the teachers we would have known at home, and he set a lot of people off on an educational journey. I stopped at the diploma having no further ambitions than that. I don't know if Frank was a fully qualified teacher or not, but I found that people in my time who had a good education had either studied for the priesthood or went into the Christian Brothers. The average Irish person couldn't afford to get schooling like that, especially not country kids. He gave confidence to a lot of people who would have needed it back then. Armed with my diploma and my American citizenship I was ready to join the boys in blue.

I started with the Tactical Patrol Unit, it used to be called Force but that sounded too aggressive so they changed the name to Unit. There were a lot of riots in the city in the sixties and this unit was able to patrol the streets without being noticed. There were a lot of Irish guys in it, including the Cassidy Brothers from Cavan. There were six of them in the police force, they also went into the bar business and owned a lot of places downtown. Then there was the Kiely's, Dan and Pat, there was a big family of them in the force too. Dan went back and is some kind of a councilman in Ballybunion now. He makes the press a lot.

There was a lot of trouble here, and the city was a dangerous place back then, but there were a lot of people hungry and poor in New York City in the 50s and 60s and the economy always plays a large part in determining the rate of crime in a place. And of course the drug trade at that time was incredible. I saw the same in Northern Ireland in the 70s when I was traveling back and forth with Project Children; the people were so poor they resorted to crime. That's why you had the Troubles. There's really no poverty in New York today. We don't have the ghettos we used to have. When I think of the places that I covered like Harlem and the South Bronx, there is nothing left of the poverty that these people experienced.

After a couple of years with the TCU, I moved on to the Citywide Anti-Crime Unit where my partner for ten years was Joe Firth, from Clare. In fact, Joe's daughter, Maureen, is a big shot with the Police Benevolent Union now. I can remember stopping off at Joe's house here in Woodlawn, on 234th Street, at the back of the firehouse, the day Maureen got a scholarship to the Bronx High School of Science. She was only a young kid, now she's put in fifteen years with the Police Department. The years fly by.

You get very close to your partner. Joe and I used to work together undercover. That time I had a beard and long hair and whatever, and down in Harlem they used to call us the two Swedish dudes. They couldn't figure out our accents, but they knew we weren't American. We'd be driving around in a yellow cab and after a few arrests in the neighborhood they'd soon get to know our decoy.

What the Department would do is examine all of the crimes committed in a given year and if they discovered a pattern they'd get us to go in and try and unearth the source. For instance there was a series of chain snatchings in the City there one time and they put out a bunch of young cops dressed up with shoulder bags and gold chains to try and catch the culprits. Same thing over there in Van Cortlandt Park where there was a series of rapes. I remember working up there with a group of girls out on the street trying to lure in the perpetrators.

At the start of a shift we turned out of Randall's Island, where we kept our equipment because it was away from the public eye, and headed off in a cab to our destination, where we waited to zoom in and make an arrest. Sometimes it was pure luck; being in the right place at the right time. They did a movie about one of the girls who worked with us, "Muggable Mary", and it was based on our unit. Mary's job was to attract the muggers who were roaming the city.

My next assignment was in a detective unit in Harlem where we ensnared homicides. At that time the city was catching between 2,400 and 2,600 homicides a year and around 125 of them were in Harlem. Now it's down to approximately 500 for the whole city. It's incredible. Of course fifty percent of those homicides were drug related, because the trade was huge here at that time, it really has dried up a lot. The white kids from Jersey would come in over the bridge to Harlem looking for narcotics and often got caught in cross fires. I spent the last twenty years of my career in the Bomb Squad from where I retired in 2002.

I was never that afraid of a gun. It's funny how things happen though because one of my main experiences with a shooting happened when I was off duty. I was down watching Coughlin's place on Sedgewick Avenue, where he was a Super, while he was gone to Ireland. One morning I called my brother-in-law, Sean O'Rourke, who lived down the block, just after two guys had pried open his door and broken into his apartment. He had hidden in the bathroom where they were again trying to push the door down and get in after him. My phone call distracted them and they fled. Sean picked up the receiver and roared, "Get down here quick." He was hysterical. I didn't make too much of it, thinking it was just a routine burglary, and that the guys were long gone. I sauntered over to his building, not in too much of a hurry, and in the meantime they had re-entered his home, so these were no ordinary burglars. As they approached his bedroom he caught hold of a statue his sister had given him and threw it at them, smashing it at their feet, startling them somewhat.

Graduate of NYC Police Department, 1969

Meanwhile I had entered the lobby, hands in my pocket, not too concerned about anything. I'll always remember this Clare man was mopping the floor, when these two guys ran down the stairs. I put up my hand to block them and one of them slashed my palm open with something silver, which I presumed was a knife, but turned out to be a twelve-inch screwdriver. In the ensuing scuffle anyhow, I had to shoot at one of them, and handcuff the other. Two days after I was shot at myself down on 100th Street and all of a sudden the department takes notice of me. How could I be involved in two shootings in the one week when some people could go thirty years without a mishap? But everyone was carrying a gun back then. It's not as bad now, even in the South Bronx and places like that; you wouldn't get as many guns.

We had a great social life. When I came out first it was the Jaeger House and then the Red Mill there where the Cross Bronx crosses Jerome Avenue. It's a jungle now, but really it was even that time too. There was a whole gang of us that hung around together. There was the Casey's, Pete Brennan, Ritchie Flood, and then the girls would be in a big group too. The dancehalls were great places for meeting people and everyone was just one big happy family. The women and the men weren't just there to date someone; they also wanted to make friends. I think it was a lot easier to meet people at that time because everyone went to the same places. Nowadays there are just bars and they're scattered all over the place. Also there was a ton of people coming out, whole families would be sitting around the table at the dance and every week there was a new face. The bar scene today is a tougher deal altogether. I feel sorry for girls nowadays especially if they don't drink or if they don't want a man who does. Where are they going to meet somebody?

I met my wife in the Red Mill; Miriam O'Rourke was her name, from Leitrim. She worked in the telephone company there on Broad Street in the repairs department. She said you'd give the guys the complaint slip and they'd drop them on the floor on the way out the door and then you'd have the people yelling at you the day after as to why nobody came to fix their phones.

But some of those companies only gave the lower paid jobs to the Irish. Back then they complained about the brogue, now they can't even get someone who speaks English. It was the same with Con Edison where a lot of my friends worked and became big bosses eventually. But they say it doesn't matter a damn now because people don't have respect for their superiors anymore, not like in our day when the boss was treated like God, he didn't have to dirty his hands.

I wasn't here that long when we got married. She snatched me out of the cradle. A lot of people got married young then. There are pros and cons. I now have a sixteen year old granddaughter, so it's nice to be still young when they're coming along. There's now a Denis Mulcahy IV, which is surprising really, as John had always been the prominent name in the family. When I took my granddaughter to our local graveyard in County Cork we could trace six generations of our family buried there.

My father came from Rockchapel, but we grew up in a little village called Meelin. We had a small piece of land and my father also worked on the roads with Cork County Council. It wasn't much of a job, not well paid, but just because he had a job he wasn't eligible for much else in the way of benefits from the State or anything. You'd be better off on the dole back in Ireland then. I think it's changed somewhat now. I went to the local National School and worked on the small farm.

There were six of us: five boys and one girl; she was the baby. She's a Mrs. McAuliffe in Newmarket now. Michael has the home place; his twin, Tom, lives up in Rockland County. John has retired from the Transit Authority and is now in Pennsylvania. Pat went home from here and raises racehorses in Rockchapel, where he inherited an aunt's farm. His son works undercover here, but his two daughters stayed in Ireland. Pat was always a farmer at heart even though he spent years with the NYPD. He is very involved in Comhaltas Ceolteóirí Eireann an organization that promotes Irish traditional music at home, even though he doesn't play an instrument. About two years ago, a Japanese film company wanted to make a movie about this young talented Japanese girl to see if she could be immersed in another culture in the course of a week. So where did they pick? Only Pat's place. His wife nearly went mad with this little one out gathering the eggs with her every morning. By the end of the week Dana, who also took part, had taught her how to step dance, sing, and play music, the whole lot. They even filmed Pat giving blood and drinking the traditional pint of Guinness afterwards, as they thought this was unbelievable altogether that a national blood transfusion center would hand out beer to their donors. Pat has a video of the movie, but of course it's in Japanese with English subtitles. It's still fun to watch though.

With my brothers, Pat and John, I started Project Children in 1975 when the Troubles in Northern Ireland were at its height. We would watch it on the TV every night and the thing that got us the most was how the little children were affected—throwing stones at soldiers, being hit by plastic bullets, lighting bonfires with bombed out cars, losing a parent to prison, being caught up in the danger and the din of marches.

We started kicking around ideas as to what we could do to help. We decided to bring some of them out here for some peace and quiet and to show them that it might be possible for them to get along in a different environment. We raised some money and we took six children out that year and placed them with host families in Greenwood Lake, New York, where we lived. It's amazing that the first six are all still friends today and were at each other's weddings.

Since then we have hosted twenty thousand children through families all over the country. Some of them have come back year after year and have ended up attending high school and college here, going on to be doctors and lawyers. Now we work with university students setting them up as interns. The Washington-Ireland Program (WIP) recruits a select group of students from Northern Ireland and places them with companies all over the United States. There's a girl living in Woodlawn now and she's just become an attorney. You see once they take the Bar Exam they can apply for visas. I will be bringing about forty students here this summer and six of them are studying Law and if they want to take the Bar they can do so and stay here legally. They are allowed a year's study overseas after graduating in Ireland. These kids have achieved goals that would not have been possible thirty years ago in Northern Ireland.

In the beginning we worked with schools, priests, and social workers. It was hard at first, as people were afraid we were raising money for guns, now we're getting funds from the U.S. federal government. I have a letter ready to be sent to the Senate Committee on Appropriations requesting funds. Among the signatories are Senators Schumer, Kennedy, and Clinton. Senator Hillary Clinton has been very good to us. She's a great lady. I went to Ireland with her husband eight times. I was on his first tour back there and was astonished at how much ground he covered, he'd wear you down. We placed some interns in his office in the White House, and Hillary has taken some too. There's a picture of me taken with him in the Oval Office. That's how I ended up accompanying him to Ireland after being picked as one of the top fifty Irish people for that year so it was a pure fluke how it happened. President Reagan was also very good to us and always sponsored a child. We would receive his check every year for $600 out of his own personal account.

The best part about Project Children though is bringing people together. When you hook people up, amazing things happen. There's a picture of Peter Rainey from Newry. He was one of the participants in our congressional program one summer and ended up playing tennis with President Clinton. He stayed at the home of Bob Kyle, an economist at the White House, and met the President when he went to work one day with Bob. I still keep in touch with Peter and visit him every time I go to Ireland. Another year Michael Keaton's, ex-wife, Caroline Douglas, hosted a kid, James Dawson, who is still friendly with their son, Sean. In fact, Sean flew to Belfast not so long ago to be best man at James's wedding. Roma Downey was also very supportive. She did a whole show of Touched by an Angel based on our work. I'm very friendly with her mother, Kitty, and talk to her all the time on the phone.

I could tell you incredible stories about my experiences with this venture. There was a family in Michigan who took this youngster one time called Paddy McGuigan. They stayed in contact for a while and then the Michigan family broke up and lost touch with Paddy. But he could never get them out of his mind, especially the woman of the house, whom he had regarded as a second mother. She ended up very down and out and was going through a very tough time when out of the blue she received a call from Paddy. He had got her number from one of the old neighbors where they used to live and decided to contact her. He sent her a ticket and insisted that she come to Belfast to visit him. She said it had been one of her worst days when she heard from Paddy and that he had turned her life around, just as she had done for him twenty years previously.

It's amazing how things have changed really. When you think of it people were willing to let their kids travel thousands of miles just to give them a better chance, even Protestants sent their children knowing they would probably be staying with Catholic families. Anything was better than staying where they were. At first we were criticized in the North for not bringing the children into the South, for not spending our money in Ireland, but this had been tried already without much success. The problem was they were brought down in big groups and the organizers lost control. The kids went mad throughout the country. Over here we place them in individual homes. We meet with the heads of household and discuss with them what they are most comfortable with. At first families were more interested in Catholic children, but then they didn't mind after a while. Sure all of the kids were the same in the end, no matter where they came from. They sometimes talk about their experiences in the Six Counties and Protestant children are surprised at the Catholics' stories about being stopped at checkpoints just because of their Catholic sounding names. I could relate to that, as when my daughter lived in Derrybeg, which was a big Catholic area, we were always nabbed at the checkpoint on the Dublin Road when we were going up to visit her. When they would hear that we were going to Derrybeg they would always detain us, whereas if we said Newry or somewhere else, we were sent on ahead. The treatment you received from the Army always depended on what area you were going into.

It's amazing really what has happened in the North of Ireland. When we started off first in 1975, the province was full of Catholic ghettos, East Belfast, the Falls Road, and Divis Flats. Then when the hi-tech computer companies came in first to the North, the Catholics grabbed the jobs in the technology industry, as they were the only ones available. The Protestants were already working in these older jobs like shipbuilding and the Civil Service that were restricted to them, and were left behind when their jobs became redundant. They did not benefit from the Celtic Tiger. In fact, the Government has just approved eight million pounds to improve the Protestant ghettos. So when the Catholics went into technology, they started making a ton of money, buying houses, raising families and doing very well. It's interesting to note too that it is mainly college students we are transporting now. That would have never happened in the 70s.

Another great achievement has been teaming up with Habitat for Humanity to build houses for low-income families in this country. It is uncanny that American people are now seeking help from the young natives of Northern Ireland, and it is a great opportunity for the latter to give back to the community that once helped them. We have chapters all over the country. The kids who work with Habitat usually have trades, but here they can hone old skills and learn new ones. They come for two months and are on leave from training programs at home.

With Habitat, however, no one specializes. All of them have to lay brick, read a blueprint, put up insulation, and more. We had a group of kids come over to build a house in Montana for a woman who was third generation Irish. She was a single mother with two kids. In two weeks they had the house finished and it was an eight-week program. Now we had to figure out what to do with them. So we approached Habitat and they had another piece of land up in Helena, Montana, beside a Veteran Hospital. The idea was to provide housing for the families of the Veterans who were hospitalized. They had the land, the materials, now they had the work force; all they lacked was the money to fund the whole project.

Some creative writer in the local newspaper wrote an article about their plight, telling them how these young people from both sides of the Northern Ireland conflict were prepared to build this shelter and within two days $33,000 was raised. They ended up building a ten-unit shelter that was opened by the Governor of Montana. It's a great experience for these kids who come from a place that was once oppressed and downtrodden and now they are helping others in the same predicament.

Another time we were doing a job up in Newbury and instead of placing the recruits with families I put them all up in a big Christian Brothers school there across the river. They had a dayroom where they could watch TV and videos, there was a picnic area, and they each had their own little bedroom. I was able to put eight kids there. There were some women who came in to cook for the Brothers and I gave them a little extra to provide for our lads too. In fact, a couple of them were from Donegal and they would take the train down to the Bronx on a Sunday and play football for Donegal in Gaelic Park. At first, I was worried about telling the Protestant kids that they would be staying in a Monastery, but of course, that didn't faze them at all. It's all about bringing people together.

Sometimes you have to keep on top of them on the plane coming over, as it takes them a little while to mix, and then you'll have the usual loudmouths who will insist on singing their rival songs and that, and upsetting the others, but usually once they settle down, they all get on great together. But, when we started first, in a typical Catholic home in the North, the father was in prison, the mother ruled the home with an iron fist, kept the kids fed and clean, sent them to the school and held everything together longing for the day when the husband would get out. Now they're from broken homes, there's no father image in the house, they're just like the rest of the world. They may have a better standard of living, but the family structure is gone now just like all over Ireland.

It has changed so much since we left.

Den and I went back after a few years, but prior to that people hardly went back at all. There was probably more money by the time we came and then of course, you had the planes. So of course we hired a car and visited all these girls from Clare and Mayo that were going back at the same time. That's what was great about over here too; we met people from all over Ireland whom we would not have met had we stayed at home. I suppose people found us changed, and we had changed too. Travel does that to you. It's an education in itself. You're thrown in with people of all nationalities and backgrounds and it broadens your horizons a little. Travel is a great education, there's no doubt about that. There was always one guy who got the place at home and the women got married and the youngest would also end up staying at home, but there wasn't enough for everybody so the rest had to leave.

We weren't poor; at least we didn't know we were poor; we didn't know there was no money. If you have food and a roof over your head you don't realize that you're poor. I suppose my mother was heartbroken when her children left. In a way it was easier to raise those big families back then because you got rid of them before the teenage, troubled years began. I was gone to England by sixteen, arrived here when I was seventeen; my wife too. Our parents only had us for the good times, the childhood years, but it's only now that I realize that they must have missed us too. I couldn't imagine letting my sixteen-year-old granddaughter go off halfway across the world, never to see her again. Indeed, I could hardly let my son go and he is forty years of age. Then, when you think of it, in Project Children they let their kids off at eight or nine for six weeks at a time, but back then anything was better than where they were.

When I left home first, I hardly knew where the North was. Then there was a bit of a connection through my wife's people, but really I didn't know a thing about it until the Troubles began. The little bit of history we might have picked up at school certainly didn't cover much about the Six Counties, let me tell you. People ask me how long are we going to keep doing it and I say as long as I have the money. After September 11, I thought the numbers would drop, but amazingly enough we got more requests than ever. I suppose when you think about it, those people are used to situations like that. They've grown up with problems all their lives. For instance, Holy Cross School in Belfast is a very troubled spot. I've been bringing children over from Holy Cross for thirty years. It is definitely more peaceful there now. Like I said, when you take away poverty you find peace.

You have men who spent long years in Long Kesh who are now back home and settled into the community and trying to make a difference once again, only this time through a more peaceful process. You have Michael Culbert, who spent eighteen years inside, now training the Antrim footballers. He drew this most amazing Map of Ireland with a Magic Marker, painstakingly including every town and county in Gaelic. He did it all by hand, with the aid of a grid, to the exact specification and I've had several copies made and distributed them all over the country here. In fact, I had a call the other day from the producers of this new movie that Colin Farrell is making, Pain and Glory, all about an Irish-American police family, and they want to have the map put on the wall of a bar where a lot of the scenes are taking place.

Michael Culbert is now a Social Worker and he works with ex-prisoners who are on drugs or whose homes were broken up because of their internment. He himself and a lot of people I know up there don't have any hang-ups because of their experiences and are now willing to help others. His wife, Monica, is very active too in Project Children. She raised her two sons in a terrible area, worked as a schoolteacher, yet donated an endless amount of time helping us while Michael was in Long Kesh. I went in to see him one time while he was on the Blanket Protest. I would get into a lot of trouble later for that when I joined the Bomb Squad. They had monitored all of my movements, most of which I wasn't even aware of, as of course they were concerned that my knowledge would benefit certain factions in Northern Ireland. I was never approached though, even though everyone would have been well aware of my background.

It was a pure miracle that I wasn't near the Twin Towers on 9/11. Every couple of years we have to do courses to keep up our certification even though half the guys who are certifying us have never been out on the streets themselves. Anyhow, we have to do it. My partner at the time, Danny Claude Richards, and myself had just put in a lot of hours at the U.S. Open and after that there was a week that was quiet so I put in my name to take one of these courses. Usually you have to give quite a bit of notice, but I called one of the big FBI boys down in Alabama, the location of the test site, whom we had taken care of in New York a few months previously, and he got me a seat in the class for that Monday morning. Otherwise it would have been my first day back on regular beat there in the West Village, about two blocks from the Towers. I would have been there in the thick of it, just like Claude was. He was last seen running back into the lobby with a stretcher for a woman who had hurt her back, my partner, Danny Claude Richards, may he Rest in Peace.

Meanwhile, down in Alabama I was worried about my two police force children, Maureen and Sean, who weren't near the scene at all, completely forgetting that Denis Jr. was actually working in the World Trade Center that day. He had been there too in 1993, when his Company had offices between the 97th and 104th floors, but after that bombing his female colleagues wouldn't return there so they moved over to the Financial Center. He was about to enter the building when he saw the second plane drive through it and he immediately turned on his heels, hopped on a boat and returned home.

Tara, who was on her way to Pace University, had just come up out of the subway, met the guys from the Bomb Squad, who got her out of there, and she ran all the way up to Eighteenth Street, where she stayed in her apartment for five days. It's amazing really, how things happen, there was I a member of the Bomb Squad, and a frequent traveler to the Six Counties in Northern Ireland, which was a hot pool for bomb makers, and I missed one of the world's major explosions taking place on my own doorstep.

I think New York is a unique place and I would never leave it. For such a big city, you can meet people here for such a short time, but become very close to them. They would help you out so much without really thinking about it. Back home it's a little bit different. It's changing there too, but I'm not sure it's for the better. Of course when you come over first you're always talking about going home, it's still home. But life goes on and you have a family. I live in a little town up in Greenwood Lake that's just like a little Irish town; it's probably more Irish than a lot of little towns today in Ireland, because we have kept up all the traditions, some of which have now gone by the wayside back there.

The seasons are great here; you always have summer to look forward to. It keeps you young; you don't realize you're aging in New York. I retired from the police force recently, but I've gone back to work now two days a week with a security company. The lure of the city just drew me back there. I love the buzz downtown, but I love to get back upstate too for the peace and quiet, so I have the best of both worlds.

I was back in Meelin recently and visited a local restaurant. This very pretty young waitress, with blond hair and blue eyes, approached my table, and I wondered if I knew her father, or who her grandparents might have been. Imagine my surprise to learn that she was from Latvia. I couldn't figure out how she found her way to Lower Cork, all the way down to Meelin, a place we had all run out of nearly fifty years before.

Interviewed at Fitzie's Bar, McLean Avenue, Yonkers, New York; April 13, 2006

L. to R. Miriam, Liam Neeson, Denis, Patti, Conor & Steven McDonald: Irish America Magazine Top 100, 1996

Mary Woods, 1962

I flew from Dublin to New York in July 1962 having traveled down from County Armagh with my mother, uncle, and grandfather. I was terribly lonesome saying goodbye, terribly lonesome. I came to my Aunt Julia. My sister, Ann, was here, but she was married, so I was still lonely. My Aunt took me down to an agency and I got a job as a kitchen maid in Far Hills, New Jersey, with a family who worked for President Kennedy. I was even lonelier down there and only stayed a short time.

My next job was with a Jewish lady with two children and she was a horrible woman, I thought, a horrible woman. She sat me down on a stool and gave me two hot dogs and sure I had never seen a hot dog before and I didn't know what to do with it. Her two little girls were there and then she had me make the bed and she stood at the foot with her arms folded, and sure I hadn't a clue how to make the bed properly, me just over from Ireland. I'd never made a bed before. Sure I muddled around and did the best I could, but she followed me around all day watching everything I did.

Then she went out and took the two children with her, but before she left she showed me my room. Sure when I saw the tiny little cell with the little bed, I knew there was no way I could sleep there. When she came back I told her I was leaving and she was shocked, but I said I couldn't stay that I knew I wouldn't be happy. I walked out the door and looked up and down the street and didn't know where I was. I got as far as 59th Street in the end and found my way home from there because Aunt Julia had showed me the way the day before. I was a bit nervous really because she was kind of old-fashioned and I thought she'd give out to me for leaving the job. But she was really nice and said that I was right to leave if I didn't like it.

I went down to the agency myself the next day and got a job with Governor Harriman's brother. When I came home and told Julia where I was going to work she was as delighted as if I'd been made Mayor of New

York. "Oh, that's great, Mary," she said, "They're the kind of people you should be working with, not those cheap ones like the other one."

The Harrimans lived a kind of a crazy life. The breakfast was served to them in silver dishes at six o'clock in the morning, so we had to be in the kitchen by five thirty. There were English and Scottish girls working there too and a couple of Irish. I was the downstairs scullery maid and it was my job to set the table for the help. There was this one from Tipperary, one of the personal maids upstairs, and every day she'd come down for lunch at the dot of one o'clock and she'd inspect the plate and the knife and fork before she used it. She'd never speak to me, but sometimes she'd go over and wash the plate again and of course I was real nervous, me only over from Ireland, and I'd be thinking I had done something wrong; that I hadn't washed the plates properly. I said to the cook one day, "Why does she do that?" And the cook said, "Because she's crazy." She was always checking her stocks and counting her money. She was a real spinsterish one and had nothing better to do, but count her money. When President Kennedy passed the Bill that all interest on savings accounts was to be taxed, she nearly went crazy altogether. She was an awful wicked woman.

Mary (left) with brother, Michael, and sister, Anne

You could work in those houses for years and never meet the people who owned them. They lived in a completely different part. I don't even know what Mr. Harriman did or how he made his living. They had these big tapestries on the walls and we weren't allowed touch to them. It was very hard for some of the girls, especially the ones that didn't get married. They became very angry working in those big houses for years.

I remember going out to East Hampton to the Harriman's summerhouse and I had never seen the ocean before. I loved the water and couldn't be kept out of it. The first day I went down there they told me to be careful not to get burned. I didn't know what they were talking about, sure I didn't know anything about the sun, and sure enough I got awfully sun burnt.

It was a great experience really when you think about it even though you were lonesome. And sure I used to be putting the dollars away. All the other girls spent their money on clothes and they'd have trunks of clothes, and it was an awful problem really when they'd be moving from job to job, but I hardly bought any. I didn't go dancing that much either; I just wasn't comfortable with it. I did go to the Laurel Eye a few times. That was in the German section—German food and German fellows. They were more the executive type and looked down on us if they thought we were maids. "Did you walk the dog before you came out?" They'd ask us. "Actually, no," one of the girls said to them one night. "I'm a pencil sharpener for Con Edison."

I think for me it was the best thing I ever did was to come to America. Because if I hadn't come to America, if I'd stayed around home, I'd never have married, I'd never even have kissed a man, never mind married one. I don't think I'd ever have done anything like that. I was here and nobody knew me. At home they were always talking about you, what you wore, who you were, and I hated it.

I was born in the village of Ballybinaby, a few miles outside Crossmaglen. My parents were both from Armagh and settled on a small farm. The oldest of four children, I was terribly bashful when I was growing up. And the many beatings I got. I remember if I got a new coat I wouldn't want to go to Mass in case people would be watching me. Or if I did wear it I'd want to sit in the back seat. I remember my father following me over to the Church and a stick at my behind every crack he could get at me. I don't know what that was; there was something in me. I didn't want anyone to know I had a new coat. My sister, Ann, was the exact opposite. She was a devil. She'd take my new coat and march up the aisle of the Church hoping everyone would see her. Ann was an awful character. She had a job in Dundalk and she'd come down the road on a Monday evening in a new suit from Modern Fashions with two big roses in the lapels and my mother would see her and run for the stick to get at her. Ann was great fun. We were completely opposite, and my mother was always comparing us.

My father was a lovely man who died suddenly when we were coming home from Crossmaglen with the cattle. He sat down in a ditch and said he did not feel well. I hailed down a passerby to give him a lift and continued on home with the cattle. He died the next day from thrombosis. My mother sent me to Navan to the French Sisters of Charity to learn economics, a fancy name for housework. We had to save the tea leaves all week and clean the rugs with them on a Saturday. After two years there I got a job with the Master who had taught me in National School whom I had been terrified of because he would beat us with a rod of Malayan rubber. The girl that had previously worked for him and his wife had got pregnant and was fired instantly. I managed to last in that household for two years until I came to America.

We had good times though growing up. I can remember the awful snowstorm of 1947. The greatest thing about it was that we were off school for weeks. We had a lot of fun sliding on the streets and the hills, and going out skating on the lake. One day the ice started to crack in the middle of the lake and people from the town had to come out and rescue us. We'd go paddling in the river too; making believe we were at the beach or something. Oh! I used love going down to the river on a Sunday. I remember having a lot of fun at the trashing, getting rides on the hay stacks and gathering blackberries in the summer time and we used to try and make jam after.

I remember New Year's night, 1957, when Sean South and Fergus O'Hanlon were shot. It came over the radio and we were all around it, listening. There was talk of nothing else for a long time. I remember the beautiful trees in the Protestant houses. The Protestants were very rich and they always had the nicest trees. We'd lie down on the grass and look up at the branches and sometimes we'd get high just staring up at the tree, which was always full of crows and jackdaws. We'd play school with the jackdaws pointing at them with a stick the way the teacher did to us in school and calling out, "One and One, Two and Two, Three and Three." Sure they didn't pay us a bit of heed, but we thought they did. We were cruel back then too because sometimes we'd rob the crows' nests and break their eggs. Then the lads would pelt us with the eggs when we were going through the graveyard. We'd drop frogs down their trousers and you'd want to see the lads leaping. You'd never see frogs in Ireland anymore, or rabbits, or cuckoos or the corncrake. The combine harvester killed all that. Sure when you heard the cry of the cuckoo long ago you knew spring had arrived.

I knew my husband from home; he was from the same place. He came out to America years later, when he was thirty three. I remember Aunt Katie calling me one day and saying, "Guess who's here, Peter Woods, why don't you come up and see him?" I went up to see him and it started from there, our little romance. It made a difference that I knew him before and that I knew his mother and everything. I felt much more comfortable and we used to have a lot of fun together. He was good for me. I was about twenty-seven when I met him. I remember the day we got married he got up on the stage and he was singing this song and then he ended off with, "Mary had a little lamb and she had a bear. I never saw her little lamb and I never saw her bear. Maybe I will tonight!" The whole place exploded. Everyone was laughing and clapping and hooting and I hadn't a clue what they were laughing at. So I asked Ann and she didn't know and afterwards she told me she would have died, that she would have ran out of the place. Then her husband, Frank, he was a kidder, he told me. He couldn't believe I didn't know. Sure we were so innocent back then. We hadn't a clue. The men weren't much better although they probably had a little bit more of a clue than we did. It was different times back then. It's gone the reverse now.

All those people are gone now. Peter is dead, as is Frank, and Ann is in a nursing home in Pennsylvania. My two brothers are back in Armagh and I still go home occasionally to visit them. My sister-in-law was very good to my mother when she was dying and I will always be grateful to her for that. Peter and I had three children. Mary lives in Pearl River, David is in Croton, and Michael moved back to Ireland. I have seven beautiful grandchildren, the youngest of whom is six months and the most beautiful, laid back baby you've ever seen. Her name is Maeve after Maeve Binchy. Mary was astray in the head about Maeve Binchy. Old age crept up very quickly. I wasn't expecting it this sudden. I still miss Peter even though he's dead three years. Still, I do believe that it was the greatest thing that ever happened, for me to come to America.

Recorded at Aisling Irish Community Center,
creative writing workshops, Yonkers, NY;
November 2005 - May 2006

At home in Woodlawn

Sean Fleming, 1963

I came to America on November 2, 1963, twenty days before John F. Kennedy's assassination. As a kid of sixteen I didn't realize the gravity of the situation. Of course, Kennedy was such a prince as far as Irish society was concerned, but I hadn't realized the depths he touched with other cultures until I saw grown men on 42nd Street crying their eyes out. They were of all nationalities and creeds—Hispanics, Italians, African-Americans—he transcended all races and religions. I was working in a small supermarket over in Queens, King Kullen, and everybody was talking about it. Because not only was John F. Kennedy dead, which was remarkable in itself, but the President of the United States had been assassinated, and that was huge altogether.

Curiosity brought me here more than anything else. I had been working in the Hotel Europa in Killarney. My home town was different than most rural areas in Ireland at the time in that it accommodated tourists from all over the world, especially Americans, and there was always plenty of work, especially during the summer season. Five miles away it would have been a different story altogether. We were well acquainted with Americans. I had always wanted to see that great country they came from. Also I had two uncles here at the time and the third one, Pat, came out on the same plane as me. He came from a big family. My mother was the eldest and he being my youngest uncle was only a year older than my eldest brother; that happened in a lot of families back in Ireland, where sometimes the nephew might be even older than the uncle. Pat and I headed straight for 3216 Bainbridge Avenue, on 204th Street, where his two brothers lived. And of course, I thought I knew everything. Like Bob Dylan, "I was so much older then; I'm younger than that now."

It was extremely exciting. As luck would have it, my uncle knew a man from Donegal, Hughie Devlin, who picked us up in a convertible at the airport. It was an Oldsmobile or a Buick or something like that, but what a great introduction to the Bronx. Bainbridge was full of Irish. In our building alone it was all Irish. Just to give you an example of what it was like at that time: We were living on the third floor and there was another group of guys on the fourth floor and one morning one of them needed a shave, so he swung out the window of his apartment, ran down the fire escape, leapt in through one of our windows and borrowed some razor blades. All of this took place without our knowing and we wouldn't have batted an eyelid at it. So there we were, three brothers and a nephew, ready to take on the world.

I had been very involved in the Irish traditional music scene before I came over, not professionally, but, nevertheless I had been playing a lot and it was automatically assumed that I would continue to do so here, which I did very soon after I arrived. At the time the city was hopping with Irish dancehalls. And no matter what type of band was playing, be it rock 'n roll or country 'n western, during the course of the night a traditional group would play for about forty to forty-five minutes and everybody would look forward to getting up for the Siege of Ennis, Stack of Barley, Walls of Limerick, and perhaps a few waltzes or what have you. Of course the Siege of Ennis was a great one for getting everybody up on the floor and you knew you were going to meet loads of women. You'd be looking down the line to see which ones you'd be swinging with and if you saw someone you liked on the other side, you'd be asking the guy beside you to swap.

The first place that I played in was the Red Mill on 174th Street and Jerome Avenue. It was owned by two guys from Kerry; one of them was Dan Kiely who is now some kind of a politician in Ballybunion, and Tim, a brother of Mickey Moynihan who has a bar up there somewhere around Katonah Avenue called the Aqueduct. The original Aqueduct was over on Aqueduct Avenue, a walking-only street off Fordham Road that covered the Croton Aqueduct, which ran water all the way from the Croton Reservoir up in Westchester down to New York City.

Tim, who owned the Red Mill, was a real entrepreneur and a bit of a character too. It only dawned on me recently how it got its name, and has nothing whatever to do with there being a mill around the Bronx. But when you think about it, it's the exact translation of that famous Parisian nightclub that housed Les Follies Bergere—Le Moulin Rouge—the Red Mill. Now wasn't he brilliant to come up with that? All those nice Irish Catholic girls long ago had no idea that they were entering a ballroom named after a burlesque cancan club. Meanwhile, Moynihan was the kind of guy that if you met him you'd think he was the parish priest. There were so many sides to him; a real character.

Anyhow these are the things I think about when I can't sleep at night. Another bright idea I came up with during a recent fit of insomnia was the name for my next album—Under the Table. No, it has nothing whatsoever to do with drinking, but is rather more cryptic like the Red Mill story. I first started singing when I was about five years old, and when the insurance man, Sean Coffey, called to the door, he would always ask me to sing him a song. What a lovely, lovely man. He's still alive. He must be in his eighties now. There's something about the way older people treat little children; if they're kind to you then you'll remember them all of your life. Sean would always ask me to sing for him anyhow and the only way I could do it was from under the table. I would sing it fine, but I was very shy, so there I'd be crouched underneath my grandmother's table bursting out The Wild Colonial Boy or something like that. So that's the title for the album I'm working on now. My last album was called Blonde because everything in my house in blond; my wife is blond, my kids are blond, the dog is blond. The dog's name is phonetically pronounced Gyre, but I don't know how to spell it. It's supposed to mean male dog in Irish; an old flame from Mayo told me that once. Our last dog, Madra, was his great, great, great grand uncle.

Anyhow I started singing at a very young age, and my grandmother always gave me a mouth organ every Christmas. She obviously saw that I had some talent. I can remember vividly examining the little holes and thinking that it would be a great place for storing sand, but I finally found other uses for it. My father played the accordion, or as he called it, the melodeon, in the parish hall in Kilcummin just outside Killarney. He kept an old, broken down one in the kitchen closet or press, as we called it, and I ventured in there one time and took down the accordion. I was very, very surprised that I could transpose what I had learnt on the mouth organ on to this instrument too.

At the time I was attending National School at the Presentation Monastery in Killarney. Of course, before that we had gone to the nuns. The first teacher I had was a wonderful, warm, soft woman; the next one was her pole opposite. She was actually the cause of me disliking school to a really deep degree and I hardly forgave her for that for nearly thirty years. I finally let it go. In the Monastery we had a Brother Eamon who loved Irish and spoke it as much as he possibly could and taught in it a good bit too, the value of which I didn't really appreciate at the time, but now being a Nationalist myself I can understand how deep that love of language can be. Then we had a Brother Finian who would have a lot more influence on my life than I realized at the time when he started up an accordion band.

Up to this I had been only exposed to the melodeon, which is played by a more traditional type of musician, whereas the piano accordion is a more classical instrument and not as conducive to the Irish music. When my parents saw the direction I was going in they were concerned that I would forget all of my Irish tunes, but I was able to manipulate this new instrument to some degree that I could manage the traditional music on it too. Brother Finian also taught us the basic theory of music, which I still use to this day.

The first time I played in the Red Mill, I just joined in with a group of musicians who were resident there at the time. One of them was a former Kilfenora Céili Band member. I never played with Joe Cunningham, but I played with some amazing musicians. Oh! I played with Joe Banjo Burke, with Andy McGann. I played with Johnny Cronin, the great fiddle player and truly an adventurous soul. He got married late in life to Maureen McGlynn who was at least twenty or twenty-five years younger than him. She was very influential as an Irish step-dancing teacher and had a lot of pupils before even Riverdance became popular. I played with Joe Nellany and Joe Madden—Joannie Madden's father—and countless others.

You see in the sixties there was a tremendous amount of Irish people here, just off the boat, and Irish music to some degree was like French wine. When a blight hit the French fields one time, the vineyards weren't affected, but nonetheless they uprooted the vines and took them to America where they were replanted and raised to maturity, and then were uprooted again and brought back to French soil for harvesting. In some ways the same thing happened to traditional Irish music; I mean it had almost died in Ireland back then; they were all into the showbands over there. James Keane will tell you that he was actually embarrassed to be seen walking down the street back home with an accordion. But here it was blossoming. It was a wonderful time. All the great musicians were over here. I got to play with some of the greatest players of all time. I mean, Joe Burke from Galway, to me, is one of the finest accordion players probably that ever lived. We were subjected to the crème de la crème of music and of course from that came another generation of absolutely magnificent players like Eileen Ivors and Joannie Madden, all children of that crop of great players that came over from Ireland. Even Riverdance when you think of it, the two main stars were offspring of Irish immigrants. We had become more Irish than the people we left behind. And it happened with other cultures too. Chinatown boomed and Little Italy, all because everybody wanted a taste of home.

The first one really to revive an interest in Irish music back there, before Christy Moore even, was Johnny McEvoy when he had that big Number 1 hit with Mursheen Durkin. He was the first guy to have a charted hit in Ireland with a folk song. Then, of course, you had The Johnston's, which Paul Brady came out of and Mick Maloney came out of, all great players, then you had Planxty and the whole lot started up again. Those guys were so good.

I was working during the day at all sorts of jobs from construction to fixing cars to painting, whatever came my way, and playing mostly at the weekends; Friday night, Saturday night; and then of course, Sunday was a huge day in the Irish circle. Sunday was probably the biggest day ever just like in Ireland. Everything was transported from Ireland. In the rural areas Sunday was the big day. So here too Sunday was the big night in the Jaeger House and the Red Mill. Then I went from playing traditional to rock 'n roll. I met two guys over in Queens, Tommy Sullivan and Martin Quinn and we started a rock 'n roll band called The Rocketeers. I was the lead singer and played keyboard, having had some knowledge from the piano accordion, Tommy played guitar and Quinn played base, and I think Tony James was the drummer. That was my first sort of sojourn into the rock 'n roll field. Our circuit was the Red Mill, the Ambassador Ballroom, which was owned by the same guy out on Queens Boulevard, the Jaeger House, and we finally wound up as the resident band in City Center, which was on 55th Street between 6th and 7th Avenue in New York. It had originally been City Center Ballet, but part of it was leased out by Bill Fuller, husband of Carmel Quinn. We played in Gaelic Park a few times, but that was sort of a different scene, as there was a guy called Mickey Carton who had the concession up there for years. Anyhow we were a bit more adventurous, and probably more cutting edge for Gaelic Park because a lot of the people up there were more into the country vein, whereas we would play stuff directly off Radio Luxembourg, like The Kinks, The Beatles, Gerry & The Pacemakers, all that sort of stuff.

Bill Fuller was one step more than a Nationalist; he was a Kerry man. And he loved the fact that I, the lead singer in our band, was also from Kerry. We played with all of the big bands back then—Brendan Bowyer, The Miami, Joe Dolan & The Drifters. My God! We played with everyone, The Royal Blues, The Kerry Blues, The Clipper Carlton, any band that was of any note at all back in Ireland was brought over at specific times of the year, and of course they packed the place. City Center was huge; they could pack about three thousand people in there. The normal procedure was that the resident band would play for about an hour at the beginning of the night, then the big band would take over and do their stint, and then the resident would end off for another half an hour or so. But, when I played, Bill would insist that the Irish band would play for about an hour first and then he'd put us on in between to give us more exposure and the big band would end off then for another hour. He'd whisper at me from the side of the stage, "Go up there, Sean, and show them how it's done." He was funny really how he approached it. So I was exposed to some of the best talent in Ireland at the time, and there were some great players, great players.

After about two years I went home on a visit, and from then on I think I went home every single year until about five years ago. Sometimes I went home five times in a year. I suppose I had the money; I wasn't pocket poor, that's for sure. Also, I didn't get married straight away like a lot of them; I was in my thirties, so I had all my wild oats sewn before that. I traveled to a lot of other places too, through the music, outside the music, and in search of music. One of my favorite spots was Montserrat, known as the Emerald Isle of the Caribbean. One of the reasons is because it is a lush, green island and also because sixty percent of the names are Irish. The neighboring island is St. Kitt's, which was used by the English as a Van Diemen's Land for Irish people who had been kicking up at home and they were transported there as prisoners, but because the islanders there didn't want them around they threw them over onto Montserrat, where they settled.

I also traveled all over the world with the Irish Tourist Board on ASTA conventions, the American Society of Travel Agents, I suppose because I had my finger on the pulse of what Irish America wanted, and also through my entertaining we could sell Ireland too. I would sing to huge audiences and for Tourism Ireland, as it was later called; this was a huge plus to have the biggest night at an ASTA convention.

I did an audition for the Merv Griffin show and got on and had the most amount of mail the first few times I appeared on it. I did seven shows probably in the space of a year and a half, which was quite a lot. Actually the first show I did I was taken out of the audience, really I was a plant, but people weren't supposed to know that at the time. Merv would pretend to pick someone at random, but it had all been rehearsed beforehand. I sang Danny Boy and I had never sung it before, ever, ever live and it went down great. People loved it. He had a nationwide audience of about two million at the time, a lot of people to be exposed to in a way, but I didn't have any management and didn't make as much out of it as I really could have in a way. Also I found out later that there were a lot of people who were not willing to help. There is a lot of jealousy in that business and people are not always willing to step up to the plate and help you, even though they would probably have made as much out of it as I did.

I was here for the best part of five years when I was drafted into the army. I was two years more than the average age for the soldiers, which was nineteen. There was even a song written by Paul Hardcastle, called 19, which was more like a rap anthem than anything else, containing statistics on the war with different voices coming in, but it was very powerful. The title comes from the fact that nineteen was the average for young American kids to go to Vietnam, whereas in World War II, it was twenty-six. One of the lines goes something like that it didn't matter that young men who have been to Vietnam came back with psychological cuts and bruises, what would bother him more would be if they came back with none. If something like that doesn't affect you, then there's something radically wrong with society. There were two ways that you could not be drafted and that was if you had a high number, or if you had inadvertently forgotten to register. There was a certain amount of allotments for each day and it went by your birthday I seem to remember, anyhow if your number was one hundred for that day; that meant that ninety-nine guys would go before you. I didn't register immediately for a couple of different reasons. First of all, I'm not very organized, and secondly, I'd seen guys come over here from Ireland and within six months they were in Vietnam. Six months! After two months basic training and four months of advanced infantry training, they were shipped out. I thought at least give me a couple of years. So I didn't go until I was twenty-one, which was good in some ways. For whatever it was worth I suppose I was a bit more mature than some of these younger kids, also I had traveled a bit. Some of the recruits were from small rural areas in America and for many of them this was their first trieste outside of their hometown, and some of these guys were so unworldly that they really

Sean (kneeling in front) with The Rocketeers Showband

had no idea of what they were letting themselves in for. Neither did I, really. That's the thing, nobody does. Nobody does.

After I had finished basic training in Fort Katlan in South Carolina, I was sent to Germany where I had one of the greatest jobs imaginable. Because I had done a lot of television work before entering the army, it was suggested to me by Merv Griffin to present myself to Special Services and to get myself into some sort of music there, as it would pull me out of other things, even Vietnam possibly. So I got myself accepted into a thirty member male chorus and all we did was sing at beer festivals and wine festivals.

It was part of some sort of a cultural connection between the German people and the American army. I had one of the greatest jobs imaginable and I was living in one of the most beautiful spots in Europe, Heidelberg. I had the best of both worlds. Then one day the Lieutenant came up to me and said, "Sean, I have some bad news for you." I thought he was going to tell me to clean out the latrine. "You've been levied for Vietnam." I couldn't believe it. "You gotta be kiddin' me," I said, "I can't go to Vietnam."

Prior to this an incident had occurred in the bomb holder where we were stationed. There was a lot of racial tension among the troops at that time, which was covered up completely and not given any attention by the media whatsoever. One night there was a race riot and I was right in the middle of it. It was the twenty-eighth of the month and nobody had any money. There was a gang of us, including a Russian guy, a Mexican guy, a Black guy from Texas, and one other guy who was stationed with us and he had just come back from Vietnam where he had been hit. Why he was still in the army was beyond me, as half of his shoulder was mown off, and they wouldn't let the guy go home. Anyhow we chipped our money together and went to the movies and when we came back 140 Black guys had stormed the barracks.

Before I knew it some of them had me cornered inside in a toilet attacking me with bunk adaptors—three feet steel pipes that are used to hold up one bunk bed on top of the other. They beat the living daylights out of me. My whole body was blue and yellow and green and whatever; then somebody shouted NC's and I jumped out the window from the scene. When I looked down there was blood flying out of me in all directions; I had a huge cut on my knee, my back was in bits; there was another cut down further on my leg; I almost lost my leg actually. When they took me to the hospital they bandaged up my leg and it acted as a tourniquet to stop the blood. Afterwards they sent me down to Garnitz in Germany, a beautiful place, to recuperate.

At this stage I was on crutches. When I came back these Black guys from Watts came to see me. You must understand that in America there was a place called Watts where there were huge riots in the sixties and some of the guys from there, militant Black guys, came to me afterwards and said, "Why they picked you is beyond us." In a way they were apologizing. And to this day I am not bigoted in any way shape or form even though they nearly took my leg, and my life, because as an Irish guy I understood. Here they were ready to give their lives for their country and they were being treated as second-class citizens. I understood too because I knew it wasn't me personally they were after. I was lucky that I didn't come out with real, real, bigoted view of the situation and I didn't, and I was lucky. That must come from somewhere deep down in Killarney.

The reason I brought that little incident up is that when I first heard that I was being sent to Vietnam, my first reaction was that I was not going. There was no way I was going. So I set about finding some way to get out of it. I went to the Chaplain and said, "These Black guys nearly killed me and they want to put a loaded gun into my hands. I don't know what direction I'll be firing in!" There was an investigation into the incident, but I mustn't have been very convincing because I ended up going anyway.

I was sent back to the States to Fort Lewis in Seattle and the night before I had one hell of a crazy night. We had heard the horror stories; we knew what we were facing. The thing about this war was that it was different than any other. In the First and Second World Wars, there were fronts, and they were fighting towards a certain area—towards Dunkirk or towards the Siege of Normandy. There was nothing like that in Vietnam, it was all skirmishes; it was more like guerilla warfare. The front line changed every day and then of course people who were your friends during the day could be your enemies at night. Some of the natives would be working inside the compound; of course they would be screened beforehand, but you could never be sure where their loyalties lay. The big joke was that you could be their "number one" GI during the day and then become their tenth GI that night. "Oh! You're my friend, you're number one," they'd tell you, but you never knew who to trust. You could have a truck load of GI's and a woman could come up and launch a grenade at it and blow the whole lot of them up. You could trust nobody, not women, children, nobody.

I do remember the immense camaraderie among the soldiers, because in a situation like that you do get very close to other humans, because that might be the last person you might ever talk to in your life and it could happen in a split second. In the wink of an eye a bullet can come along and blow someone's head off. I saw a lot of death, but I didn't observe that much actual dying on the field itself, but the first guy I shared a tent-half with didn't come back. When you went out in the field you had basically nine days rations, you had an M16, you had four rounds of ammunition, and you had a tent-half. The very first guy that I shared my tent-half with didn't come back. He was killed. The second guy didn't come back and the third guy didn't come back. That was three guys that I knew, not to mention all the thousands that I didn't' know at all.

When we went out in the boonies, as it was called, we carried a lot of things—our personal stuff, army stuff, a rifle, 400 rounds of 60-caliber machine gun ammunition, and then another half of a 50-caliber machine. I was carrying about 90 lbs of stuff and it was 110 degrees and it was 99 percent humidity for a month solid. Solid. Everything that you had was wet. And the water that you had to drink was basically rice paddie water, full of buffalo piss and that, and you had to drink it with iodine. And the guys who didn't take the iodine, who thought they were above the foray, got the most severe dose of diarrhea imaginable. Then the rations were also gastronomically challenged so that put more pressure on the bowels, but if you took precautions you were safe enough.

The thing was you never knew where the firing was coming from. You'd be out there in the middle of the biggest bush you could imagine. That's where you had to be, because you dare not go on a trail that had already been used, because all of those were booby trapped. If you saw a trail you had to not use it; you had to whack your way across with a machete to make a new trail.

Our job was to set up search and destroy missions. About fourteen or fifteen of us would go out and set up an NDP—a night defensive position—and then maybe four or five would go out on search and destroy. We were not just searching for the enemy. We would look for anything at all belonging to the Viet Cong, even rice cachets, and destroy them. Then of course there were the Hoi Chanhs who were recruited by the program Chieu Hoi to deflect. In effect they were young Viet Cong that came over to our side for whatever reason. Some of these kids were only fifteen or sixteen years old. Vietnamese people aren't big to start with, but these kids were so tiny, and they were our point men, right on the very front of our line, and they knew every single area we went into. One time we took a prisoner, a young nurse, and this little Chieu Hoi, as we called them, this little fifteen year old kid, said just give me a knife and I will take her away and find out anything you need to know. Such was their way of life. Human beings have an incredible capacity to adapt to whatever is expected of them.

Were we scared? Like hell we were. The first time we went out on the field, we were transported by five Huey helicopters. In each helicopter there were ten fifty caliber machine guns and ten GIs and we were dropped into this area at the same time and simultaneously the fifty machine guns started spraying immediately. You cannot imagine the incredible noise and chaos that ensued, as we didn't know if we were attacking or were under attack. I thought it was the end of the world and I couldn't imagine anything being more terrible than that.

Then we were left there for thirty days. We had run out of rations about three or four days before the end and you dare not even eat a piece of left over chocolate you found on the ground, as it was just too dangerous. So of course there was a huge fear factor attached to the whole thing. Firing a rifle was the least of your worries. Every single second from the time you became conscious at the break of day until you became again unconscious that night for whatever sleep you were going to grab, every single second of every waking moment was taut with tension. And this went on for thirty days. When you got back to camp for a three-day R&R, rest and recuperation, it was a rude awakening to try and become part of some sort of reality again.

After one month, it was November, the Monsoon season, when it never stopped raining; I approached Special Services again with the idea of putting on a Christmas concert for the troops; anything rather than going back into the field. I had found an old beat-up guitar, which I really had never played before that and I taught myself a few tunes and I went up and sang for the kids in the MASH unit. Now these young kids were barely this side of death. When I went into that unit for the first time, I was stopped in my tracks, because death was all around me; there was blood coming from every direction. They would have just arrived in from battle, these young, American kids, and I had to make a conscious decision to walk past them, because I knew if I didn't, I would never be able to do so again. I walked through the melee and took up my guitar and sang a few songs for these fallen troops and I went back there every day I possibly could, and sang for them. I did that every day that I could possibly do it.

One day the First Lady General of the United States Army happened to be passing through at the particular time I was there; she saw what I was doing and she wrote a letter down from the Pentagon, through the ranks, not straight to me, but through the ranks which was an unbelievable way of doing it, everybody knew that this letter was coming towards me and everybody read before it got to me. What she said was that I was doing was more beneficial than anything else I could be doing. So they pulled me out of the field permanently. It was unbelievable. I was pulled out of the field to sing.

But then what they had me do was even more dangerous even though I was no longer behind a gun. I would be taken away, just me and a pilot, in a Huey, a helicopter with one propeller, to the most remote places. In fact, these places were so isolated that the only way we knew how to find the guys was from smoke signals that they would roger out to us. I was allowed take my rifle with me for protection, but the armory in the compound didn't open until six o'clock in the morning and we were usually gone before that. We were ordered to hand up our gun every night, as they were afraid when guys had a few beers that something might happen, but I would hide mine under the bed, as there was no way I was going out in the bush without my rifle. And I would play my guitar for them and sing for awhile; We Gotta Get Out of This Place. We'd thump out that great hit from The Animals, and then take off again to the next spot. We traveled from one place to another continuously for the next five months singing - "We gotta get out of this place,"- anything at all that would touch them for that short while and release the tension. "We gotta get out of this place, if it's the last thing we ever do!"

In a way, music saved me, not only physically, but it saved my sanity too. Praying was out of the realm of my way of dealing with Vietnam, but

I'm sure that religion came into it somehow. Of course they facilitated all religions in the Army and they sort of prompted you to keep it going as they didn't want to be responsible for you to be losing your faith. For me religion is just a calisthenics for spirituality, whatever your religion is it keeps you fit spiritually, but some people mistake spirituality for religion. They talk about religion when they mean spirituality.

I never got involved in the drug scene. Maybe it was my Irish attitude to drugs. Maybe it was my music and all the songs I was writing in my head; but mainly I think it was because it was very necessary for me to remain conscious and aware of everything that was happening at all times. If I didn't, it would not only be detrimental to my own safety, but to many others around me. I did not want to be distanced from the situation at all.

There were a lot of facets to coming back. Probably the first one that hit me was how ungrateful the American public was to people who had put their life on the line for this, their adoptive country. For whatever reason I went to Vietnam, I still haven't come to grips with what the reason was, perhaps it was a swashbuckling affair. My way of looking at things is that the world is mine and I wouldn't like to jeopardize any border or someone's chance to cross over a border and I didn't want to swipe America off my list as a place I couldn't go to. It certainly wasn't too much in the philosophical vein, even though I have some clue as to what is going on in the world, I don't have a real in-depth idea of why people go to war, I don't think anybody does really, because even if you do, somebody else comes along with another theory and debunks your idea. But the nucleus of my belief would be something along the lines that good or bad I feel that America might really have been trying to give these people a leg up to be able to fend for themselves. Whether it's a naïve way of looking at things or not, I don't know, but it was the best I could come up with when I was involved.

It's the same today. I can see certain similarities between Vietnam and Iraq. Even though I'm not a supporter of the regime that's in power in America now, I have to say that I agree with President Bush in that it would be a wonderful thing to have democracy in Iraq so that people can make their own decisions based on their beliefs and not because they might be chastised by the government. It's just not the right time and it's not the right way of doing it.

The other thing that hit me after coming back was that it took me a long time, probably years, to get rid of that feeling of not being in a war zone and not having a gun close at hand. It almost made me feel naked. And even to this day helicopters have a sort of an eerie feeling for me because that's all you could hear in Vietnam. For the first couple of years I would duck for cover if a helicopter hovered overhead. It's a very intense thing to put yourself that close to the edge like that. You're so close to death at any given time that you become acutely aware of every little thing, of every thing that goes on in your head, in your body, to the people all around you. It's a very, very intense awareness and it's difficult to get rid of that and some people can't ever get rid of it and that's why they end up in hospital. Even twenty, thirty, forty years afterwards they wake up screaming. I didn't have it as bad as others because I didn't actually see my friends being blown to bits.

The thing that sometimes I find really hard . . . this could take me some time . . . every time I think about the kids . . . to see a small child's body melt away . . . that's the one thing I think that hit me the hardest. Sometimes I saw them hit by napalm and their bodies instantly melted. Napalm has a high heat degree. They burnt the enemy really. When it hit them, the only way I can describe it really is that it melted them away. And you would see them hobble all over the place and it was just horrendous. Of course, there were a lot of kids around the American compounds.

I remember one compound in Trabong, which was in the highlands. After we had eaten, all of the leftovers were put in a truck and the minute those trucks went outside the kids would swarm around it like flies and the GI's who had their jobs to do would just be kicking them out of the way. Then the truck was taken to an area and they'd pour what was called C4 on top of it. C4 was an explosive device that could blow up a house if suppressed by a blasting cap, which was then released. By lighting a match it could be used to burn stuff. Sometimes we used it out on the field to heat up the rations, and this is how they got rid of our scraps. They burned them. And this is what these kids were after: food. Sometimes I look back and wish I had done something about it, but of course the road through life is paved with good intentions. But if I'd only suggested to the GIs to give over the left-over rations to the children, we would have made more friends and less enemies than all the bombs that were thrown in the name of democracy or freedom or whatever the hell it is we go to war for.

When I came back I had to basically restart my career from scratch, and I mean from scratch. Two years is a long time in show business and people forget about you very quickly. I had to start off all over again with an acoustic guitar playing in this little place called, ironically, Danny Boy's, and I went from there to Flanagan's on 66th Street, where I met my wife, to Flemings on 86th Street where I opened my own place. I played resident there with the Sean Fleming Band for so many years.

My wife, Lisalot, is from Sweden and we have three children. The oldest one, Dillon, is a very deep thinker, a straight A student, who's turning out to be a real nice young man. He has taken up running recently and we're delighted about that as he's usually the kind of guy who would read nine books in a week. Anders is next. He's one of these gifted kids, a wonderful athlete and a fine drummer; he's just pure poetry in motion. Then there's Elin, the little one, who plays Gaelic football with the Rockland girls' club. They have quite an affinity to Ireland.

They all have their Kerry jerseys, even though we are not really steeped in it up here. In fact, recently it was Dillon's birthday and he asked for the usual things like an I-Pod, but he also asked for a book about the IRA. They're more engulfed in their Swedish heritage, they're all bilingual and they spend every second summer there. Dillon speaks Swedish almost without an accent. He is also good at French, and Anders excels at Spanish, but when you have two languages the third one comes much easier.

My mother must have been absolutely terrified when I was in Vietnam. To this day I couldn't probably get to the depths of her anxiety. When you have children of your own you realize how petrified you can be at times for their welfare. Lisalot often says to me "if anything happens to those kids you can just get a padded cell for me," and I feel the same way. I lost a brother when he was only twenty-three years old just at the prime of his life. He had been here for a while and then went on to England where he was to go on a motorcycle trip around Europe with some friends. He took the motorbike out on a test drive and never came back. It was the freakiest accident. He had hit the side of the curb, which in itself wouldn't have been so bad except for a small gate had just been erected to prevent children from running out on to the road and it burst his liver. I often think though what a way to go. He must have been on top of the world in this monster of a bike and what a way to go out.

When I heard the news, I just dropped, my legs went from under me and I curled up like a baby. In some ways it was probably the saddest feelings I ever had, because it was sadness without apology. I can only imagine what it did to my mother. She died ten years later from cancer and I often think it must have stemmed from the shock of that. There were ten of us, five and five. I'm second from the top. One brother lives about five minutes from here, another in Port Washington, and another in Chicago. The sister next to me came over here, got married, the marriage broke up, she has one daughter and she's back in Killarney.

My father was first steward on Killarney Golf Course; my mother was the cook. We lived in the clubhouse and my oldest brother had taken his time coming along so my mother thought I would too so she was out on the course when she got the pain that announced my arrival. We weren't exactly poor, though hardly rich either with ten children. Those times in Ireland I remember my father telling me there was the haves and have-nots. In the golf club there was a lot of snobbery and the players dictated how thing were to be run. They decided how much everything was and he would have to stay until they left late at night and be there early in the morning for the next crowd. He had no say in anything and he said you just couldn't make money the way they orchestrated things. Nowadays it's completely different as there is much more of a middle-class in Ireland now.

He would also work at all sorts of things as well as fulfill his duties as Steward. When I think about him hopping on an old rusty bike and hobbling along an old country lane about three miles into town where he would work for maybe twelve hours at a time and have to hobble back home again; really it was slave labor. He worked in a garage fixing cars; he did paint jobs; anything for extra money, but it was a pittance really. Then the first really new deal you could call it that came to Killarney was the Liebherr Crane factory, where my father got a job. He raised his pay from five pounds a week to twenty pounds every two weeks; he raised it one hundred percent really when you think about it. And I can remember the first time he came home with that twenty pound in his hand and it was very exotic really, but he was beside himself, really beside himself and then they opened Hotel Europa and both of them were opened by Liebherr and that was the greatest thing ever to happen to Killarney.

Last year I invested in property out in Montauk, Fleming's Tipperary Inn, with Steve Harley who is a magnificent drummer. He's played with everybody, Elton John, Paul McCartney, but he's equally a gifted human being. He's got something really special. There's a guy who's running it for us, another partner. In a way Montauk is very similar to Killarney in that it's a seasonal town and very dependant on tourists. In a way I've come around the full circle. I am still playing music, not in New York so much anymore, but mainly along the East Coast. We could be anywhere from Florida, Philadelphia, the Jersey Shore, and Washington DC, and the odd gig in New Hampshire, Maine, even Phoenix; it depends on where it comes in. Somebody asked me to play at their daughter's wedding in Ireland this summer so I worked out a few other things that will coincide and we'll make a trip out of it.

I have written a poem about Anders' soccer coach who is dying of Lou Gehrig's disease. Maybe it's because I was in Vietnam that I think really heroes come in all shapes and sizes. This man is wilting away to nothing and he's still there, he's there for the kids at every game. He is in a wheelchair and the only way he can communicate with the players is through a computer device attached to his head, which he taps with a wand like instrument and it strikes out whatever word he wants to relay. I would love to have some sort of benefit for him, as we're surrounded here in Nyack by celebrities and I am sure they would all pitch in. My poem is called On No Less a Battlefield. And for me it says that everybody has their own battlefield and heroes come out of all places. For this man it is the soccer pitch and he is a hero in that he didn't chose to hide away and wait for death, but he is out there showing the kids not only how to play football, but how to live life in the face of all adversity. It just shows you how things affect us all of our lives. A lot of my imagery and vocabulary comes from war, which illustrates how powerful Vietnam was in my life. One's experiences in life can have a positive or a negative effect and I try and take the positive with me everywhere I go, as I am an optimist to a fault.

Interviewed at his home in Nyack, New York;
May 03, 2006

Agnes Delaney, 1964

When I think of it now, it is fitting I was born in the village of Ardnagall. The name means "hill of the foreigner" and once I left the village in the parish of Tuam, County Galway, I too became a foreigner.

Ardnagall was originally part of a 2,700 acre estate owned by the Bodkin family who were both English and Catholic. The Bodkins acquired the estate in 1759 and lived in Ardnagall. They later built a Georgian house in the next village of Kilclooney. Then came the potato famine in the 1840's. The poverty, death and immigration that resulted meant there were many years when tenants were not able to pay the rent. Eventually, the Bodkins went broke and left Kilclooney.

In 1884, the Irish Land Purchase and Settlement Company bought the estate for 43,000 pounds. It was thought to be valued too high, so it took many years for things to be settled and for the land to be divided. In today's market, one half-acre site is worth more than the entire 2,700 acres was back in 1884. And after many years of neglect the house has now been fully restored by a local family.

In 1906 my father's family and three other families were granted a bog, a twenty-six acre holding and a new house each in Ardnagall. The farmhouses were all built alike, with slated roofs, three bedrooms and a large kitchen. When more of the estate was divided we acquired about ten more acres. Dad was about eleven when he moved from the next village and he often said they thought they had moved into a "palace." My paternal grandfather died before the move to Ardnagall. My paternal grandmother lived to be in her nineties. My parents did not marry until 1935 and that was after Dad's mother died and he was free to do so.

The marriage was an arranged "match." Mam was thirty-five and Dad was forty-three. Their common denominator was Tom Garvey. Tom was a friend of my father and married to a cousin of my mother. Mam came from Lavalleyroe - - a village near Clunfad in County Mayo - - with a cash dowry to marry a man she had only met a few times. The dowry guaranteed that her name was put on the property.

Mam was the seventh of ten children born into a large religious family. Her first cousin was John Cardinal D'Alton, Archbishop and later Cardinal of Armagh from 1946 until his death in 1963. Mam's uncle was Msgr. Edward D'Alton, who wrote books on ancient Irish history. He was also instrumental in helping my Uncle Michael get an education and a job in the Civil Service. Uncle Michael worked as a Customs Officer in Dublin. During World War Two he would send us tea and other necessities that were rationed. The neighbors often told me how grateful they were to my mother for sharing the tea. Five of Mam's brothers emigrated. Two went to Australia and were killed in a mining accident in their 20's. Three more went to London. One — Uncle Ned — returned to settle in the home place. My uncle Martin and two sisters never left. My aunts married locally and both died from complications of childbirth. Mam helped with the raising of the children.

As for Dad, he was youngest of seven. Two of his brothers moved to England. One of those uncles who was in the old IRA, was conscripted into the British Army during the First World War and he deserted. He was captured and shot. The other died in England, at a young age. Dad's two other brothers and his two sisters went to America around the turn of the century. One sister eventually returned and married locally. The second became a nun in a cloistered order in Troy, New York. She never returned and died in her 50's. One of his brothers had hurt his leg playing football before he left for America, got gangrene during the long journey and died. He was buried at sea. After Sr. Mary died, Dad lost contact with his brother.

In addition to the matchmaker Tom Garvey, the two families shared an allegiance to Ireland's struggle for Independence. The men on both sides were involved in the struggle. I remember shopping in Tuam with my Uncle Martin one day and he proudly produced his IRA pension book to make a purchase, without question it was accepted. Dad would tell us stories of times he was "on the run" and had left my grandmother home alone and how he worried that she would be killed by the Black and Tans. He always hoped that he would see a United Ireland in his time. Later, when he got old, he changed it to "in our time." But he died without his wish being realized. Ironically, Dad died on my adopted country's 200th anniversary of independence — July 4th 1976.

The farm was off the main road, so it was a quiet and peaceful place to grow up. We also had land near the Bodkin's old Georgian house and used to go in there to pick apples. We all lived such simple lives back then with very little money or new clothes, but we were fortunate to always have plenty of food. We lived off the land and neighbors helped each other. I remember we had a horse that died giving birth to a foal. We were all so upset. The horse was badly needed on the farm and I am sure was hard to replace. When I was about five an elderly bachelor in the village died. He had his last few pounds sewn into his undershirt. It did not take the men of the village, including my father very long to find it and give him a good all night Irish wake with his own money!

I am the youngest of six children, or as my mother would say she was blessed with six children. We were all born within eight years, at home with the help of the local "midwife." Dad was over fifty when I came along and Mam was forty-three. My brother Tom told me that he remembered the day I was born, Dad took my brothers and sisters down the field and when they returned they found out they had a sister. Another baby girl didn't cause much excitement as they already had a thirteen-month old sister.

The kitchen was the center of our home. It was where the meals were eaten, the fire was always going and the cooking was done on the open fire. Mam did not work much outside the house. She preferred to spend her Sundays reading the newspaper and listening to the radio — when we eventually got one.

There was a lot of walking in Ardnagall. We walked to school and walked to Mass. We went to Mass in Milltown because it was nearer than our parish, Tuam. When I was very young we traveled by trap until one frosty Sunday morning, the horse slipped and the shafts of the trap broke. After that, we walked the three miles and sometimes cycled.

My parents were different in temperament and ways. Dad could be impatient and obstinate, but at the same time, he was more outgoing and sociable than Mam. He liked to go to town and meet up with the local farmers for a few pints — especially on a "fair day." At my mother's request, I sometimes met up with him in Grogan's Bar and Grocery in Tuam on a Saturday afternoon and we would cycle home together. I remember enjoying meeting those farmers. I liked listening to them talk, as they were always arguing about politics or farming. But I suppose I really liked the few pennies they would give me to buy magazines to read.

Dad was the boss. He made the decisions and held on to the purse strings. He worked the farm and we all helped when we were not in school. It was hard manual work and he did not have much patience if you didn't pull your weight. It was on those green fields that we learned valuable lessons about life, responsibility and hard work. My favorite farm chore was making the hay and bringing it back to the house where we would make large haystacks in the garden. Dad was hard working and wanted the best for his children. He constantly "preached" that we should have a trade and save for a "rainy day." I never quite understood that, as it rained a lot in the west of Ireland!

Aged 17 (England)

Mam on the other hand, was patient, quiet and accepting. She did not visit neighbors very often and she didn't go to town except for church and shopping. We learned to knit and sew during the long winter nights. She was very religious and insisted we say the rosary every night. She accepted everything as God's will, believing that her life on this earth was to be endured and that her reward would be in Heaven. She rarely saw her own family after marrying and moving to Galway, though her brother Martin would cycle the twelve miles to see us. He would always give us half-crowns, so he was definitely the favorite.

I attended Strawberry Hill National School, which was in the parish of Dunmore. The school was old, and cold. And even though we students brought the turf ...it was the teachers who stayed by the fire. We didn't have that little luxury. I have fond memories of my years there and my teachers, especially Sean Purcell. He was Ireland's greatest Gaelic footballer and he was my teacher for my last three years. I remember in 4th class, he gave me 'Gulliver Travels' to read. He was in his twenties at the time, was a good teacher and nice to all the students. He remained a friend of mine all his life, and I often thanked him for kick-starting my life-long love of reading.

I remember walking home from national school one day and seeing the ESB putting down the poles to bring us electricity. Mam considered it such a luxury to have instant good light to read by. Dad bought a radio in Tuam and that brought in the outside world as well. Mam liked to listen to Irish plays on Sunday nights. I first heard Elvis Presley on that radio on the "Top Twenty" program from Luxemburg. He remained one of my favorite singers. I was in Ireland in August 1977 when he died and I cried when I heard the news. My children wanted to know if Elvis Presley was related to us.

When I was thirteen, Dad took me into the Mercy Convent in Tuam to register for secondary school. He also bought me a new bicycle for the six-mile journey each way. Secondary school wasn't easy for me as most subjects were taught in Irish, my least favorite subject. And those nuns could be mean, not abusive, but they had little sympathy for the country girls who cycled in long journeys. We were often cold and wet from the six-mile ride in, and the nuns made us stay that way until we dried out, only to cycle home again. It was on the journey home every evening, with all the other students that attended the various schools in Tuam that I learned a lot about life. It was the most fun part of my secondary school education.

As teenagers we would go to the local dance hall in Milltown. During Easter a marquee was put up for a Carnival. Great bands played under that tent for a week. Easter Monday we had the Races. It was a great day out with all sorts of amusements for the whole family. We also went to dances in Tuam, Ballyhaunis and Tooreen during the summer months. I loved to go dancing and listen to the big band. On a Sunday night we would all be getting ready, drying our hair at the open fire and thinking we looked smashing when my father would bring us down to size, saying "Good looks won't boil the pot". When we were ready, we would have to wait for him to give us the six shillings for the dance. Here he would say, "Well, isn't it a nice piece of bacon that would buy?" At that moment I didn't care if I never saw a piece of bacon again! He would be counting out the coins as he smoked his Walnut Plug tobacco by the fire and would recount how in his time he'd go out with a shilling and still have change at the end of the night. He told me years later that he often needed the money, but he still didn't want us to be left at home when all our friends and neighbors were going to the dances.

When I was sixteen, my brother Tom was home from England and I begged him to take me back with him. I was tired of school and tired of Dad stopping me from going to the dances during the school year. I already had two sisters nursing in England and would watch them come home to visit with new clothes and money. Unfortunately, I had neither! With reluctance, Dad let me go to stay with his nephew and family. I was able to get an office job after learning shorthand and typing in the Mercy Convent. The job was easy but the money was small — six pounds a week. I learned early to manage my few pounds and to participate in Birmingham's social life. There were several dance halls there that catered to the Irish and there was no Dad to prevent me from going dancing any night. All I needed was the money to go and the energy to get up for work the next day. My brother Tom, a carpenter by day, was a bouncer in the Harp, so we went there often.

Despite seeing my siblings all the time, I returned home to visit my parents often. First the train to Holyhead, then the boat to Dun Laoghaire and down on the train to Tuam. The boats were in very bad condition and would be crowded with young Irish people. But we had no worries. We were young and having great fun, especially traveling home for the Christmas holidays. During one holiday break in 1963, my life changed.

I remember, I was in the kitchen, looking out the window at the mountains far away, including the top of Croke Patrick, and I thought about going to America. I had looked out that kitchen window hundreds of times as a child, asking Mam what was beyond, and she would say, "America." I was restless for a new adventure and returned to England determined to find a way to get to America. One dreary January day I was looking through a newspaper and an advertisement called out to me "An American Family Invites You." It was an ad for a nanny for a family in New York. I immediately wrote to the agency in London for that position. There was an exchange of letters and pictures and it all looked so beautiful! Big houses, lots of sunshine...I could hardly wait. Six months later I had my Green Card from the American Embassy in London, so I was ready to see what was beyond those mountains.

I returned to Ireland one last time to say goodbye. The neighbors were happy for me, giving me addresses of their relatives in America –

some in Boston, some in Chicago. The neighbors may have been happy...but Dad was not. He even tried to arrange a marriage to keep me close to home. The "match" was a local man who looked about 40. He had returned from abroad and bought a farm. My parents were a 'match', so Dad naturally thought this arrangement was a great plan. The potential husband was very interested, but I wasn't ready to settle down on a farm and repeat my mother's life. I left my father and the 'good catch' in Grogan's bar in Milltown on my last Saturday night and went off to a dance. I didn't want to hear about what a great life I would have. Later in life, I understood why Dad didn't want me to move so far away. All of his brothers and sisters left and only one returned. Mam was upset as well, but did not try to stop me. But I am sure she prayed for my safety.

When July 6th 1964 arrived, Dad hired a hackney car and came to Shannon Airport with me. I had never seen him so sad as we said goodbye. I was as excited as he was forlorn. I flew to London, changed planes for New York, and found myself on a flight full of young girls just like me emigrating to work for American families. It was so hot when we arrived and I was completely overdressed in polyester. The clothes stuck to me as I made my way to the arrivals hall. I also noticed police officers with guns and that made me uneasy. I stood there as all the girls met their prospective employers. I had a photo of my new family, but couldn't see them anywhere. Eventually the crowd thinned and I was still alone. I sat on my suitcase and wondered what to do. Eventually, I went over the desk and asked to have the family paged; foolishly thinking they might not recognize me. The counter lady looked down the list and found my name. She told me that I was staying in a hotel for the night and flying to Hyannis Airport the next day. She handed me the ticket and before I could ask a question, she called the hotel and within minutes I was there. I still had no idea why the family didn't show up or where Hyannis Airport was. I spent my first night in America in a hotel room at Kennedy airport. I don't remember being scared at all. I think I was too young and too innocent at the time. The next day, I flew to Hyannis. The family expected me a week earlier and had already rented a vacation house on Cape Cod. I suspect the little four year-old was disappointed – expecting a playmate, not a minder. But I had a great time at that beach house. We went to the ocean every day and ate out in restaurants every evening. They bought me summer clothes and made me feel welcome. They also showed me where President Kennedy's family lived. On the trip back to New York, they stopped in Newport, Rhode Island to tour the 'Breakers Mansion', which was once the summer home of the famous Vanderbilt family. I had never seen anything so big — not even in pictures. The doghouse was big enough for a person and the dining room could seat more than one hundred people! The tour guide was telling us that back in the 1920's, all the very rich families would have "poodle parties." The chauffeur would pick up each dog, in a bow-tie, and drive to whichever house was hosting the party. I just couldn't believe what I was hearing, as dogs in Ireland were usually kept outside in order to help on the farm.

Eventually, reality set in. We arrived at the house in a posh neighborhood in Bronxville, New York. I was put up in the maid's quarters next to the kitchen, and soon learned the woman of the house expected me to be the maid — to cook and clean. I couldn't do either. I thought my job was to mind a child and I wasn't even sure that I was qualified to do that! As the youngest of six, I was usually the one with a book in my hand instead of a broom. I could not understand why this woman wanted me to vacuum and dust rooms that were not even being used – and were so clean already. Not to mention, I had never seen a vacuum cleaner. I grew up in a farmhouse with a cement kitchen floor! She then discussed making meatloaf. I had never even heard of it. As the days went on, I felt so lonely and all alone. I missed my family and friends so much that I was beginning to wonder if Dad's idea of the 'match' wasn't so bad after all.

On my first day off, my employer took me into Manhattan by car. He dropped me on 5th Avenue up in the 60's and told me to walk down and see St. Patrick's Cathedral, the other sights and eventually go to Grand Central station and get on a train back to Bronxville. I followed his directions to St. Patrick's. Then I found Saks Fifth Avenue Department Store. Wandering around, I picked up a scarf worth $50.00 — more money than I had to my name! I quickly put it down and left. Instead of shopping I spent the afternoon looking up at the skyline. The buildings were enormous, the weather was beautiful and I was completely taken with the sights and sounds of New York City. I did not want to return to Bronxville.

Just two weeks after arriving, I had a chance to cure my homesickness. My employer called me in to the living room one evening and told me that it would take his wife too long to train me properly, and they were willing to send me home. I was on a one-year contract and owed them money, but they offered to pay my fare to Ireland. I was lonely and tempted – but not ready to leave. I made contact with a girl from Dunmore I met in England and swapped Bronxville for the Bronx.

After Cape Cod, suburban Bronxville and watching '*Hawaiian Eye*' on television in England, my first impression of the Bronx was a bit of a let-down. But there was one bright spot — the 'Red Mill' dance hall. I went there on my first Saturday night. The 'High Spots' were playing and I was transported back to the dance halls of home. I was so happy and excited to be back in the company of other young Irish people. It felt like I had been in America for a year rather than just a few weeks.

I got a job the next week. It was at Western Union Telegraph Company and I did all kinds of office work. I started out making $60.00 a week and by the time I left five years later I was making $120. I worked my budget on the envelope system, where I put some aside each week for the rent and other bills. I spent the rest on clothes, a social life and saved a little for Dad's famous 'rainy day.' I liked my job as I worked with a lot of young American girls who were just out of high school. They took me to visit their families and took me shopping. I spent my first Thanksgiving with an Italian-American family in Yonkers and couldn't believe that they spent all day eating.

Around Christmas time I met up with Mary Lynch at the Red Mill. I had known her from my Mercy Convent days. I moved to Inwood with Mary and her cousin Noreen in January 1965. We lived on a fifth floor walk-up on Academy Street. What a great Irish neighborhood it was! You were always meeting new Irish people or bumping into old friends in the street, at Inwood Park and at Good Shepherd Church.

The social life back in the 60's was very good. We went dancing a couple of times a week and always ended up in the Red Mill on a Sunday night. I also liked City Center as they had great music and big crowds. During Lent, Ireland's big bands would come over and play at City Center. It was the place to go on a Saturday night. I didn't go to Gaelic Park that much, maybe a couple of times a year when certain teams were playing, instead I preferred the beach. We would go by train to Rockaway Beach and the bus would take us to Orchard Beach. We also spend time visiting friends, playing cards, going on dates and of course reading was always part of my life. After about a year, I settled into life in New York and never wanted to return to England.

There were some bumps in the road. I remember when my fellow Irishman Mike Quill put us all walking in January 1966 during the great transit strike. The city was nearly brought to a standstill. Shortly before that there was a power outage and I read *Gone with the Wind* by candle-light. During the summer of 1966, I returned to Ireland for six weeks. My parents were delighted that I hadn't changed. I gave some serious thought to returning home the following year. I met a fellow in the Seapoint Ballroom in Galway and we had a great few weeks together. He couldn't believe that I didn't drink or smoke. I promised him that I would return the next summer. We wrote for a while, but I had forgotten him before the year was out.

My brother Tom and I bought a television for our parents that summer of 1966. It was the first one in the village. Initially, Mam didn't like it but couldn't live without it as the years went on. The local farmers would come in on a Monday night to watch Michael Dillon's 'Farmer's Journal'. It became great company for them, as did the telephone for my mother. My children helped their grandmother make her first call to me in New York in 1987.

In the late 1960's, I attended Frank O'Connor's GED preparation class down on 23rd Street. O'Conner was a teacher from Co. Kerry. Hundreds of young Irish people took advantage of his GED classes. He always asked the new students to write an essay about their hometown and we would read them out in class. I wrote about Tuam with its sugar factory, many schools and famous football players; Sean Purcell and Frank Stockwell. I also included that when Galway won the All-Ireland football final in 1956, Sean Purcell took the Sam Maguire cup to our school and we all drank orangeade out of it. I did earn my GED, but then put my studies on hold for a while.

During those years, I was well aware that there was a war raging in Vietnam by watching television and through my job at Western Union. Sending telegrams was the way a lot of communication was done back then and I would eventually see copies of the wires pass through my desk. I would ask my American colleagues what the war was all about. Most would usually shrug their shoulders and say they didn't know. I began to read American history and about our involvement in Vietnam. I was against the war, believing the cost in human life was too high. I saw

Robert Kennedy march up 5th Ave. in the St. Patrick's Day parade in 1968. The thing I remember most was his tan and his incredible smile as he waved to the crowd. I supported his run for President, as he was against the war. Three months later he was killed. I was in England in 1963 when his brother, President John F. Kennedy, was shot and I remember how upset everyone was. I took an interest in American politics after coming here and became an American citizen in 1969. Through my son, J.P, I had the opportunity of meeting former President Bill Clinton in 2005. I had been a long time supporter. I also met Senator Hillary Clinton on a few occasions. I did not support going to war in Iraq, as again, the cost in human life would be too high and it is.

At a friends wedding in the spring of 1967, I met my future husband, Austin. We got engaged at Thanksgiving and married the following June. I moved from Inwood to 201st in the Bronx to St. Philip Neri parish. It was also a very Irish neighborhood. Several of my friends got married around the same time. Back then most people got married in their early twenties and had children right away. Our first child was stillborn. It was a sad, lonely and confusing time for me. It was decided that I not see my son before he was laid to rest and I've often regretted that I wasn't strong enough to insist on seeing him. Here I was so young, so far from home and facing the first real tragedy of my life. Even though I had a husband with me, it was my mother that I missed and wanted. I can still remember being in Union Hospital in the Bronx. It was a Saturday evening and several friends came to see me. They were young and didn't know what to say, I didn't know what to say either, so we all said nothing. I wrapped my fingers tightly around the top of the sheet and all I wanted to do was pull it over my face and make everyone and everything disappear. Needless to say, I didn't.

It was my next trip home that July that brought me back to myself. It was so comforting to return to the house I was born in, to sit by the fire with a cup of tea with my parents and feel safe and secure again. We had our next three children very quickly, three in three and half years. J.P. was born in 1970, two years later Ann Marie and the following year Dermot. As young mothers didn't work as much then as they do today, we had a great support system. We would go to the Yonkers parks and swimming pools, walk to the Botanical Gardens and go shopping on Fordham Road. I also returned to Ireland nearly every summer so that my children would know their family. My brother Michael, who never married, was such a good uncle to my three. He had a donkey and cart and he would let them go around the fields and have great fun playing "taxi." They became totally immersed in farm life in Ardnagall and also in Kilnock, County Mayo, where their aunt and many of their cousins lived. They were able to write long essays on what they did during the summer holidays on their return to school.

As adults, J.P., Ann Marie and Dermot are proud of their Irish heritage, which I encouraged. J.P., an attorney, works for O'Dwyer and Bernstien, lives in Manhattan with his wife Melissa. Ann Marie a restaurateur and wine connoisseur, who has lived in Ireland over the years in Mayo, Dublin and Kilkenny, now works and lives in Manhattan. Dermot is also in the restaurant business in New York, is married to Jennifer and they also live in Manhattan. Raising children is the hardest job I've ever had, but watching my three graduate high school, go off to college and make their own way in life, has made it all worthwhile. Their teenage years were a challenge for me to keep them on the 'straight and narrow'. Thankfully, we all survived. I spent many happy hours watching them play all kinds of sports. I was sorry to see Dermot give up the Gaelic football when he became a teenager, but he went on to play American football in both high school and in college. I am so proud of them and very happy to have two wonderful daughters-in-law.

My marriage ended after ten years as we both had changed and grown apart. It was a painful time for me, as I did not have many friends in the same position. I wondered how this could have happened to us. We had married for 'love'; and yet my parent's, whose marriage was a 'match' had stayed together. With the help of some counseling I began to feel better about myself, and my future. I was talking to a friend in Ireland the following year, and he asked what I was going to do now, without even thinking, I said, "I am going back to school." And with the same resolve I had to move to England at sixteen and New York at twenty, I was now just as determined to get a college education.

My first step was registering at Lehman College in 1979. It was very hard in the beginning, as I was out of school for many years. I struggled through with a lot of support from friends and faculty in the Adult Degree Program and graduated in 1984 with a BA in Psychology. I was then accepted at Columbia University, not even knowing that it was an

Ivy League school. I graduated from there in 1987 with an MS in Social Work. Through my job at United Hospital, I obtained an MS in Health Care Administration from Iona College in 1990. Dad would have been proud and surprised if he had lived to see me graduate. Mam was and showed my graduation photos to everyone who visited her. Those ten years that I spent going to school in America were the best years of my life. School became a much-needed outlet from raising young children. Attending lectures and listening to professor's helped me forget all about my many responsibilities at home for a few hours each day. I would often stop in the cafeteria before returning home and there would be crowds of students hanging out, smoking marijuana and drinking coffee. I would have liked to join in sometimes, but the reality was that I had three small children returning from their school. Lehman College was supportive and fun with a lot of emphasis on class participation. I had not been used to that in Ireland. As a result, I encouraged my friends to also attend school here. Women tended to return to school more than men, as they are willing to put in the time and make the necessary sacrifices.

I moved from the Bronx to Yonkers in 1980 and to Bronxville in 1984, coming full circle, back to where it all began. I have never regretted coming to the U.S. It has given me opportunities to grow, work, study and travel. I have many great friends who have always been a great support to me over the years. I always had a good social life and continue to like dancing, music and the theatre. I also have been fortunate to have good health. In 1996 and again in 1998, I had an amazing opportunity to work on a ship where I traveled around the world. It was such a great experience to see so many countries and experience different cultures. I visited Vietnam on one of the trips and was glad to see that country at peace. As well as returning to Ireland regularly, I have visited many other countries and hope to continue to travel.

Emigrating, especially to New York, gives you the opportunity to meet people from all over Ireland and the world. The negative side is that you don't see your family as often and your children grow up without grandparents and other relatives close by. I lived in Galway City for six months in 1998 and it is where I spend most of my time when I go there now. As Gaelic football has always been part of my life, I was delighted to be in Croke Park in September 1998 to see Galway win the All Ireland football final.

In 1987, I returned to work in the Health Care field concentrating in hospitals, clinics and nursing homes. I am currently the Director of Social Services in a nursing home. It is very rewarding to work with the elderly, as they are often neglected and lonely. I have also worked with people with AIDS for many years. I have been involved with the Aisling Irish Community Center since 1997. It is a great center that helps so many people. We are fortunate to have such an organization in Yonkers and more fortunate to have the support of the local community and the Irish government.

I am delighted with the prosperity in Ireland today. It makes me so proud that such a small country has achieved so much, especially during the last twenty-five years. Long may it continue. We were poor and deprived for centuries. It was also a more closed society. Most problems were rolled under the linoleum. The Catholic Church was dominant and had control of almost everything. They could tell you who and what to vote for from the altar. Still, there was great respect for the Church and everything was accepted as God's will. Those days are almost all gone now. I always liked when we had the 'Stations" (Mass in the house). A couple of villages were part of our station group so it came around to our house about every ten years. I went home in 1990 to help prepare for the big event. It was such fun painting and getting the house all ready for the Mass and the party afterwards. All my family and the neighbors were there. The party went into the night and my mother sat by the fire enjoying it all. We ended up having a great singsong. George Garvey sang the 'The Bridle on the Wall' to everyone's delight. Sadly, it was the last happy event in our home. My mother died in October 1991.

Most of the people I grew up with emigrated to England, Australia or the United States. The oldest son usually stayed home to care for the parents. My oldest brother Michael was no exception. He never left, developed arthritis before he was thirty and suffered many a day after that. He died when he was fifty-four in 1992. It was just nine months after my mother died. My sister Bridie who was a nurse in London, died in December 1992 as a result of complication's from a Liver transplant. My other brother Tom died in 2002 in London at the age of sixty-three. My oldest sister Mary returned from England many years ago and married locally. My sister Kitty also returned from England and lives in Roscommon. I have many nieces and nephews in Ireland that I keep in contact with. When I visit Kilclooney graveyard, I know more people buried there than I do in the local villages. I like to walk around and remember them.

In all the years that I lived in Ireland, and all the trips I made home, it never occurred to me that one day, the house I was born in would be closed up. It is, as are several houses in the village, including three of the four that were built in 1906. When I went home the year after Mam and my brother Michael died, the house did not feel like 'home' any more.

When I look at nineteen-year old girls now, they seem so young. I think back on that day long ago when I was looking out the kitchen window and deciding to leave all that was familiar to me and travel 3,000 miles on my own for people I had never met. I often wonder where I got the courage and determination. It was my parents who gave me my wings and for that I am grateful. An old man, Pat Keavney who lived across the field from our house would always come in to see me when I came home on holidays. He would tell me about his sisters going to America back in the early 1900's and that they never returned. He would get sad remembering them. I would try to cheer him up, explaining that it was hard to come home during those early years and how easy it is to fly now. He never accepted it and would say to me "it's the nature within you that brings you home" I suppose he was right. I have always kept close ties to Ireland and cherish the happy memories I have of my childhood growing up in Ardnagall.

I still remember when I was about three, my sister Bridie, who was about five, followed our older sister and brother down the fields to bring home the cows. They did not know she was behind them and she kept going. She went through the bog and ended up about three miles away in another village. A man from that village was bringing home turf and his son heard the child crying and he took her to his home. Meanwhile all the men went out with lanterns looking for her and all the women stayed home and said the rosary. The word went around and she was brought home and more prayers were said. It was considered a miracle she did not drown in the bog. That story is still told in my village, Ardnagall.

August 2006

Joe Flannigan

by Brian Lynch Johnson

I spend the hours just sitting here. It's been the same from year to year.
With a drunken hand I lift the glass, waiting for the hours to pass.
No kinsman here to shake my hand. A lonely heart in a lonely land.
The nightly ladies pass me by casting o'er a hoorey eye
But Lord that whiskey's good tonight.

The TV's on to no one's heed, each one here with a different need.
To live or die I have no will, while I can hand my dollar bill
And order scotch from across the shelf for me to drink and forget myself
For Lord that scotch, that scotch is good tonight.

The ashtray's full to overflowing, fag after fag and me not knowing.
Flashing neons light the place often showing up my face.
On the soggy bar the money's laid, two hundred bills I just got paid
From working on those buildings high, piling blocks up to the sky.
But Lord that whiskey, that whiskey's good tonight.

Then the barman with a dirty rag wipes the spot where I dropped my fag
He tells me now I've got to go and hands me my coat for the falling snow.
I ramble towards the swinging door. I stop, I glance across the floor.
All those people having fun, each one with friends but me with none.
I struggle on the wall my brace as the pelting snow chops at my face
The smell of whiskey off my breath shows signs of warding off my death.

I ascend the stairs flight by flight, no man to bid me the time of night
Fumbling forward through the door I find myself upon the floor
I struggle on and light the light, those dam grey walls what an awful sight.
I bury my head between my hands was I cursed because I left Ireland.
They told me stories of famed Broadway, one of the reasons I came this way
But three thousand miles is a woeful journey to know it is a fabled story.

My friends in Ireland think it's great to pack their bags and emigrate.
To see what we call the Land of the Brave, how small their minds of an early grave.
They think that death is a motionless body, if they could see my soul now, O lord what folly

I spoke Gaelic once with all the blas, but its all gone now Lord what an awful loss.
My soul is turned in wild disarray, and its getting worse from day to day
There's nothing left save what you see, all else is dead inside of me.
But Lord that whiskey, that whiskey's good tonight.

On Greyhound buses riding West I'd read of Synge or Casey best
I'd see oul Fluther loud and clear or Maurya's face shed a silent tear.
Every bus stop looked the same, no matter where, how strange the name.
Then I'd bundle up on snowy nights when my world became a world of lights
And I'd conjure thoughts of long ago as my four-wheeled house moved through
the snow.
The hours and miles would pass me by until a light shone in the sky
And my world of lights would disappear as that damn dawning sun drew
ever near.

It's long since I've seen my parents, don't know if they're still apparent
Or maybe lying 'neath an emerald sod and pleading at the throne of God
For him to help a long lost son that the Godman's blood long ago had won.
Or maybe they are fingering beads atoning for a lost son's deeds
Asking Mary's help in praise to see if she'd a lost soul raise
And lift him back on wisdom's track or take the devil off his back.
For there's nothing left save what you see, all else is dead inside of me.
But Lord, that whiskey, that whiskey's good tonight.

You see I'm bowed but not with years
You see I shake but not from fears.
You see I mourn but not the dead
'Twas on different stuff my soul was fed.
You see my life I've learned to hate it
But now, but now thank Christ it is consummated!

Brian Johnson, a native of Banagher, County Offaly, is a member of the Franciscan Brothers of Ireland. He went to California in 1967 and came to New York in 1969 where he taught in Cardinal Hayes High School in the Bronx until 1981. He then became Principal of St. Philip Neri school in Bedford Park where he remained until his departure from the U.S. in 1999.

While in New York, Bro. Brian was actively involved in the Irish community helping young immigrants with housing and employment. He was also very much associated with the NY GAA where he played hurling and football with the Offaly and New York teams.

Since 1999 he has worked with the rural poor in Kenya and among other things directs a Secondary School and a Polytechnic Institute. He is also engaged in several poverty elimination projects in that country.

Brian has a great love for Irish literature and culture, and has had several poems published and one play produced.

Glossary

All-Ireland	the All-Ireland Senior Football and Hurling Championships held annually in Croke Park is the premier competition for these games in Ireland
Ancient Order of Hibernians (AOH)	Irish-Catholic fraternal organization founded in New York in 1836 primarily to assist Irish immigrants
An Óige	Gaelic word for youth; also youth hostel organization in Ireland
AT&T	American Telephone & Telegraph Co.
AWOL	military term – 'absent without leave'
Bedford Park Shamrock Club	started off on Decatur Avenue and is now in St. Brendan's on Bainbridge
bialy	bagel/English muffin combination
Black and Tans	a paramilitary force employed by the Royal Irish Constabulary from 1920-21, to suppress revolution in Ireland
Blanket Protest	Provisional IRA and Irish National Liberation Army prisoners held in the Maze prison, Northern Ireland, wore modified prison blankets instead of uniforms of convicted criminals
Blueshirts	popular name for supporters of Fine Gael party in Ireland
BMT	Brooklyn-Manhattan Transit Corporation
camogie	a Celtic team sport – women's variant of hurling
Caledonian, The	a traditional Irish set dance from County Clare
Catskill Mountains	known simply as the Catskills are situated in New York State north-west of New York City and west of the Hudson River
ceílí	Irish step dancing to live traditional Irish music
City Center	New York City Center, built in 1923
Civil Rights Movement (Ireland)	The Northern Ireland Civil Rights Association founded in 1967 pressurized the Government of Northern Ireland to grant their demands
Civil War (Ireland)	conflict between supporters and opponents of Anglo-Irish Treaty; June 28, 1922 – May 24, 1923

Cobh	port town in County Cork, Ireland. Of the 6 million emigrants from Ireland to the U.S, 1848 – 1950; over 2.5 million departed through Cobh
craic	Gaelic word meaning fun or sport
Croke Park	principal GAA stadium in Ireland located in Dublin
Easter Rising	rebellion staged in Ireland, Easter week 1916, by militant Irish Republicans to win independence from the United Kingdom by force
EL	elevated subway trains
Eucharistic Congress	Roman Catholic gatherings of ecclesiastics and laymen for the purpose of celebrating the Holy Eucharist. The 1932 Congress held in Dublin was hugely significant in asserting the Irish Free State as a leading Catholic nation
FCÁ	An Foras Cosanta Áitiúil – Irish Army reserve force
feis	Gaelic word meaning traveling festival; usually of Irish dance, music and culture; includes competition
Fianna Fail	currently largest political party in Ireland
Fine Gael	currently second largest political party in Ireland
five and ten store (Woolworths)	The F.W. Woolworth Co. was among the first stores to sell discounted goods at fixed prices, usually five or ten cents; also the first to display merchandise for the shopping public to handle
fleadh	festival of Irish traditional and dance
Flemings	a bar owned by Sean Fleming on 86th Street, NYC, between 2nd and 3rd Avenues
Free State	The Irish Free State was an independent republic made up of 26 counties; forerunner of today's Republic of Ireland The remaining 6 counties of Ulster in Northern Ireland are part of the United Kingdom
GAA	Gaelic Athletic Association, an organization focused on promoting Irish sport
Gaelic League	founded in Dublin, July 31, 1893, for the purpose of keeping the Irish language spoken in Ireland
Gaelic Park	principal GAA stadium in NYC, West 240th St., Bronx.
Gaeltacht	Gaelic word for Irish speaking regions in Ireland
Gander	town in Newfoundland

Garryowen, The	ballroom in London
GED	General Education Diploma for adults who have not completed High School
Holyhead	port town in Wales, famous for ferry that links it with Dun Laoghaire, a port town in County Dublin, Ireland
Home Rule	an Act passed by British House of Commons granting Ireland national self-government within the UK
hurling	outdoor team sport of Celtic origin; administered by GAA; and played with sticks and a ball
Hyannis port	village on Cape Cod peninsula; southern tip of State of Massachusetts
Idlewild	original name for John F. Kennedy International, New York's premier airport
ILIR	Irish Lobby for Immigration Reform
Independent:	Independent System (IND)
IRA	originally Irish Volunteers (1913); then Irish Republican Brotherhood; later Irish Republican Army (1916) who aimed to remove British rule in Ireland by armed force. Sometimes called Old IRA. Now a paramilitary group intent on removing British rule from Northern Ireland
Irish/Gaelic football	form of football played mainly in Ireland
IRM	Immigration Reform Movement
IRT	Interborough Rapid Transit NCO
Jaeger House, The	New York City ballroom, opened 1953
Jahn's	ice-cream parlor chain
JFK	John F. Kennedy, President of the U.S. 1960-63; also name of principal New York airport – JFK International
Jimmy K's	bar on Katonah Avenue, Woodlawn
12th of July	anniversary of Battle of Aughrim celebrated every year in Northern Ireland
JC Mac's	bar on 238th Street & Broadway, the Bronx
Kennedy/McCain immigration reform bill	devised by Senators Edward Kennedy and John McCain to facilitate future legal immigration to the U.S.
leaving certificate	commonly known as 'leaving cert' is final course in Irish

	Secondary School system, and culminates with leaving certificate examination
Maze Prison	known colloquially as H-block or Long Kesh; situated near Lisburn, County Armagh, Northern Ireland
McKeon's	bar/restaurant on McLean Avenue, Yonkers, NY
melodeon	old Irish word for accordion
Month's Mind Mass	celebrated in Ireland one month after a person's death
musician's union	The Local 802, Associated Musicians of Greater New York, are part of the American Federation of Musicians and the AFL-CIO
November's Eve	the night before November 1st, All Soul's Day
NYPD	New York Police Department
NYU	New York University
Orange Lodge	a Protestant fraternity based in Northern Ireland called after Protestant Prince William III of Orange, who succeeded Catholic King James II to throne of England
Orange Parade	held every year on July 12th; to celebrate victory of King William III at Battle of Aughrim (1691), which confirmed Protestant supremacy of Ireland
Páirc Uá Chaoimh	Gaelic Athletic Association stadium in Cork city, Ireland
pioneer	The Pioneer Association was established in Dublin (1898) to combat alcohol abuse in 19th Century Ireland. Members wear a pin and are known as pioneers
Project Children	bring children from Northern Ireland to American homes for vacation
publican	owner of bar, or pub as it is known in Ireland
Public Works	The Department of Public Works is responsible for the physical upkeep and maintenance of all properties and roadways belonging to its respective city
Public Safety Act of 1923	Public Safety (Emergency Powers) Act, 1923 For more information go to http://www.irishstatutebook.ie/ZZA28Y1923.html
Punch Bowl, The	bar on 238th Street and Broadway, the Bronx
Red Mill, the	Bronx ballroom
Redmonites	followers of John Redmond, leader of the Irish Parliamentary party (1910-1918), opposed to physical force nationalism

Republican	opponents of Anglo-Irish Treaty (1921) signed by Michael Collins and David Lloyd George, British Prime Minister
ROK	Republic of Korea
Rory Dolan's	bar/restaurant on McLean Avenue, Yonkers, NY
Rosie O'Grady's	bar/restaurant at 800 Seventh Avenue, NYC
Samuel Gompers	Samuel Gompers Vocational & Technical High School
Schrafft's	East coast chain of restaurants established by Frank Shattuck in Boston (1898)
Scoil Eanna	bilingual school founded in Dublin by Irish poet and revolutionary, Padraig Pearse, and brother, Willie (1908)
Seapoint Ballroom	built in 1949 in seaside village of Salthill, County Galway
Shannon	Shannon Airport, located in County Clare, Ireland
Six Counties	the six counties of province of Ulster, Ireland, which still remain under British rule
Stouffer's	chain of restaurants started in Cleveland, Ohio, by Abraham and Mahala Stouffer (1922)
Super/Supers	superintendents of the building
tender	a workboat or service boat
tog out	dress up/get ready for
Transit Authority	The New York City Transit Authority (NYCT) was not created until 1953; the Metropolitan Transit Authority (MTA), created in 1968, oversees the NYCT. For a history and timeline of rapid transit in New York City, go to http://www.mta.info/nyct/facts/ffhist.htm
Troubles, The	term used to describe period of sporadic communal violence in Northern Ireland involving paramilitary organizations; the Royal Ulster Constabulary; the British Army and others from late 1960's to late 1990's
Union Jack	common name for the flag of the United Kingdom
USO	provides morale, welfare and recreation-type services to Uniformed U.S. military personnel
Van Diemen's Land	original name for island of Tasmania, Australia
War of Independence	or Anglo-Irish war was a guerilla campaign mounted against the British Government in Ireland by the Irish Republican Army that resulted in the creation of the Irish Free State and Northern Ireland

Glossary of Names

Adams, Gerry	Irish Republican politician and abstentionist Westminster Member of Parliament for West Belfast. President of Sinn Féin, largest nationalist, republican or pro-Belfast Agreement political party in Northern Ireland in the 2005 UK general election
Barry, John	Commodore John Barry. Born in County Wexford Ireland in 1745, Barry worked his way up from cabin boy to a senior commander. Eventually allying himself with the colonist's cause during the American Revolution, he came to be known as the "Father of the American Navy" For more on Commodore John Barry go to http://www.ushistory.org/more/commodorebarry.html
Bowyer, Brendan	lead singer and trombonist with legendary Royal (Irish) Show band
Chieftains, The	traditional Irish folk band
Clancy Brothers	Irish singing family who popularized their native music in U.S.
Clifford, Archbishop	Archbishop of Cashel and Emly in County Tipperary, Ireland
Clipper Carlton	famous Irish Show band of the fifties
Darby, Seamus	County Offaly footballer last minute goal in the 1982 All-Ireland Football Final knocked Kerry's chances of the title for five years in a row
Delahunty, Mick	leader of well-known Irish Orchestra in the 40's and 50's
DeValera, Eamon	(1882-1975) one of the most dominant political figures in early 20th Century Ireland and its President from 1953-1975
Devlin, Bernadette	Northern Ireland republican political activist
George, David Lloyd	a Welsh statesman who guided Britain through World War I postwar settlement as the Liberal Party Prime Minister, 1916-1922
Kelly, Sean	President of GAA in Ireland
Lynch, Jack	fourth Taoiseacht (Prime Minister) of Republic of Ireland, serving two terms: 1966-73 and 1977-79
Madden, Joannie	whistle player and flutist; leader of traditional Irish music group – Cherish the Ladies

Makem, Tommy	traditional Irish musician and folksinger who performed with The Clancy Brothers in the 70's and then formed a duo with one of the brothers - Liam Clancy
McEvoy, Johnny	Irish country music singer for last four decades
McGann, Andy	Irish fiddler
McManus, J.P.	Irish entrepreneur and businessman
Moore, Christy	(born 1945, in Newbridge, County Kildare) popular Irish folk singer and guitarist; one of the founding members of Planxty
Morrissey, Ruthie	singer with The Mickey Carton Band in 50's & 60's New York
O'Donnell, John Kerry	leased Gaelic Park from City of New York in 1941
O'Shea, Kitty	married woman whose affair and marriage to Charles Stuart Parnell, 19th Century Irish political activist, ended his career
Quinn, Carmel	Irish singer based in New York
Ring, Christy	legendary hurler for County Cork in 50's and 60's
Roach, Hal	Irish comedian
South, Sean	Irish rebel from Limerick, shot in Armagh 1957; memorialized in Song – 'Sean South from Garryowen'
Wolfe Tones, The	Irish folk group

AS SLOW OUR SHIP

As slow our ship her foamy track
  Against the wind was cleaving,
Her trembling pennant still looked back
  To that dear Isle 'twas leaving.
So loath we part from all we love,
  From all the links that bind us;
So turn our hearts as on we rove,
  To those we've left behind us.

When, round the bowl, of vanish'd years
  We talk, with joyous seeming, -
With smiles that might as well be tears,
  So faint, so sad their beaming;
While mem'ry brings us back again
  Each early tie that twined us,
Oh, sweet's the cup that circles then
  To those we've left behind us.

And when, in other climes, we meet
  Some isle, or vale enchanting,
Where all looks flow'ry, wild and sweet,
  And nought but love is wanting;
We think how great had been our bliss,
  If Heav'n had but assign'd us
To live and die in scenes like this,
  With some we've left behind us!

As trav'llers oft look back at eve,
  When eastward darkly going,
To gaze upon the light they leave
  Still faint behind them glowing, -
So when the close of pleasure's day
  To gloom hath near consign'd us
We turn to catch one fading ray
  Of joy that's left behind us.

Thomas Moore (1779-1852)

ACKNOWLEDGEMENTS

We would like to acknowledge the Government of Ireland, Department of Foreign Affairs (Irish Abroad Unit) for their funding of this book. We are also grateful to the Irish Consulate of New York, Tim O'Connor and David Healy, for their continuing commitment to the Aisling Irish Community Center. A special word of thanks goes to Patricia Hamill of Heron Moon Press who read the manuscript and offered a thorough, creative and invaluable editorial service. We are indebted to Nuala Purcell, our photographer, who spent endless hours capturing the essence of our storytellers in her snapshots. We thank our Executive Director, Orla Kelleher, and Administrative Assistant, Maura Jordan for always being there to lend a hand. We wish to express our appreciation to Glucksman Ireland House, and to those who offered their time and expertise, including Patricia Grogan, Patrick Grogan, J.P. Delaney, Tony Quinn and Larry McCarthy. We sincerely thank the Board of Director's for their confidence and support. Finally, this work could not have been completed without the Center's 'Young at Heart' group whose patience, willingness to share, and sense of humor is exemplary as to how life should be lived and remembered.

All of the proceeds from this book will go to
the Aisling Irish Community Center.

GREEK LINE

GENERAL STEAM NAVIGATION CO., LTD., OF GREECE

8-10 BRIDGE STREET, NEW YORK 4, N.Y.

..................CLASS

WESTBOUND PASSAGE CONTRACT TICKET

№ 931552

(cover)

This passage contract ticket is issued subject to all terms appearing on the front and reverse sides of passenger's receipt and passage contract ticket (Page IX and cover) including numbered clauses 1 - 27, also clauses 5 a and 26 a

Della Boyle (Hennessy) and fellow passengers on board the SS Corinthia, White Star Line, Cobh to New York, 1926. Courtesy of her daughter, Sr. Christine Hennessy